EXCELLENCE
BY DESIGN

EXCELLENCE BY DESIGN

TRANSFORMING WORKPLACE AND WORK PRACTICE

TURID H. HORGEN
MICHAEL L. JOROFF
WILLIAM L. PORTER
DONALD A. SCHÖN

JOHN WILEY & SONS, INC.

New York • Chichester • Weinheim • Brisbane • Singapore • Toronto

Copyright © 1999 by Turid H. Horgen, Michael L. Joroff, William L. Porter, and Donald A. Schön. All rights reserved.

Published by John Wiley & Sons, Inc.
Published simultaneously in Canada.

This publication is designed to provide accurate and authoritative information in regard to the subject matter covered. It is sold with the understanding that the publisher is not engaged in rendering legal, accounting, or other professional services. If legal advice or other expert assistance is required, the services of a competent professional person should be sought.

Library of Congress Cataloging-in-Publication Data:

Excellence by design : transforming workplace and work practice /
 Turid H. Horgen . . . [et al.].
  p. cm.
 Includes index.
 ISBN 0-471-24647-6 (alk. paper)
 1. Work environment. 2. Work design. I. Horgen, Turid H., 1944–.
T59.77.E93 1998
658.3′8—dc21   98-7020
                                                   CIP

Printed in the United States of America.

10 9 8 7 6 5 4 3 2 1

To Don, our friend and colleague

You had to leave before our work was done.
What you left us who remain behind was a path
    from which
to see distinctly the remarkable within the ordinary;
to enjoy the observation of everyday life as a composition of profound questions;
to explore the complexity of professional practice
    by learning to approach the object of our studies in free flight.

Contents

Preface

This book has its origins in the authors' professional practice and in their association with the Space and Organization Research Group (SPORG) of the Massachusetts Institute of Technology's School of Architecture and Planning. Many of our ideas were shaped over a number of years by interaction with colleagues from SPORG.

SPORG was created in 1990 to explore the interdependence between physical space and organizational behavior and capability. It draws from the heritage of the fields of architecture, management sciences, and organizational development. Faculty, students, business managers, and design practitioners who join SPORG activities learn through formal research, participation in corporate and institutional workplace projects, and reflection about practice through seminars and workshops.

Donald A. Schön, our late friend and colleague, deserves a major share of the credit for the vitality of the SPORG program. His keen intellect, curiosity, and special view of how organizations behave and how professionals learn from practice provided much of the glue that has bound together successive waves of students and faculty.

At the heart of the group's working process have been the SPORG seminars, which continued without interruption throughout the time of our research. Some of these sessions focused on particular themes or concepts that we discuss in this book—for example, the meaning and function of space in relation to work practice, the integration of spatial, organizational, financial, and technological dimensions of the workplace, and the art of using tools for workplace and organizational transformation. Other seminar sessions focused on particular case studies. In many instances, seminar participants included the organizational leaders and workplace professionals who were key actors in the cases discussed.

Interaction between SPORG and the world of workplace-making has been a two-way street. The envelope game, an intervention strategy and concrete design game described in Chapter 5, is an example of how the group's interaction over time created a tool that has since been taken into practice.

Participants in and contributors to the SPORG seminars included John Habraken and Sandra Howell, professors emeriti of the Department of Architecture, MIT; Charles Kukla of the Integrated Manufacturing and Product Development Group at Digital Equipment Corporation; Crispin Miller, a former instructor and doctoral graduate of MIT's Department of Mechanical Engineering; Zack Rosenfield, architect and principal of NBBJ; Sheila Sheridan, director of facilities and services, John F. Kennedy School of Government, Harvard University; Jacqueline Vischer, principal and founder of Building-In-Use; Gregory Zack, former director of Xerox's Design Research Institute at Cornell University; and Craig Zimmring, professor of architecture, Georgia Institute of Technology. David de Sola, Suon Cheng, Bonne Smith, Barbara Freeman, Anne Townes, Arlene Kisiel, and Xiaofang Tu, all students at or recent graduates of MIT's School of Architecture and Planning, also participated in SPORG seminars, and in some cases collaborated as research assistants in the preparation of case studies.

Richard Luecke provided editorial advice, and the reams of transcripts we mined as our data (from seminars and from some of the case study fieldwork) were prepared by Nora Lynch Smith. Zsuzsanna Gaspar prepared the final renderings of the concept diagrams for the book.

The contributions of the Takenaka Corporation of Japan and its personnel deserve special acknowledgment. A generous gift from that organization supported our research. SPORG has also benefited greatly in several other ways from its association with the Takenaka Corporation. Mr. Takashi Shimanuki, general manager of the Office of Facilities Planning and Management, provided the grant on behalf of Takenaka and hosted several valuable research seminars in Japan with his staff and corporate managers. Ichiro Yoshida, manager of Takenaka's Office of Facilities Planning and Management, participated in discussions that shaped our thinking, helped us to explain our ideas to our Japanese colleagues, and helped us clarify these ideas and test their relevance in other national and corporate cultures. In addition, two research assistants in our group, David de Sola and Suon Cheng, served as summer interns in Takenaka's Office of Facilities Planning and Management, gaining the opportunity to observe how Takenaka's staff approached spatial programming and to engage in dialogue about SPORG's evolving ideas.

Even the term *process architecture,* which we use to describe our approach to workplace-making, must be credited. It borrows from a term that describes the practice of a number of Norwegian architects and planners.

Introduction

This book introduces a new approach to creating workplaces, called *process architecture,* that can improve work practice and transform organizations. As an approach to workplace-making, process architecture engages a wide array of stakeholders in rethinking the dynamic relationship between work processes and the spatial, technological, financial, and organizational environments within which these processes occur. This approach can be applied to the design and redesign of all forms of enterprises—factories, service centers, offices, laboratories, schools, and health care institutions—and at all organizational levels. Its value is apparent wherever shifts in an organization's environment place new demands on work processes, or whenever the organization refocuses on its core mission or restructures its task systems.

Practitioners of process architecture cannot be identified by degree or professional certification. They may be business managers, architects, organizational development specialists, or employees with a stake in the outcome of workplace transformation. These *process architects* understand that effective workplace-making requires collaboration between stakeholders with different interests, freedoms, and powers. They recognize that success demands that professionals from diverse fields blend their expertise and that those who do the work of the organization—people who hold local knowledge of the way the workplace works—must be part of workplace design. They know that contentious organizational issues must be confronted directly in the process of workplace change, and not swept under the rug.

Process architecture is both radical and familiar—aspects of its practice are part of other approaches to workplace-making and many of the tools it relies upon are in common use. Its underlying assumptions—its approach and particular way of using tools—make it different from the usual practice of workplace-making. Many current approaches were crafted in a time of greater stability, when the future was assumed to be largely a continuation of what was familiar and when organizational decision-making was more hierarchical and easier to predict. Process architecture is created for the needs of today's business landscape, where organizations and work processes are subject to continuous change, where the new technology of work changes rapidly and in often unpredictable ways, and where there is uncertainty about even the future of the enterprise.

This book presents the features, benefits, and challenges of process architecture through comprehensive explanation of the approach and framework with cases from the field. The cases include commercial offices, hospitals and nursing homes, educational institutions, and research laboratories. Chapter 1 describes the unstable environment in which most organizations are attempting to meet the challenges of workplace-making. It also includes a complete case study of a company that has met the challenge successfully. This case involves an operating unit of a major eastern bank that had to rethink its physical workplace even as it transformed its business strategy and its processes for satisfying customers. The case lays out many of the practical problems and opportunities that organizations confront when both work and workplace are simultaneously changing.

Chapter 2 reveals the conceptual framework of process architecture and its key elements. The first of these is the metaphor of the game. Workplace-making involves different practitioners and stakeholders whose partly cooperative, partly antagonistic interactions greatly determine the quality of the outcome. The game metaphor provides a useful context to describe these interactions, the practice of process architecture, and the roles of various players. This chapter also covers the fundamental objectives of the process architecture approach—dynamic coherence, uneven development, design inquiry, and collaboration—as well as the tasks and challenges facing contemporary workplace professionals.

Chapter 3 presents two cases that illustrate the way work can be redefined through the process of workplace-making. The first case looks at how the scientific laboratory radically changed after the introduction of high technology. The chapter takes us next into a hospital setting, where a design consultant, nurses, and administrators attempt to integrate space, technology, and work practice to create economies of effort and better care for patients. One of the striking features of this case is how workplace development led to a new and more important role for nurses in the management of patient care. Both cases illustrate what we mean by *uneven development,* a situation in which a change in one dimension of the workplace creates pressure for change in another. They also underscore the need to set aside stereotypes that can hinder the productive transformation of work and workplace.

Chapter 4 describes the design game and the people who play it. Using four short illustrative cases drawn from various kinds of organizations, it explores the interpersonal and political dimensions of workplace-making. These cases provide insights into the challenges that any group of workers, managers, and workplace professionals is likely to encounter, and the way effective process architects can understand and transform the game to secure better outcomes.

Process architecture includes a number of tools that practitioners have found useful. Several of these are described in Chapter 5, which also includes three case studies involving the ethnographic analysis of work practices. This reveals the social networks of interaction, or communities of practice, through which workers tackle emergent issues. Other tools, such as concrete design games, attempt to surface and test the objectives, agendas, and preconceptions of all players in order to pave the way toward beneficial transformation of the game.

Most companies now recognize the contributions that communications and team-based learning bring to the creation of new products and services. Chapter 6 takes us inside a research and technology center of the Xerox Corporation. There a team of lab workers, facilities managers, and outside consultants struggles to configure one group's office, laboratory, and auxiliary spaces with the goal of improving R&D productivity. Initially, each party sees the problem—and the solution—through a different lens. Through dialogue and intervention, the team manages to achieve consensus in a workplace experiment that is still evolving. Through the history of the overall process—the initial conditions, the collaborative evolution of ideas, and the dramatic result—this case illustrates key features of process architecture.

The final two chapters of the book reflect on previous chapters and cases. Chapter 7 assesses process architecture's ability to transform work and the organization, and what it requires of its practitioners. Chapter 8 deals with learning process architecture, focusing on practices, skills, attitudes, and values and how they can be learned by both individuals and organizations. Learning, we argue, is not a one-time event; rather, it is an activity that must take place continually, in different contexts, and in different combinations. The experiences of several protagonists in earlier cases are used to illustrate how learning can occur and how it can be blocked. We discuss the relationship between individual learning and organizational learning, and how learning can be planted and take root in an organization.

1

Workplace-Making beyond the Stable State

istory is replete with examples of *workplace-making* where organizations have sought to reshape the workplace to meet the demands of a changing economy. During the Renaissance, designers gave enduring civic art to the merchant families of Europe—even as they built accommodations for enterprises of commerce and manufacturing. In the early twentieth century, American engineers and architects created ambitious plans for buildings that were monuments to the industrial power that flourished in the wake of the pioneering initiatives of Frederick Taylor and his followers. In the mid-twentieth century, German designers created the "landscaped office" in order to combine, in the words of one group of analysts, "scientific management principles . . . human relations thinking which promoted a related and status-free form of layout . . . and cybernetics . . . the concept of the office as a kind of communication device or control system."[1] And the 1970s saw significant efforts by Scandinavian designers to create more humane and engaging workplaces oriented toward the requirements of the semi-autonomous work group.

This same desire to reshape work and the workplace continues today, but with a more acute sense of urgency as organizations attempt to respond to technological innovation, industrial competition, and the structural and political changes in the modern world. As we cross the threshold to the twenty-first century, new approaches to structuring workplaces are emerging in the design of all forms of business and service organizations—factories, offices, laboratories, service units—as they strive to survive and succeed in an increasingly unstable environment.

This rethinking is occurring—from individual workstations to team spaces, from single buildings to whole portfolios of buildings. However, in these turbulent restructuring processes, many workplaces simply fail to support business functions as productively as they could. The failure is compounded by the fact that the process through which workplaces are created does not contribute as much as it could to developing organizations that can respond quickly to a changing market. Synergy between spatial and electronic support for work is limited, and opportunities to support productivity through workplace redesign are missed. In some instances the very process of creating the workplace exacerbates existing organizational fragmentation. Even more important, the potential to use the process of workplace-making—and the attention that the organization focuses on this effort to transform work and the organization of work—remains largely unexamined.

Underachievement in the making of workplaces and a lack of capacity for change have a long history among American businesses and institutional organizations. In many cases, this underachievement has gone unrecognized. In others, it has been accepted as relatively inconsequential. In still other instances, the organization may be unready to effectively address transformation; design professionals and their clients may think they have a reasonably clear idea of the organizational purposes to be served by workplace design, when in reality the creation of facilities goes forward even as underlying organizational issues remain unresolved.

THE NEW WORLD OF WORK

Workplace-making is particularly challenging in the new world of work—what we call *the world beyond the stable state*.[2] This is a world that many businesses, non-profits, and government organizations have already begun to experience, and one that the rest of the work world will surely encounter before long. In this world, established values and assumptions are continually challenged; new competitors appear from unexpected locations; product life cycles grow shorter;

deregulation undermines the old order; innovation sweeps established products and services aside; and customers demand greater speed, quality, and cost effectiveness. Even effective solutions have only transient value.

Early signs of the world beyond the stable state were detected thirty years ago in patterns of industrial competition, technological innovation, and structural and political change. But this world was not widely recognized then, nor was its name recognized as something central to organizational development and survival. Over the past fifteen years or so, this has been corrected. The imperatives of organizational change and learning are now proclaimed in every forum concerned with management consulting, and organizational design.

There is an interesting progression in how organizational change has come to be seen over the last fifteen years or so. At the beginning of this period, the language of organizational change tended to stress the company's need to adapt to a rapidly changing environment. Later, perhaps in the mid-eighties, the language began to shift (as in the writings of Russell Ackoff) toward stressing the organization's responsibility for—and capability of—the design of its own future. More recently still, the language has come to emphasize the need for organizational learning.

This unstable environment has tested the mettle of even the most adaptive and agile organizations. Corporations of all types and their employees are being pushed to new levels of performance—if only to stay in the game. Successful organizations find that challenge never ends and that responding to a changing environment on a continuing basis is imperative.

Organizations—in business, industry, government, and the non-profit sector, in the United States as in other countries—are now responding to increasingly turbulent environments in many ways: rethinking business mission and strategy; reengineering work processes; striving for higher quality and increased efficiency; and turning to less hierarchical forms. These organizations are pruning core staff and adding more part-time and contract workers for greater flexibility and lower total cost. Team interactions across product, functional, and geographic boundaries are now in vogue. Corporations large and small are creating alliances and joint ventures—often with erstwhile rivals—in record numbers.

Today organizations are seeking new forms of balance between central authority and local autonomy. Bureaucracies and hierarchies are broken apart; responsibility and decision-making authority are being pushed down to lower levels and outward to peripheral locations where the boundaries of the organization meet the customer directly. Demands for individual expertise increase while at the same time expertise is diffused across members of cross-functional teams. *Value added* has become a corporate mantra and a key metric to justify retention and advancement of workers, managers, programs, and facilities in thousands of organizations worldwide. The instability itself contributes to the spiral of change and to a work environment that calls for radically new thinking about workplace and organizational design. The research findings of the Space and Organization Research Group (SPORG) prove that there is an undeniable link between workplace and work process.

Strategic Development of Working Places

A causal arrow connects organizational transformation to changes in the workplace: The new world of work should logically be reflected in new workplaces and new ways of designing them. When the organization as a whole is challenged to rethink its central mission, assumptions, and strategies, then everything about the organization is equally subject to challenge—including the spaces within which the organization operates and the manner in which those spaces are created. One positive consequence of the unstable world is the desire to depart from stereotypical work practices and organizational design. Doing this opens up the question of what work and workplace can and should become—and the relationship between changes in them and the organization. Workplace-making in this situation is not simply about designing and building physical space. It is, in fact, a four-part process that begins with the first awareness of the problematic situation, includes understanding of underlying conditions and objectives, goes on to develop a new work environment, and proceeds to maintain, manage, and redesign the relationship between the environment and its uses throughout its life cycle. When we refer to *workplace-making,* we refer to the entire process.

Activities in this process need not occur in sequence, and frequently the process is iterative and messy. Nevertheless, the term *workplace-making* connotes the idea of unfolding in time, with a beginning (the design problem) and an end (the design product). Of course, the end of such a process characteristically generates a new beginning, because new problems or new opportunities arise out of the solutions to old ones.

Relationships between workplace-making and organizational transformation are complex, multilayered, and reciprocal. Factors conducive to continuing organizational change—both those broadly related to the loss of the stable state and those specifically related to the transformation of work—lead management and employees to rethink how work and the workplace should be defined, designed, and organized.

Organizational change implies changes in work process, the organization itself, and the work and business environment. But this is not the only significant relationship between workplace-making and organizational change. The development of a new or modified workplace—or the process for creating it—may precede a more comprehensive shift in organizational life and work, and may then provoke or enable that larger and more significant shift. Thinking about the work process influences workplace design. But, just as often, emerging concepts about the workplace influence, shape, and sometimes create patterns of work and organizational systems. The elements of the workplace-making process may also help an organization to reframe the way in which it understands the work processes of an operating unit. Workplace-making in this sense becomes a powerful means of organizational intervention, capable of enabling the organization at large to enhance its capacity for change.

THE FOUR DIMENSIONS OF WORKPLACE

Conceiving the workplace as a strategic element in the enterprise requires a shift in how we view the workplace itself. Traditionally the workplace is viewed as a physical container for work. Its design is influenced by considerations of cost, work processes, and organizational culture. But the workplace as a strategic element of the organization is more than this: It depends upon the internal compatibility—indeed, the active mutual reinforcement—of spatial, organizational, financial, and technological arrangements. The relationship is represented in the SOFT diagram in Figure 1.1 (see also Color plate 1). The workplace at the core of the diagram has four dimensions—spatial, organizational, financial, and technological—symbolized by the four corners of the square. These dimensions are interdependent and in a dynamic relationship with one another. A change in one demands change in others. The result creates opportunities otherwise unachievable. Approaching the workplace through these interdependent dimensions usually suggests solutions that might not otherwise be considered.

The objective, then, is to achieve a dynamic coherence between the work and these four dimensions of the workplace. For example, when a team of information systems technologists sets out to improve the work of engineers responsible for dealing with breakdowns in a chemical plant, the team members' first thought was to install computer technology.[3] This technology would provide the engineers with

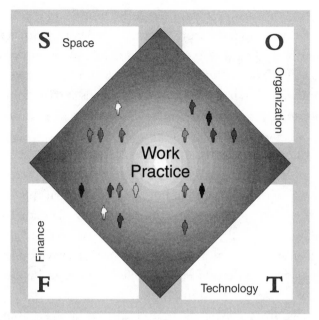

Figure 1.1 The four interdependent dimensions of the workplace.

feedback from sensing devices and easy access to the plant's engineering drawings, which were housed in a separate building. This, the systems technologists believed, would solve the engineers' problems, linking together the engineering control room and the far-flung operations of the plant. In effect, information systems would make physical distance irrelevant and aid the breakdown team in its work.

Prior to implementing this solution, however, the technologists carefully studied the organization of the control group, its mission, and how it went about its work. In doing so, they discovered situations where spatial proximity seemed to be unavoidably important. The controllers, they learned, depended heavily on an "intuition of the place"—how it smelled, what was heard, what experienced operators were seen doing. Feedback from sensing devices provided another piece of information, but one that simply added to other things the engineers were learning and needed to know. In the absence of direct learning from the production floor, the computer-generated information was too abstract. Control engineers, it was found, were most comfortable when they had many types of information at hand. The analysts also learned that a breakdown brought together individuals representing many divisions and disciplines; these individuals needed a space in which to assemble to examine charts, drawings, and pieces of material and to discuss the many different pieces of data that might point to causes of the breakdown.

The simple preconception of the designers, in this case, was very much at odds with the more complex reality of what the controllers needed to do their jobs. And having gotten to the actual situation through diligent analysis, a team of designers and controllers devised an integrated spatial-technological solution that provided both real-time information via computer-controlled sensors and opportunities to "feel" the actual production process.[4]

This brief story describes an iterative or uneven approach to seeking coherence between workplace and work process. If designers treat coherence as a static relation to be achieved (for all practical purposes) once and for all, then they miss the dynamic, open-ended, and provoking processes that are characteristics of actual workplace development and its reciprocal relationship with organizational transformation. If they treat integration as seamless, comprehensive development of all relevant dimensions of the workplace—a development process that, in our view, no real organization is capable of delivering—they miss the bumpy process of uneven development by which actual transformations of workplace and larger organization are achieved.

To conceive of the workplace in this broader way, we need to break free of established stereotypes of workplace design. Doing so, however, is easier said than done. Old images of the workplace persist, even as the patterns of work change.

Approaching the workplace-making process through the interdependent dimensions suggested by the SOFT diagram requires new ways of conceiving the practices associated with the activities of the professional groups occupying each corner. These professionals hold different and frequently incompatible understandings and modes of communication. Processes and tools are needed to bridge different frameworks, values, and professional languages (*adjacencies, bandwidth, return on net assets, throughput*) that naturally complicate decision-making about the work environment, generate ambiguities and mis-understandings, and make it difficult to coordinate disparate activities (Figure 1.2). Approaches need to be devised to surface conflicting objectives and viewpoints brought into the workplace-making arena by stakeholders with different interests, powers, and freedoms. To gain the most fruitful collaboration among all the professionals involved, the individual stages of workplace-making—from project creation to ongoing habitation—need to be brought into a continuous, interrelated stream of development and boundaries between separate workplace professionals need to be blurred or eliminated.

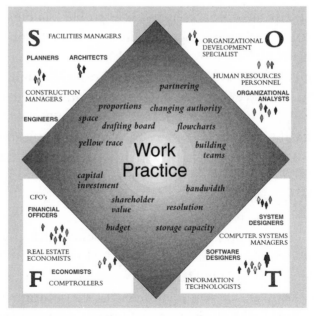

Figure 1.2 Different competencies need to communicate to optimize the workplace.

OPTIMIZING THE WORKPLACE
THROUGH COLLABORATIVE ENGAGEMENT

The following case study of the securities processing center for the Bank of Boston provides one example of custom-designing space to support the work of the business.[5] Here, where physical spaces were created hand in hand with the redesign of the entire business unit, we see workplace-making in an organization positioning itself in a turbulent business environment. How the bank's management responded to a business problem provides an interesting case of business reinvention and the part that workplace design played in that important process. It also reflects many of the issues we have just raised and will continue to address in subsequent chapters.

The Securities Processing Center

In 1988, the Bank of Boston had a major problem in one of its operating units. Its securities processing division was losing market share and profitability. The view of the bank's top management was that the division would have to be either fixed or unloaded.

Securities processing is a highly competitive business between major banks, trust companies, and other financial services firms. Unseen by the general public, this back-office business handles millions of stock transfers, dividend and interest payments, shareholders' services, and other operations every business day. Without these services, the operations of brokerage firms, mutual funds, and pension plans would grind to a halt.

The corporations and institutional investors that pay securities processors are selective and demanding: They want to know that shareholders and bondholders receive timely and accurate service when they buy or sell their securities, that the securities themselves are safely kept, and that dividend and interest payments are made on time and to the right payee, as well as other important data.

The keys to market success and profitability in this competitive business are service quality and internal efficiency—fast, low-cost, error-free operations. The Bank of Boston was an unprofitable player in this business. If these goals could be attained—and soon—the securities processing division would not have to be sold off. However, there simply wasn't room in the tough East Coast banking environment for a unit that couldn't carry its own weight. The bank's senior managers assigned Peter Manning to the task of cleaning up the mess and gave him a short timetable for producing results.

Fixing the Mess

Peter Manning had the right instincts for the job. An accountant by training, he saw the division's problems through the lens of efficiency and control. He called in Coopers & Lybrand, whose consultants, working with the bank's internal staff, audited the division's procedures. They examined over five years of records to map the division's current work processes. These revealed the root causes of the division's service and profitability problems: poor tracking of services, lost or misplaced documents, and transactional errors.

Having identified what appeared to be the main problems, Coopers & Lybrand was authorized to solve them through the application of just-in-time (JIT) methodology. Originally developed by the Toyota Motor Company in the mid-1970s, JIT is a management method that emphasizes the elimination of waste and the continual improvement of business processes. Initially, JIT was applied to materials inventories; the basic concept being that materials, either in the stockroom or on the factory floor, would be replenished exactly when needed and in the quantities required. Thus, the components supplier would deliver 100 starter motors just as 100 starters were scheduled for installation on the line. Ideally, those starters would never see the inside of the automaker's parts stockroom, but would be delivered directly to appropriate workstations on the factory floor.

Best suited to operations containing repetitive tasks such as product assembly, JIT is a demand pull system triggered by upstream customer orders. Those orders pull materials and finished output through the system as needed. Operations expand and contract as demand requires. The result: less material (and cash) tied up in inventory and the space required to hold it. Successful JIT practitioners eliminate their stockrooms entirely.

Coopers & Lybrand had extensive experience in just-in-time management. Using its initial analysis of the bank's processing operations, it began to apply JIT methods to Manning's "mess." At the time, no other business had applied JIT to paperwork processing. The results were less than satisfactory: Despite visible improvements, securities processing operations remained inefficient and control of documents and work in process was still a problem. Because work activities were organized around products (dividends, stock transfers, etc.), work for a given customer could end up being routed through product-based systems in several different locations. At each step, costs in time, labor, and materials were added. The need to maintain controls in these separate settings contributed further to the bank's costs. Coopers & Lybrand had optimized the current work design, but that design was deeply flawed.

Manning soon recognized that incremental improvements to the current suboptimal system would not turn the division around. He would have to throw out the mess and build a new system from the ground up. "We've got to rip these businesses apart," he told senior bank managers, "and see how they can be reconfigured in ways that make control sense and financial sense, where we can make a profit." By 1989, Manning had gained the administrative support and the resources to make that happen.

Restructuring the Business

Initial analysis and his own instincts provided Manning with a vision of what the reconstructed business would be like. It would be an "accounting factory" in which all securities processing would be done entirely under one roof. Activities originally clustered around separate products such as shareholders' services, corporate trusts, mutual funds, and pension administration would now be grouped around functions such as record keeping, accounting, and transaction execution. This function-based accounting factory would be designed from the bottom up to optimize efficiency, control, transparency of operations, and flexibility. It would be based on just-in-time principles and would be the benchmark operation for other back-office businesses. It would also be a clean and orderly work environment in which "we knew before we went home each night . . . exactly where each piece of work was [located]," and in which all processes and procedures would be transparent. Furthermore, the new operation would be a model workplace to which prospective customers could be brought with every confidence that they would leave with the intention of giving Bank of Boston their securities processing business.

Manning's factory model was not a new idea—that model had been around for almost a century in the world of manufacturing—but it was unique in the securities back-office business. Still, there were clear analogies between manufacturing and paperwork processing: The work of the division, like that of an assembly plant, addressed a large set of repeatable operations, and different products had different processing requirements. To the extent that individual tasks in this factory could be specified, simplified, measured, and made "goof-proof," efficiency and service quality would surely improve. But Manning's concept was more modern than Tayloresque. His would be a flexible factory in which different operations could expand or contract to accommodate varied work flows, a perennial problem for securities processors.

Having sketched this vision of the accounting factory in broad strokes, Manning and his colleagues soon recognized the relationship between the work and the workplace: Their physical facilities were inadequate to the task. When the project began, the division and its 1400 employees were scattered across 11 different New England locations, the majority in the Boston vicinity. For the most part, the spaces within these facilities fit the mold of clerical hell: The great bulk of employees worked in cramped cubicles at desks piled deep in paperwork and documents. Not surprisingly, the employee turnover rate ranged between 25 and 30 percent. The work itself was organized around particular services—stock custody, stock transfer, and so on—instead of around unifying functions.

Teams formed to analyze current tasks and processes and to formulate new ones recognized the relationship of form and function in their current arrangement and how the existing facilities layout would hamstring their ability to restructure the business for greater quality and profitability. If business processes needed to be redrawn on a clean slate, why not get rid of the existing eleven facilities and start with something new, designed to support the new business arrangement?

A New Single Space

Although the bank would have preferred to build a new processing center from scratch, there simply wasn't time. Manning had little more than two years to show results. The decision was made to vacate the existing facilities and rent a two-story building in an office park in the town of Canton, Massachusetts. Located along Route 128 southwest of downtown Boston, the site would provide access to employees suited to the kind of flexible workforce required by the new business strategy: educated mothers seeking part-time work and students. Eventually the Canton facility would be staffed by 800 bank employees, a major reduction made possible through work redesign.

Both the layout of the building and the redesign of the work would address four requirements laid down by Manning: efficiency, flexibility, visibility, and control.

Efficiency

Realigning processes from a product orientation to a functional orientation simplified work, reduced processing steps, and diminished the potential for costly, time-wasting errors. Coopers & Lybrand's contribution was a minimalist, value-added approach that eliminated anything other than the minimum amount of equipment, systems, material space, and employee time absolutely essential to add value to a production service. Efficiency was enhanced through functional teams. In the stock transfer area, spatial designers supported this approach through team "pods" like the one shown in Figure 1.3. Here the several tasks associated with stock transfer were handled by a team that worked in visual and verbal proximity. Not all tasks were suited to this type of configuration, however, and many followed more traditional arrangements.

Flexibility

Bank of Boston's accounting factory would need to accommodate changing customer demands for types of service and volumes of service; experience had shown that both shifted on a seasonal or even a daily basis. This required flexibility in both labor and space. The labor element of the equation could be met through the division's traditional reliance on part-time employees, but spatial flexibility represented a new challenge. In Manning's words, "We wanted something we could make ten times the size overnight."

Nancy Harrod, project designer for the Canton facility and a principal designer at Sasaki Associates, Inc., came up with an initial design to support Manning's flexibility requirements. Brainstorming with others shaped and reshaped this design until the planning team had a

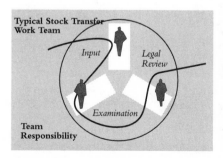

Figure 1.3   Innovative workstation for the new stock transfer team.

work space layout that made rapid reconfigurations of floor plans easy, fast, and inexpensive. Partitions could be moved by no more than two maintenance people, and desks on sawhorse supports became "electronic picnic tables" (Figure 1.3). To support efficiency in the work process, the designers developed a team station for stock transfer made up as a pinwheel of three electronic tables. Each workstation is prewired and equipped with a computer, a table lamp, and an adjustable chair. The woman in the picture is receiving the information she needs in paper form, and is working through the computer. There is no printer, no telephone, and no filing cabinet, and personal lockers for shoes and purses are not located at the workstation.

Harrod's workstation mock-up and easily reconfigurable floor layouts created a need for an equally flexible infrastructure of electric, phone, and computer cables. The flexible workplace could not function if this infrastructure were hardwired. An ad hoc team of internal staff and outside designers solved this problem by means of hanging cable trays that resembled track lighting (clearly visible in Figure 1.4). Cabling could be pulled to the prewired work surfaces as needed through flexible black industrial hoses, eliminating the time and costs associated with changing power outlets and patching carpets and permitting desk configurations to be easily changed.

Visibility

Inefficiencies and problems with control in the old processing business had been traced in part to spatial barriers that blocked visibility between supervisors and workers. In the words of Jon Stein, manager of the new Canton operation:

> All the people who were doing work sat in one room, the supervisors sat across the hall in another room, and the managers sat down the hall in two other offices. And guess what? The managers never spoke to the supervisors, and the supervisors spent most of their time talking on the phone, I'm sure, and were never out on the floor.

Figure 1.4 Infrastructure for the electronic tables.

This situation was changed in the Canton facility. Figure 1.5 shows before and after views of the typical processing workplace. In the new design, managers and supervisors were placed at the center where they could visually observe the problems and opportunities experienced by their employees. Emphasis was placed on keeping everything in plain sight. Clear lines of sight, minimally enclosed offices, and uncluttered, open work surfaces made this possible.

Control

Managerial control is a critical element of any work process; control is needed to assure the timing and quality of any product or service. In the Bank of Boston case, control and visibility were closely related. Visibility assured that supervisors could control both the processes

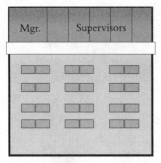

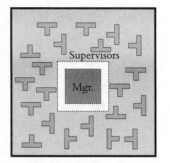

Before
"Manager in the corner office, supervisors on the phone all the time, nobody knew what went on on the floor."

After
Manager and supervisors in the middle of the floor, workers in functional, flexible teams.

Figure 1.5   The arrangement of space in previous locations and in Canton.

and products of work. The new work environment was designed to be as paperless as possible. This would not only reduce costs but enhance control of whatever papers (stock certificates, powers of attorney, etc.) there were. Fewer pieces of paper were simply easier to control. Spatial design also made document control more error free. In the traditional arrangement of work cubicles, credenzas, and cubbyholes, papers had countless opportunities to be lost or misplaced. As Jon Stein explained: ". . . those papers are worth money. And in a standard panel system there are loads of places to get paper lost."

In the interests of visibility and control, the Canton facility was designed with the following features: (1) a minimum of enclosed offices with low (66 inches) or no partitions; (2) desks on sawhorses to ensure that everything remained visible and papers could not be misplaced; (3) no desk drawers or personal storage at desks to reduce the risk of losing certificates and other valuable paper; (4) no printers, telephones, or filing cabinets at workstations; (5) locked wire wastebaskets; and (6) lockers for employee personal items such as shoes and purses.

Although proximity and visibility were primarily intended to facilitate control of operations, they also enhanced communication among the members of functional teams (Figure 1.6). Gail King, who developed the software for the new system, put it this way: "Move people closer together. Take down the barriers between them. Allow people who are doing the work to communicate directly with each other at the moment of transaction as opposed to in a circuitous fashion."

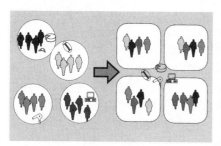

From organization by product to organization by function

Just-in-time adapted to workspace deployment

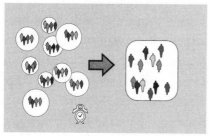

Efficiency

Minimal equipment, material and space

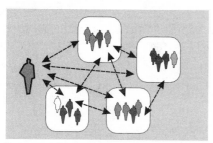

Process control: Transparency of operations

STRATEGIC PRINCIPLES

Clear lines of sight: minimally enclosed offices, clear and open work surfaces

SPATIAL COUNTERPARTS

Figure 1.6 Strategic principles and their spatial counterparts.

Workplace as Merchandising Display

From the beginning, Manning visualized the new Canton services center as a showcase for JIT securities processing, the paperless office, and the transparent production process—a place where prospective customers could see efficient, flexible operations in action and leave confident that their business would be in good hands. In this sense the facility itself would become a marketing tool for selling Bank of Boston's securities processing services to new customers. As Manning explained:

> We concluded quickly that the thing closest to the heart of a chairman of the board or a president or a general counsel is how well his shareholders and debtholders get treated by the bank that processes their work. So we said, if they could come in here and kick the tires and we let them talk to the operating people—the people who would be handling their account—that's pretty powerful stuff.

With that in mind, the bank began to schedule tours once the new business was up and running—something that had never been attempted by any of its local competitors. Every week featured a tour for prospective institutional customers, followed by a one-and-a-half-hour meeting in one of the facility's conference rooms. When customer teams emerged, they would find that one of the securities transfer teams had rearranged its space to accommodate a different type of activity. Prospective customers were promised that their operations would be up and running within thirty days of notification, a tactic the bank considers directly responsible for major sales to such telecommunication giants as PacBell and NYNEX.

In short, the Canton facility became a stage for work where employees were the actors and customers were the audience.

Outcomes

When the design was fully implemented in early 1990, Bank of Boston's new Canton facility had achieved most of its objectives:

Construction costs	The new facility housed the entire set of securities processing operations. It was rented and remodeled in the summer and fall of 1989, just at the peak of the hot real estate market. Total costs, including furnishings, were roughly $9 million, or about $45 per square foot.
Personnel	Employee turnover, which ran at 25 to 30 percent before the move, dropped to about 10 percent. How much of this change is directly attributable to the improved working environment and how much to an economic recession in Massachusetts is not clear.
Financial results	Investment in the building and costs of renovation came to $10 million, which translated into $1.5 million per year in depreciation and amortization. Taken together, workforce reduction due to consolidation and improvements in efficiency produced savings in payroll and benefits amounting to some $9 million per year. In addition, the move freed up 60,000 square feet of space; this was rented out to other divisions of Bank of Boston, yielding $1.5 million per year in rental income.
Business performance	During the first year of operation, activities increased in volume by 80 percent. Within four years, the center became a profitable division of the Bank, and one of the top five such organizations in the United States.

The Bumpy Road to Success

The Canton project led by Peter Manning is a remarkable success story. It achieved what every business restructuring aims for: improved processes, higher morale, higher revenues from fixed resources, greater profitability, market share expansion, and cost reduction. These are remarkable results, but obtaining them was neither easy nor painless. Bank personnel and outside consultants worked under high pressure and enforced speed. The course of progress was not a smooth, linear ascent, but was marked by uneven development, discontinuities, surprises, tension, and difficulties. It was messy and uncertain. From the beginning, hundreds of employees knew their jobs were in jeopardy—even as dark clouds of recession gathered over the local economy.

Forward progress was followed by unanticipated setbacks; design moves made in earlier stages created or revealed problems and dilemmas that had to be resolved later on. Many of these difficulties were detected and corrected during the design process, but others remained hidden until the workplace was inhabited. In managing this messy process, Manning and his colleagues had to solve the following problems:

- Because the project was on a fast track, they had to redesign the work process, the organization, and the physical facility at the same time. This made the task more difficult but created the potential for an integrated approach to workplace development.

- The types of expertise necessary for the combined restructuring of the business and its work environment had to be mobilized. Some of these existed within the bank; others had to be imported. Consultants who had not worked together before had to be coordinated in a smoothly functioning team.

- A smooth transition from one phase of the turnaround to the next had to be managed without the loss of essential information, capability, or organizational direction.

◉ Although the vision of the new workplace (the accounting factory) was established, the details were lacking. Manning and his team had to work out detailed specifications even as they responded to unanticipated problems.

◉ The process was vulnerable to risks and conflicts of interest.

Solutions to these problems called for teamwork, managing of uncertainty, training, a fluid and interactive design process, and learning. Peter Manning provided vision and leadership and assembled a team composed of internal managers and employees along with outside consultants to handle the design and implementation of the new facility. Three distinct constituencies inside the bank participated in planning the reconstruction of the securities processing business: the facility management group, employees who were going to work in the new environment, and a management team created to guide the transition. This third group, the Wings Team (an allusion to the bank's eagle symbol) was composed of managers from the existing securities processing sites, along with other individuals seen as good problem solvers. While all three of these groups functioned throughout the process, their roles changed as the process unfolded: In the early programming and design, all three groups were involved. In design development, when the details of the workstations were being set, the Wings Team and the facilities managers served as the main links to the designers. During construction documentation and administration, the facilities people moved to center stage.

Among the internal participants, Gail King played a key role in developing an in-house software system, Delta Vantage, and for this purpose she had done a great deal of work flow analysis. She was asked to take on a one-year assignment as one of the project leaders for the move to Canton. As she said, her systems development work fit well with the JIT work flow analysis: "Now that we know it works this way, we could rack it out, change it, and not have to reinvent the software wheel we just finished putting the whitewalls on."

Manning augmented the core internal team with outside consultants. Coopers & Lybrand was carried forward from the first phase of
the project. Other consultants who appeared in the second phase
included Rosabeth Moss Kanter of the Harvard Business School,
whom Manning described as a "spiritual advisor"; a demographics
consultant; and Andersen Consulting, which helped design a computer control room. Sasaki Architects was selected by a committee
that included both bank facilities personnel and analysts from Coopers & Lybrand. The Sasaki group was selected largely because of its
team approach to problem solving and project management.

Some consultants, like Kanter, worked for only a few days;
others, including Coopers & Lybrand analyst Scott Petersen and
move coordinator Arnie Westphal, worked regularly throughout the
process and eventually became full-time bank employees. Manning
did not feel wedded to any one of these consultants. As he put it:
"Everyone had a different role. No one firm supplied everything we
needed."

Manning sought to convey the image of the accounting factory
in such a way that team members could play out their roles within a
common framework. He expected them to understand the broader
goals of the business, but left them free to use their expertise, in
cooperation with others, to determine the many details of the new
workplace. As he put it:

> If we have experts on our staff, like our facilities people, we
> expect them to understand our business. And then what do we
> owe them? We owe them support. So when they recommend this
> or that, [such as to hire] Sasaki or whomever, we listen to them and
> we go with it, because that's their business . . . I'm not going to
> have my line business executives overrule the space people. If they
> said this is the amount of space or this is the budget, that's it. And
> if it means that my office is this size, that's the way it is.

The activities of Manning and his three major teams are
described graphically in Color plate 2. There the project is shown

with its two time-based stages on the horizontal axis and the major activities on the vertical axis.

Managing Uncertainty and Risk

The project posed a variety of risks and created a climate of uncertainty and fear. People everywhere are ambivalent about or fearful of change, and the Bank of Boston personnel were no different. There was a great deal of justifiable fear of job loss and dislocation. There was a certain expectation that everyone should be promised a new job within the firm, but this expectation was not supportable. As Manning saw it, the choice was between closing the business (and losing its 1400 jobs) or maintaining it as a going concern, and he used the threat of closure as a means of gaining commitment: ". . . if businesses are drowning . . . you throw them a life raft, and you say, 'I want to save your business, the 800 jobs.' " Six hundred jobs would be lost, but, as Manning said, "a lot of those we were going to lose anyway, because they didn't want to move. . . . We had an internal posting program, so if they didn't want to move they could get a job somewhere else in the company."

Manning wanted to broaden the base of commitment to the Canton project in the face of the risks the project posed. As he saw it: "I was way out front by myself. And I didn't want that. I wanted ten or twelve of us [managers] way out front." To develop commitment, Manning brought in Harvard Business School professor Rosabeth Moss Kanter, a widely recognized leader in the field of change management. Kanter organized an off-site meeting designed to build Manning's team of change agents: "She gave us the spiritual courage to try change." Kanter's two-day workshop emphasized role modeling and training in personal risk-taking. Manning described the process:

> Some people were very entrenched and not eager to create change. Change meant taking personal risks. So my line executives did various crazy things to show to their people that they weren't

afraid of change. One of them composed a tune about the move to Canton. Another formed an Elvis Presley group and sang to his people in a theater in the Burlington Mall. Everyone did something crazy that showed personal risk-taking; these set an example and a tone that people shouldn't be afraid.

During the workshop, Kanter also created a process for mobilizing employees to make the move to Canton. Her approach was to bring people to the site and engage them in the design of its amenities. The participants discussed the possibility of incorporating a health club, walking trails, barbecue grills, and other features into the site.

Training

Employees had to be trained in the JIT production methods to be used at the new facility. Eight hundred Bank of Boston employees, plus the Sasaki architects, attended a one-day Coopers & Lybrand course on JIT. Meeting in the morning in groups of thirty, the participants heard short presentations on the basic JIT ideas. In the afternoon, they were asked to play a game, the intention of which was to build team skills. Members of each group of thirty were divided into teams, given Lego blocks, and asked to produce a sailboat. They were to design, at the same time, the sailboat and the organization and physical setting for its production. Each group was free to set up its own team organization and invent its own process, so that everyone could see how different ways of organizing the work flow and physical environment would affect production. The game went through four to five rounds; Coopers & Lybrand instructors then discussed the differences in the approaches, thereby demonstrating the meaning of JIT. (The sailboat game is described in detail in Chapter 5.) Participants in the training sessions were also introduced to a method for pulling work teams toward the pace of the most efficient performer. This was to counter the tendency of work teams to downshift to the pace of the least efficient member.

Managing a Fluid and Interactive Design Process

The design process for the Bank of Boston project was inherently unstable: Work flow, the members of the design team, and facilities plans were all changing at once. For example, the Wings Team, which was supposed to help guide the project, was in the process of being reorganized; new members would appear and others would be reassigned even as the team struggled with its work. In the meantime, managers were having to incorporate employee groups from existing locations slated for closure. The design process was not, as Gail King pointed out, clean and sequential. "We'd meet in one group one week, and the next week we'd go to the follow-up meeting and they'd say, 'Oh, this is the new manager, and in the restructuring they've reassigned so and so, whom you met with last week.' "

To accommodate this flux, the architects worked in long, highly concentrated periods of time. Coopers & Lybrand had written volumes of reports about the work processes, their spatial needs, and the staff requirements from a banker's point of view. The architects used that information, but instead of writing formal programming documents describing all the relationships between work activities and spatial needs, they went right into schematic layouts on tracing paper, which they used to clarify goals and decisions as they developed. As Harrod explained:

> We had different teams with different areas they were working on that they would go and meet with people and make new drawings on yellow trace, and then go back and revise them as the bank was going through these changes, in order to move the project ahead.

Learning from Surprise

Not all design solutions proved to be successful once the new workplace went into operation. In several cases, they produced disturbing surprises. Yet even in these instances, Manning and his team were usually able to diagnose and fix the unanticipated problems, which reflected for the most part a mismatch between the design solution and the way work was actually done.

One of those mismatches involved the designers' attempt to apply JIT uniformly to all parts of the securities processing operation. Initially, JIT was applied to all aspects of the work flow and the new spatial environment; one of the consequences was the elimination of personal filing space. The entire facility was supposed to run on an impersonal basis, in the sense that account files were to be centrally located so that anyone who received a phone call from a customer could obtain the relevant file and deal with that customer's problem or request. This arrangement worked for stock transfer, but it did not work for stock custody. In stock custody, satisfaction depended on the customer's trust in a particular bank representative; to the customer, that employee was the bank. Thus, if a customer was comfortable in working with Susan, and confident in her ability to solve problems, that customer would always ask for Susan. In the eyes of JIT, however, employees should be interchangeable, and this meant that the customer was unlikely to be served by Susan each time he or she called.

During the programming phase of the project, some employees had indeed complained that the proposed JIT design would not work for stock custody. But their concerns had been dismissed as reflecting unwillingness to take risks with unfamiliar solutions. Moreover, the full-scale mock-up and the testing area for JIT had been set up for transfer, not for custody. In the end, the design team learned that the stock transfer and stock custody businesses required different spatial solutions. Because the telephone work of custody personnel called for a certain amount of acoustic privacy and personal storage, their area had to be equipped with private space for personal filing cabinets and telephones.

A second problematic outcome of the design process had to do with the symbolic meaning of office space. The size, location, and accoutrements of space have long been used to symbolize different levels of organizational stratification. The new design eliminated that symbolism to a substantial degree. Some were pleased, but not others. As Stein pointed out, the "pink-collar operations staff were thrilled [with the new workspace], because they'd never worked in an office that seemed like fun." But white-collar MBAs in the marketing department resisted the leveling effect of a design that arranged all desks in undifferentiated groupings. The head of marketing worried that he would not be able to recruit college-educated MBAs if they knew they'd be sitting at the designers' high-tech sawhorses and not in their own offices behind traditional desks. Ultimately, the bank conceded. Workstations for the marketing people became larger, with higher partitions, and the style of the fabric on the partitions became more conservative—"Brooks Brothers" fabric, as the designers called it.

Finally, there was a puzzling surprise, still unresolved, about the advertised proximity between supervisors and workers. As planned, the workstations of the line managers and supervisors were all located out on the floor, distinguished only by having more accoutrements than the others. But it was striking to the researchers who observed the site on several occasions that few of these workstations seemed to be occupied. Perhaps the workers were managing themselves. Or perhaps, at least for stock transfer workers, such management activities as job assignment, clarification of directives, and instructions for reporting were not coming face-to-face from supervisors but were being transmitted by computer.

REFLECTION

The Bank of Boston case illustrates how spatial and technological arrangements, work practices, and work organization were co-invented, and how they were integral to the reformulation of business strategy. The co-invention of a restructured workplace and business organization calls for a design process of a special kind. Of course, the Bank of Boston version of that process bears the marks of its particular organizational situation, but it also demonstrates some very general principles.

Discontinuities—across phases of the project, organizational boundaries, professional disciplines, and interest groups—are inherent in any such process. Yet, in spite of the dangers posed by these discontinuities, the process must function as though seamless if it is to be effective. This case shows how such apparent seamlessness can be achieved.

Clearly, Peter Manning's leadership was essential. However, the case reveals more specifically what that leadership entailed:

- A strong vision of the future workplace based on deep knowledge of the work to be done
- A willingness to perform the restructuring of work and workplace on a do-or-die basis
- Strong, central control over the complex and rapidly changing context set in motion by the need to change everything at once, but, at the same time, an ability to obtain broad-based commitment to the vision
- A willingness to leave specialists free to work out their own solutions within a common framework of goals and constraints

In this case, success was also predicated on Manning's ability to orchestrate teams of multidisciplinary specialists drawn from within the organization and from other sources. The selection and deployment of these teams was carried out in such a way as to draw on organizational knowledge of the detailed patterns of work, moving specialists in and out of leading roles as required by changing needs, and to preserve continuity from one phase of the process to the next.

Of course, the project's success depended on the capabilities and commitment of its many participants. Manning could encourage, but he could not make things happen by himself. Participants brought a number of tools to the process of remaking the division, including (1) production tools—work flow analysis, software design, and JIT methodology; (2) architectural tools—the tracing paper and rapid mock-ups; (3) training tools—the sailboat game; and (4) Kanter's design dialogue.

Finally, the Bank of Boston case illustrates organizational learning. When the project worked as planned, it reflects both the preexisting expertise and the online learning of many participants. When it did not work as planned, it reveals, for the most part, the ability of the participants to detect and adjust to misguided design assumptions.

The decision of the Bank of Boston to create a JIT office environment reflects an organization that was ready to reconceptualize its workplace strategy as it reconceptualized work patterns. In this it is unusual. More frequently, organizations seek a facility solution based on projections heavy with assumptions about the continuity of past behavior, even though the group that will use the space may still be grappling with unresolved organizational issues.

Normally, a story like this would simply involve just-in-time reengineering or one of the many other process improvement methods that have filled so many business books in recent years. This case, however, has another important dimension: It shows how the integration of process improvement and workplace design can radically restructure business strategy. Here a fairly traditional search for more efficient production methods was found to be an inadequate response. Managers and employees had to think about restructuring the entire business; the development of a new workplace went hand in hand with that effort.

This story represents an example of how, in this time beyond the stable state, managers and members of an organization joined with an array of professionals to rethink how work and the work environment should be defined, designed, and organized, and how each of the professional groups worked together with all who had a stake in the outcome of the project. The story has the elements of an approach to workplace-making that we call *process architecture,* discussed in the following chapter.

2

Concepts of Process Architecture

P eter Manning, leader of the Bank of Boston security processing group, and the design team he assembled completed their
work with a great sense of satisfaction and pride. They created
a new workplace for a new way of working. However, even when
workplace-making goes well, it rarely goes smoothly. Workplace-
making is subject to uncertainty, surprise, conflict, and confusion.
Potentially disruptive forces are always present; but such forces can
contain the potential for new ways of seeing things and can force
the emergence of creative alternatives. In the Bank of Boston case,
for example, one key participant pointed out that whereas an outsider might see workplace-making as a "nice neat set of steps," the
insiders were simultaneously engaged in many different activities: consolidating four divisions into one, developing a new facility, and
redesigning both work flows and organizational hierarchy. These
insiders were, in this person's view, "scurrying around with ninety-
seven things going on at once" (Color plate 1).

Workplace-making refers to the entire process of creating or
modifying a workplace. Expanding on our earlier definition, it begins with the first awareness of a problematic situation, goes on to
develop a new work environment, and then proceeds to maintenance, management, and redesign of that environment throughout its
life cycle. This process includes the activities of programming, design,
building, maintenance, management, and renovation. These activities
need not occur in rigid sequence. Nevertheless, the term *workplace-
making* connotes the idea of unfolding in time, with a beginning (the
design problem) and an end (the new workplace in use). Of course,
the "end" of such a process characteristically generates a new beginning, because new problems arise out of the solutions of old ones.
When we speak of designing a workplace, we refer to the entire
process or to any part of it—the production of a whole building or

the solution of a particular building problem, such as space allocation or lighting maintenance.

In many cases, the outcome of workplace-making is quite different than what was planned or anticipated, leaving occupants of the space and workplace-making professionals alike puzzled, distressed, and frustrated. Each of these parties experiences the frustration that results when the workplace "does not do what you want it to," even after a great deal of time and effort. Almost everyone who engages in workplace-making can point to unsuccessful outcomes that simply cannot be explained. The antidote to these puzzling outcomes is a new framework for shaping and guiding workplace transformation. We call this framework *process architecture.*

Process architecture shapes and guides the workplace-making process. Its goal is a dynamically coherent workplace, which we define as one in which work and workplace are joined in a potentially reinforcing relationship. Each changes according to its own rhythm, and each affects the other. The term *process architecture* implies that working toward workplace transformation is itself subject to careful design and craftsmanlike execution. It is cast against the backdrop of the organization in which the work occurs, technologies that support the work, the individuals who do the work, the physical environment, and the way the work is done. Many, if not all, of these factors may be changing more rapidly than our ability to design and construct workplaces to accommodate them. Everything that impinges upon the transformation of the workplace may itself be changing. At first glance, this would seem to create a hopelessly unmanageable situation.

Process architecture equips stakeholders to anticipate and adjust to the effects of changes. Process architecture does not approach its final destination in a linear path of logical steps. Rather, it triangulates between many shifting reference points, most of which are clouded in uncertainty and complexity. It anticipates surprises, dangers, and opportunities at each step, and even seeks these out as constructive influences. It advances no final workplace solutions. Because it operates strategically, process architecture can accommodate shifts of tactics without losing consistency with its higher-level purposes.

Process architecture contrasts with the approach to workplace-making that depends upon technical-rational expertise. To people trained in that approach to workplace-making, process architecture seems alien. The technical-rational approach, which has analogues in many other professions, contains a particular view of professional knowledge and a complementary way of framing the professional's role and relationship with clients and other stakeholders (Color plate 3). This view of professional knowledge is consistent with the formulation put forward by Everett Hughes, one of the founders of the sociology of the professions.[1] The professional, in this formulation, holds specialized knowledge in matters of social importance—a knowledge of technique based on systematic understandings of objective phenomena. On the basis of this esoteric knowledge, society allows the professional to exercise social control in the domain of his or her expertise. The technical-rational approach to the practice of the workplace-making professions depends on the assumption that the professional can know in advance, at least conceptually, what the results of his or her activities will be. Of necessity, this view rests on conventional interpretations of the client organizations as the professional imagines them to stand today. Technical-rational practitioners tend to hold stereotypical views of the workplace (What is an office? What is a laboratory?). This set of assumptions makes it possible to think mainly in terms of routinized measures and rules of thumb, such as using per-square-foot requirements without worrying much about requirements for *what*. Only secondary consideration is given to an organization's likely future evolution; even then there is a tendency to make straight-line projections from the present.

Furthermore, individual stages of workplace creation, from initial conception to ongoing habitation, tend to be imagined and practiced as autonomous tasks that are assigned to different types of professionals, sequentially performed, and relatively compartmentalized from one another. Differences among professional groups complicate decision-making about the work environment, generate ambiguities and misunderstandings, and make it difficult to coordinate disparate professional activities. Without ways of bridging the gaps between the perspectives and lexicons that members of each group bring to the table, it is difficult to balance multiple values and resolve conflicting viewpoints—processes essential to the development of a dynamically coherent workplace.

The technical-rational approach does not offer possibilities for closing these gaps, preferring to define interests and professional territories narrowly. This makes the integration of spatial, organizational, financial, and technological aspects of the workplace—never an easy challenge—all the more difficult, especially when the organization of work and its technological supports are becoming increasingly intertwined and changing in ways that are difficult to anticipate. These dynamic conditions call for change in the approaches of workplace professionals, their self-concepts, and their ways of practicing.

THE METAPHOR OF THE GAME

Workplace-making involves many different practitioners and stakeholders whose partly cooperative, partly antagonistic interactions greatly determine the quality of the outcome. To make sense of these interactions and their impacts on workplace quality, we are drawn to the metaphor of the game, which provides an extremely useful context for the practice of process architecture. The power of the game metaphor derives from the fact that games are simple, transparent, and understandable counterparts of the complex, often more confused, and more opaque social processes that occur in real life: war, diplomacy, business, politics, and workplace-making. Games help us to understand and anticipate the outcomes and the development of particular situations.

The metaphor of the game is one of the most powerful organizational constructs of the twentieth century.[2] In the early 1960s, French sociologist Michael Crozier introduced a theory of bureaucratic phenomena based on games of interests, freedoms, and powers played by the occupants of roles in formal organizations. In the late 1960s, policy analyst Eugene Bardach wrote *The Implementation Game,* drawing (consciously or unconsciously) on Crozier's ideas to explain the often distorted processes of policy implementation. War games, and business games modeled on them, have long been staples of research and analysis at institutions from the U.S. War College to the Harvard Business School. From the 1970s onward, the planner Richard Duke invented simulation games as tools for research and education in the fields of planning, policy, and administration. In the 1980s, architect John Habraken and his students introduced a series of "concept design games" geared toward exploring the nature of the social process of architectural designing.[3] Today it is difficult to find a branch of social science, economics, political theory, planning, or management that has not been touched by the metaphor of the game.

In the most generic sense of the term, a game is a social activity in which multiple actors, occupying defined roles and operating within a shared system of rules and a conventionally defined context, seek to achieve desired outcomes. The everyday games that inspire the game metaphor are playful social activities, conventionally set off against real life, in which the actors, as individuals or teams, engage in structured win/lose competition. In sedentary games of amusement, such as chess, Monopoly, or Go, rules indexed to a physical setting—a *game board*—constrain the roles of the actors, their freedom of movement, the moves they are permitted to make, and the definition of winning.

The power of the game metaphor derives from the fact that these conventional games are simpler, more transparent, more readily understandable counterparts of the complex, often more confused reality of war, business, politics—and workplace-making. When we see real-world activity as a game, we automatically think in terms of a mixture of constraining roles and rules of play, together with a degree of freedom of individual action that creates, within some encompassing order, a core of uncertainty and unpredictability. Interesting games, like interesting conversations, are combinations of order and disorder, constraint and freedom, predictability and uncertainty.

Workplace-Making as a Design Game

We use the game metaphor to explain, analyze, and anticipate the unfolding of any workplace-making process. The game is thus a diagnostic tool that enables players—workers, managers, owners, and workplace professionals—to perceive their roles more accurately and to play them more productively. This can be done either while the game is in process, or retrospectively, to learn from past experience how workplace-making either succeeds or goes astray. The metaphor of the game works in the ways just described because there is a correspondence between the interactions of players in games of amusement and in the real-life games of consequence in which we all engage. For this reason, too, playful games of childhood and youth serve as preparations for the serious activities of adult life. American managers are trained for their adult roles in youthful games of football, baseball, or soccer, and many believe that the battle of Waterloo was won on the playing fields of Eton. Most games are zero-sum games—one player wins at the expense of his or her adversary. Interest has begun to grow, however, in games that seek not to invent winning strategies within established rules of play but to change the rules so that the players can achieve mutually satisfying outcomes. These games emphasize negotiation, cooperation, and competition.[4]

We describe the game that emerges in the workplace-making process as a *design game*. This game is a bounded circumstance within which competition for resources, management of processes, and innovation occur. It represents a microcosm of the larger organizational game of interests, freedoms, and powers in which that larger game may be played out. Nevertheless, being a more bounded circumstance, it affords players the opportunity to experiment with increasing their freedom of action, the results of which they may take back to their everyday work.

Stakeholders in the Design Game

The design game features a large and highly differentiated cast of characters: workplace professionals, building users, owners, corporate managers, contractors and subcontractors, regulators, and neighbors, among others. These multivariate players generally hold different images of the workplace, pursue different and often conflicting objectives, and seek to protect their respective interests.

The traits individual players bring to the game have three principal roots. First, the individuals have professional orientations that carry distinctive professional languages and values. Second, they have personal styles that determine how they set and solve problems and how they create and respond to interpersonal relationships. Third and most important, they come from different organizations or divisions within the same organization, and they occupy specific roles and positions of authority. All three of these factors impose attitudes or norms that influence the players' ways of dealing with change. And all three influence how they play out their roles in the design game.

PROFESSIONAL LANGUAGE

The professionals who occupy the four corners of the SOFT diagram often use different terms to describe their understandings, methods, objectives, and criteria for success. These differences often generate ambiguities and misunderstandings that make the coordination of activities by specialists more difficult. In the absence of a common language, or ways of bridging the gaps, communication among specialists is often limited and unreliable. Professionals in the design game also express themselves through different media. For example, architects and engineers speak through drawings, financial officers through memoranda and spreadsheets. Administrators employ regulations and guidelines; system designers express themselves through technical memoranda and network diagrams.

PERSONAL STYLE

Personal styles influence how people approach problems, how they negotiate, how they make decisions, and how they interact with others in a common design process. Some players are active and explicit in pursuit of their objectives; others are passively aggressive. Some work cooperatively to achieve coherence among multiple organizational objectives, while others single-mindedly pursue individual goals. Many different schemes have been developed to impose some order on the proliferating variety of personal styles that influence how people approach issues, negotiate, and make decisions, as well as how they interact in a design game.[5]

ORGANIZATIONAL ROLE

The design game inevitably throws together people who occupy different organizational positions and roles. These juxtapositions are not always harmonious. Furthermore, different organizations vary with respect to how they deal with change.[6] The cultures that exist within organizations influence the abilities of their members to address and resolve problems. Thus the roles members occupy in these organizations are heavily inflected with behavioral attributes and performance expectations.[7] There are also power differences among players. Some players inevitably have more power than others; in some instances, power shifts in the course of the game. Players also differ in how they exercise power or react to the power of others.

In order to balance disparate objectives and resolve conflicts of values, we must bridge across the different languages, styles, and organizational roles of the players in the design game and learn to see more acutely how these factors enter into decision-making about the work environment. We should caution, however, that these diagnostic perspectives are heuristics that aid in learning more about the participants and should not be seen as stone tablets brought down from the mountaintop. The potential danger in their use is that they might freeze the views of individuals rather than letting those views (and behaviors) evolve over the course of the workplace-making process. The challenge for process architecture is to harness counterproductive patterns people bring to the workplace-making process and turn those patterns into positive forces.

The Game Board

We have found it useful to think of the players in their relative positions on a conceptual game board. The game board helps us understand players' positions in the game, their relationships with one another, and their self-interest. It also helps us understand when and how a variety of tools can be used effectively. Participants see the game board as a mirror, making them more aware of their current behavior and helping them think about more effective roles for themselves. The matrix in Color plate 4 shows how players may be arrayed on this board as *instigators* or *recipients*. Instigators play key roles in initiating a workplace-making project. Recipients are those affected in some way by the project—people with a legitimate stake in the outcome. Clearly, the two categories are not mutually exclusive: Owner-residents of a building may function as both instigators and recipients. In the Bank of Boston case, instigators included the top bank officials who posed the elimination of the securities business, as well as Peter Manning. Recipients included the professional and administrative staff of the divisions that were consolidated in the new facility.

The horizontal axis of this matrix—passive to active—represents the degree to which the participants take active roles in the process; the vertical axis—isolated to collaborative—indicates the degree to which players act in unison. As we pinpoint the roles instigators assume, and chart how their positions in the matrix change over the life of a project, it becomes possible to see developments within any particular design game and to compare one with another.

Playing the Game

Most games have winners and losers: Some players get more than others—and at the others' expense. Accordingly, architects, contractors and subcontractors, owners and managers, facilities managers, and building users may try to win or to avoid losing, adopting unilateral strategies of play. These strategies are generally counterproductive for the project as a whole. For example, a business unit might not be able to expand, or complementary business activities might not be able to co-locate to carry out an important research and development project.

There are many different styles of play in a design game, and these styles may be adopted by any player from time to time. Effective play, according to the norms of process architecture, requires that these differences be recognized and put to productive use. The objective is not to eliminate diversity or conflict but to harness them in creating a team that can make more productive decisions. When differences lead to conflict, it is easier for one party to dominate the others and for some actors to impede exploration of alternative ways of framing problems. When unresolved conflict among players persists, it causes confusion about the meanings of success, blocks organizational learning, and leaves many players baffled, if not downright angry at the lack of progress in workplace development.

The process architect can and will play many roles in the design game. Like the queen in a game of chess, he or she is able to engage other players in many ways. The process architect observes and diagnoses the situation; he or she may also engage the other players directly, both through collaboration and confrontation. Indeed, process architects have different ways of thinking about and acting out their roles. And those roles may shift from project to project. In one project, the role of the process architect may be to detect the agendas of key players and their criteria for success. In another, he or she may employ the Myers–Briggs test or something similar to help players understand their different decision-making and communications styles. In yet another case, the process architect may act as a sounding board, drawing out other players in ways that make their positions more public and accessible to negotiation and change. Regardless of the role he or she assumes, however, the process architect sees workplace-making as proceeding by means of engaging in dialogue, exposing false beliefs, eliciting underlying assumptions, dealing with conflicting ideas, aiming toward principled conflict resolution, and developing a new and productive synthesis. The process architect is not the only player who may assume a different role in the course of the design game. Experience indicates that any player can change his or her role or assume several roles.

Transforming the Game

More uniquely, the process architect sees transforming the game as integral to his or her professional approach. While others may take the situation and set of players as a given, or accept the problems of the current environment as stated, the effective process architect will challenge assumptions, bring in people with a legitimate stake in the workplace-making project who had been previously excluded, help others to change their roles, and create opportunities for players to see the problem in new ways—that is, the process architect will reframe the problem and help others to do so as well.

Process architecture places a high value on co-inventing multiple aspects of the workplace through the active and collaborative involvement of building users, workplace professionals, and other stakeholders. This does not make the design game disappear; rather, the style of play becomes more dynamic. Different perspectives inform and influence one another, leading to new directions and paths for discovery. Different ideas intersect, as did the ideas of the accounting factory and the transparent workspace in the Bank of Boston case. And one idea may move the process along different developmental paths simultaneously.

A dynamic, collaborative process of workplace design requires open and reliable communication among game players and an atmosphere conducive to discussion and resolution, where conflicting values can be placed on the table, confronted, and shaped in new ways. Real collaboration is hardly possible when the conflicting interests of important stakeholders remain below the surface or when communication among the players is fragmentary or distorted.

The design game can be transformed for the better or for the worse. Using the game board, it is possible to map projects as well as people. Compare the two diagrams in Color plate 5, which reflect contrasting situations. In the first diagram (of the Ainsley project, see Chapter 4), a project was dominated by a single instigator who chose not to engage many members of the stakeholder group. Instead, the instigator pursued his own vision of a prestigious building, and his actions had a substantial impact on the cost of the building, even forcing sacrifices of space and quality onto the inhabitants. The arrow points to the lower left corner of active but isolated decisions on the part of this important instigator. In the second diagram (of the Xerox project, see Chapter 6), the arrows point upward to the left top corner, where active collaboration was achieved by all involved in the project.

A LAYERED FRAMEWORK FOR PRACTICE

Because of the integration of all aspects of workplace-making, from the most detailed to the most general, we like to think of the practice of process architecture as operating within a framework consisting of three layers. The first is a conceptual *approach* to professional practice; the second is composed of *intervention strategies;* and the third contains

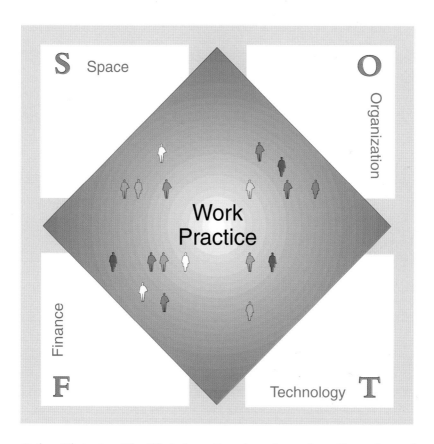

Color Plate 1 *The Workplace.* Four interdependent dimensions of the work environment—spatial, organizational, technological, and financial—constitute the workplace. They are in a dynamic relationship with one another: A change in one demands change in others.

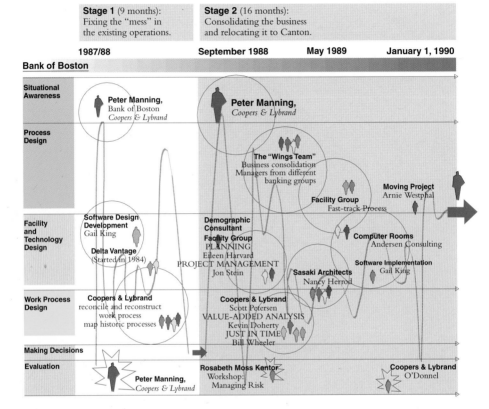

Stage 1 (9 months): Fixing the "mess" in the existing operations.

Stage 2 (16 months): Consolidating the business and relocating it to Canton.

1987/88 | September 1988 | May 1989 | January 1, 1990

Bank of Boston

Situational Awareness

Peter Manning, Bank of Boston *Coopers & Lybrand*

Peter Manning, *Coopers & Lybrand*

Process Design

The "Wings Team" Business consolidation Managers from different banking groups

Moving Project Arnie Westphal

Facility Group Fast-track Process

Facility and Technology Design

Software Design Development Gail King

Delta Vantage (Started in 1984)

Demographic Consultant Facility Group PLANNING Eileen Harvard PROJECT MANAGEMENT Jon Stein

Sasaki Architects Nancy Herrod

Computer Rooms Andersen Consulting

Software Implementation Gail King

Work Process Design

Coopers & Lybrand reconcile and reconstruct work process map historic processes

Coopers & Lybrand Scott Petersen VALUE-ADDED ANALYSIS Kevin Doherty JUST IN TIME Bill Wheeler

Making Decisions

Evaluation

Peter Manning, *Coopers & Lybrand*

Rosabeth Moss Kantor Workshop: Managing Risk

Coopers & Lybrand O'Donnel

Color Plate 2 *Bank of Boston: building the inside-outside team.* Peter Manning assembled a team of internal managers and employees, as well as outside consultants, to handle the design and implementation of the new facility. Three distinct constituencies inside the bank participated in planning the reconstruction of the securities processing business: the facility management group, employees who were going to work in the new environment, and a management team—the Wings Team (an allusion to the bank's eagle symbol)—created to guide the transition.

The Technical-Rational Approach

The consultant sees his or her role as gathering information from the occupants in order to build a basis for informed decision-making by the management. The management makes the decisions and implements the results. The feedback loops, from the occupants through the consultant, are of passive character. The function of the data is to validate or eliminate already-made notions or ideas, not to design new ones.

The Participatory Approach

The consultant sees him- or herself as someone who engages the occupants in describing the functionality of the new workplace. In this approach the consultant still acts as the only acknowledged expert, and the evaluation and the design are done solely by the professional, based on information gathered from the participants.

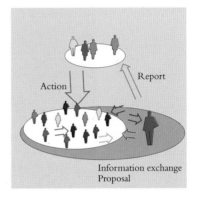

The Co-Design Approach

The consultant engages the stakeholders in a collaborative design process for the new work environment. The consultant relinquishes the sovereignty of being the sole expert, and is willing to confront his or her own expertise as designer with the recipients' specific expertise in how work is done. The consultant responds to the messiness such a situation creates, developing a problem-specific interaction with the client system.

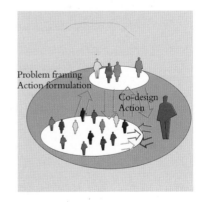

Color Plate 3 *Different professional approaches.*

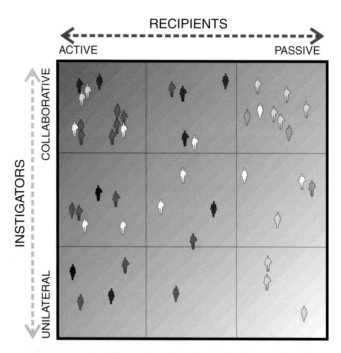

Color Plate 4 *The game board and the players.* Players are arrayed as instigators or recipients. Instigators play key roles in initiating a workplace project. Recipients are those affected by the project.

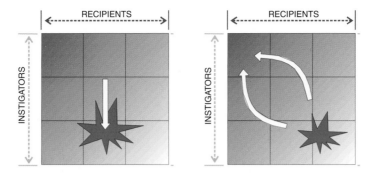

Color Plate 5 *Transforming the game.* The two diagrams reflect contrasting strategies and their outcomes. The first shows a project dominated by a single instigator who chose not to engage members of the stakeholder group. In the other project, active collaboration was achieved after an initial set of conflicts had blocked progress.

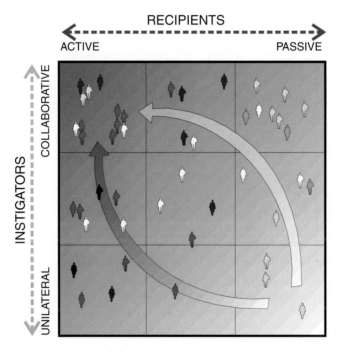

Color Plate 6 *Moving toward active collaboration.* The process architect creates a framework within which instigators can take a more collaborative stance in the process of problem framing and resolution, and, at the same time, recipients can participate more actively in the game. Shaping a creative tension between the instigators and the recipients is a necessary step in formulating and realizing an innovative workplace-making process.

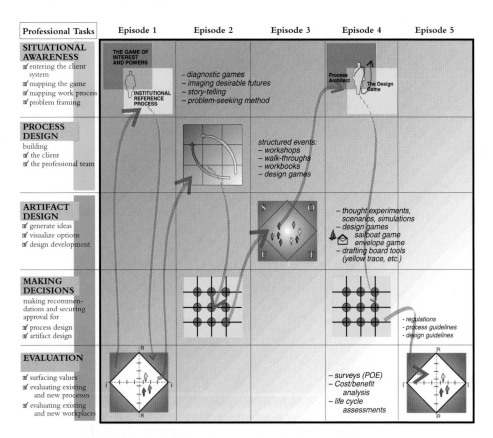

Professional Tasks	Episode 1	Episode 2	Episode 3	Episode 4	Episode 5
SITUATIONAL AWARENESS ☑ entering the client system ☑ mapping the game ☑ mapping work process ☑ problem framing	THE GAME OF INTEREST AND POWERS / INSTITUTIONAL REFERENCE PROCESS	– diagnostic games – imaging desirable futures – story-telling – problem-seeking method		Process Architect / The Design Game	
PROCESS DESIGN building ☑ the client ☑ the professional team			structured events: – workshops – walk-throughs – workbooks – design games		
ARTIFACT DESIGN ☑ generate ideas ☑ visualize options ☑ design development			S O R I	– thought experiments, scenarios, simulations – design games sailboat game envelope game – drafting board tools (yellow trace, etc.)	
MAKING DECISIONS making recommen- dations and securing approval for ☑ process design ☑ artifact design					- regulations - process guidelines - design guidelines
EVALUATION ☑ surfacing values ☑ evaluating existing and new processes ☑ evaluating existing and new workplaces				– surveys (POE) – Cost/benefit analysis – life cycle assessments	

Color Plate 7 *Tasks and challenges of process architecture.* In a design game, one event triggers another. The process might start with evaluating a given workplace; this in turn could lead to an event where the problem is reframed. Then a process can be designed to create a new workplace.

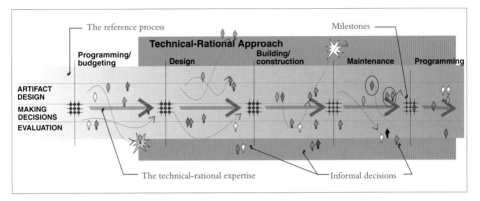

Technical-Rational Approach

The reference process is the set of institutional procedures intended to guide workplace-making. In *the technical-rational approach* the workplace-making process is regarded as fixed. Sequential milestones define a rigid skeleton for a specific workplace-making project. The technical-rational expert approaches professional tasks serially, progressing from one to the next. Informal decisions and design take place outside the outlined project plan and unrecognized by the reference process.

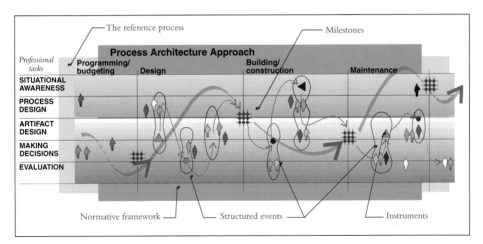

Process Architecture Approach

Process architecture provides a normative framework for designing *a strategy of intervention* that emphasizes collaborative engagement of all stakeholders and that addresses professional tasks simultaneously. This approach incorporates the informal and spontaneous activities that take place outside the technical-rational approach and connects them with the institutional reference process. Structured events focus the efforts of the design process, opening up the participants for new situational awareness, redesigning the process, and making decisions for the next steps. Each event is designed to move among several professional tasks as it progresses. The events are constructed from a repertoire of tools and instruments assembled by the process architect.

Color Plate 8 *Contrasting the approaches.*

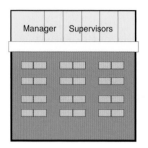

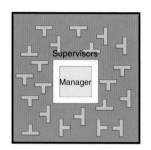

Bank of Boston: From Office to Support System for Work
The traditional pattern of spatial arrangement is to locate the manager in the corner office and the supervisors in offices remote from the core of activity of the business. Bank of Boston relocated the managers to the very center of the work.

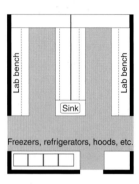

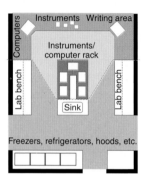

University Research Laboratories: Rethinking the R&D Environment
The stereotypical configuration of the wet lab represents the world of research before the introduction of digital tools that monitor and control experiments and analyze results. The laboratory of the future integrates the computer with the other critical tools of the scientist.

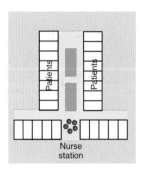

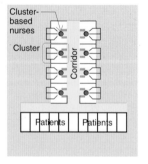

Cluster Design: Rethinking Health Care Facilities
The evolving cluster design represents an integrated set of spatial and organizational solutions to the problem of providing optimal health care to patients. The new spatial invention creates an opportunity to reexamine and redefine the traditional work process.

Color Plate 9 *Workplace transformation and typology of space.*

tools that consist of professionally structured events and the instruments employed within those events. These three make up a nested hierarchy where each layer is affected by the others. The integrated use of all three defines the practice of process architecture.

Approach

The first and most fundamental layer is composed of the principles and values that provide a normative, professionally sanctioned structure for the workplace-making process. Like the Samurai Bushido code or the code of chivalry adopted by King Arthur's Knights of the Round Table, the process architecture approach is fundamental to the way an organization or individual thinks and acts. It is committed to engaging stakeholders collaboratively in the enterprise of workplace-making, to drawing upon them for the expertise they can contribute to that process, and to maximizing the benefits that they can achieve from the workplace-making process. At the same time, it is committed to linking workplace-making to organizational and institutional, and, if possible, societal development.

When a design game is played within the approach of process architecture, it has four fundamental characteristics. (1) It moves toward the objective of dynamic coherence. (2) It extracts benefits from uneven development. (3) There is an ongoing process of design inquiry. (4) Its participants are collaboratively engaged.

Let's discuss each of these characteristics.

DYNAMIC COHERENCE

Dynamic coherence is an evolving match between the changing work process and its workplace environment. Dynamic coherence depends upon establishing a relationship among the four principal interdependent environments for work: spatial, organizational, financial, and technological. When an organization sets out to transform its work process, it commits itself to a transformation of all of these four dimensions of its work environment.

UNEVEN DEVELOPMENT

Effective workplace-making follows a path of uneven development in which innovation in one aspect of the workplace creates new potentials or demands for innovation in other areas. For example, the rapid development of corporate intranets, groupware, and video conferencing technologies has outpaced development in how companies are organized and how their workspaces are arranged. The mere fact that the technologies now exist compels change in the other areas in order to fully tap their potential to support work.

The process of uneven development is akin to what economist Albert O. Hirschman called *unbalanced growth*.[8] In his early writings on economic development, Hirschman argued against the comprehensive growth theorists of his time, pointing out that if developing countries were capable of progressing simultaneously on all fronts they wouldn't be undeveloped in the first place. Rather, Hirschman thought, development should proceed naturally—and by policy—through initiatives in one area that create pressures, demands, or incentives for development in others. A gap, bottleneck, or tension in the economy stimulates growth and development elsewhere because of the mechanisms that connect one area of the economy to another. Indeed, it is difficult to think of progress in any human endeavor in the absence of an unbalanced situation.

In seeing situations as unbalanced and recognizing that the imbalance can be utilized in order to effect change, the process architect recognizes opportunities to achieve substantial improvements in workplace-making.

DESIGN INQUIRY

Uneven development of a workplace is a situation in which intelligent human beings, engaged in transaction with their environment, create a new or modified artifact through collective thought and action. This process, however, does not fit the familiar technical-rational approach: It does not begin with a clear objective and proceed systematically, through increasingly specific choices, toward a final design. Rather, like a pinball game, it follows a bumpy course, bouncing back and forth between participants, to its final resolution. Innovation in one area (e.g., technology) gives rise to unanticipated tensions and difficulties. These, in turn, may be addressed, and perhaps resolved, in new rounds of concerted thought and action. We call this process *design inquiry,* a term borrowed from the philosopher John Dewey.[9]

By inquiry, Dewey means something more than the colloquial notion of investigation. For him, inquiry is a process of intertwined thought and action that begins with doubt about a situation that is confusing, complex, or full of conflict: a "messy" situation.[10] The process of inquiry moves through thinking and doing to a definition of the problem and to its resolution through action. Problem resolution, in turn, generates new doubts, which must be addressed through further rounds of the same inquiry process.

Dewey conceived of the inquirer as *within* the situation and in transaction with it. It was the situation that he saw as inherently doubtful or problematic. Such situations block the free flow of action; they come labeled with the description of a problem to be solved. To get from a messy situation to a solvable problem, one must engage in problem-setting. Both problem-setting and problem-solving are, as Dewey saw it, inherently social activities.

Stretching Dewey's definition, we could think of design inquiry as a term describing the kind of inquiry that consists of making an artifact—either a tangible object (a building), an intangible object (a work routine), or a technological product (a computer-based system for sharing information coupled with instructions for its use). By definition, design inquiry takes place under conditions of complexity and uncertainty. *Complexity* means that many variables are in play at once; these variables are interrelated such that a move intended to satisfy one is likely to have unintended effects on others. *Uncertainty* refers to an inability to make sense of a situation—because we confront more information than we can handle, because the available information is too sparse to support a sound conclusion, or because the environment is changing in ways we cannot predict.

Whatever its starting point, design inquiry is a rolling process in which now one, now another of many interdependent facets of a problematic situation passes through a zone of imbalance. Design moves made on the basis of one view of the problematic situation generate new phenomena. Thus, over a period of time, individuals play the design game. Diagnosis and mapping of their experiences in the game lead naturally to a new or greater understanding of problems, constraints, resources, and so forth. That understanding spurs a reframing of the problematic situation, which leads to some form of transformation. Like an expanding spiral, this cycle of playing, understanding, reframing, and transformation continues over time.

The concept of design inquiry is a very general notion of how we make sense of the world around us. It can be seen in many human activities where thinking and doing come together: how a child plays with a set of blocks, or how a physician deals with a patient. Discovery, experimentation, and invention are parts of the process. In process architecture we distinguish two paths for design inquiry. The first is searching for dynamic coherence between a changing work process and its workplace; the second is achieving an understanding of how to benefit the organization as a whole through the workplace-making process.

Within a given workplace, a change in work practice or in an aspect of the work environment calls for further changes in the others. In the Bank of Boston case, managers of the stock and securities processing division introduced new software for the stock processing operation. More or less in parallel with this, Coopers & Lybrand consultants introduced their just-in-time production methods. In combination, these innovations transformed the stock processing operations, enabling Peter Manning to implement his new image of the business, the accounting factory. This new image of the operation led to the formulation of new specifications for space, technology, and organization in the work environment—later realized in the bank's Canton facility.

Cases presented later in this volume highlight the role played by new spatial design ideas in the reshaping of the technological support and the organization of work, and also show that any one of these environments for work[11] may be the arena in which change is initiated. In examples such as these, an initial round of design inquiry into a specific feature of the work situation generates a tension, and an opportunity, that leads to a new round of design inquiry. This does not occur, however, unless the potential for further change is perceived by people in the system and converted to active demand. Facilitating this process is one of the most important contributions of process architecture.

The dialectic of design inquiry also plays a role in the larger process of organization development. Here is an idealized description of such an organizational design dialectic:

Initiating the cycle is an imbalance between performance and expectation—performance of the workforce and expectation, for example, on the part of the leadership. This sense of imbalance may result from a growing, generalized perception of shortcomings in the spatial and technological conditions for work, a breakthrough in work practice whose implications cannot be tolerated within existing spatial and technological conditions, a loss of position in the marketplace, or a perception of a new market niche into which the company ought to move.

The next phase uncovers the potential for change by looking inward through assessment of previously latent dissatisfactions and awareness of the potential for improvement in both the spatial and the technological conditions. It then uncovers potential by looking outward to the new external conditions the work group is supposed to meet. In order for the group to become aware of the potential for change, this process of uncovering is necessarily accompanied by imagining possible interventions into the spatial and technological conditions of the workplace. These design possibilities are an integral part of the discovery process.

The last phase is modification of work practice in ways that improve it within the newly enlarged potential of its spatial and technological conditions. These interventions will solve some problems and create others. The process architect does not shy away from interventions that create new problems, but instead uses them to propel the next episode. Once the potential of the changed spatial and technological conditions has been realized, the same cycle of imbalance may begin again.

COLLABORATION AND ENGAGEMENT

For the process architect, workplace-making requires levels of collaboration and engagement that exceed the usual norms of the workplace professions. This does not require one set of players to give up its agenda or cede power to others. What it does require is a process of the type shown in Color plate 6, in which all the players move from passive to active involvement and from unilateral to collaborative design inquiry.

When key stakeholders are active and involved, the process is more responsive to the needs of the organization and tensions among participants tend to be productive. Our cases suggest that a design process consistent with these norms yields superior outcomes. Intervention should therefore aim at mobilizing efforts to make the process active and collaborative, moving it from the dead-end, lower right quadrant of the matrix into the vital, complex, and often combative top left quadrant.

Tensions and disruptions can be productive, but only if they arise within an institutional framework strong enough to support them. That framework must feature open communication and trust that legitimizes collaborative inquiry and mobility in the roles people play. Beyond these very general requirements, the boundaries between different disciplines and professions and between professionals and workplace users must be flexible and porous.

Workplace professionals must make a place at the table for members of the workforce as well as managers, and help both groups to articulate and develop design ideas, synthesize those ideas, and create alternative design principles from which they can make informed choices. Such collaborative involvement in the design or redesign of a workplace makes the most of all participants' knowledge of work practices. If participants are engaged in developing a new design, they are more likely to be committed to its implementation; even more important, they learn how to improve work and workplace on a continuing basis.

Just as workplace professionals bring different approaches to a given project of design inquiry, so the stakeholders who enter into that process display a variety of attitudes as to how they will try to shape the project or allow it to shape them. Some actors may come with open minds, displaying a willingness to accept whatever procedures are laid down by the formal rules of the organization or the dictates of the workplace professional. Some may bring their own approaches. Others may begin with a wait-and-see attitude, holding off their decision as to how they will play until they see how the process unfolds and how the others behave. The stakeholders must recognize these conflicts in approach, find ways to surface them, and introduce the essential elements of process architecture.

Before practitioners of different disciplines of workplace-making can collaborate effectively, they must learn to transcend the boundaries of their specialized compartments. Space professionals must learn enough about the expertise of their counterparts—the business unit manager, the information systems specialist, the logistics expert, and so forth—to understand what each has to contribute to workplace design. This is no easy task.

Top leaders of the organization must take their share of responsibility for process design and project outcome; that is, they must be collaboratively engaged in matters that have to do with their position and authority in the organization. We have seen few instances where a workplace-making process is effective in the absence of leaders of the organization taking responsibility. In the Bank of Boston case, Peter Manning's role serves as a prototype of leadership, demonstrating close connection between the functions that need to be fulfilled by that leadership (for example, mobilizing resources around a unifying image of an accounting factory) and the functions delegated to process managers.

Intervention Strategy

Process architecture can start whenever an organization detects a problem or opportunity and chooses to open itself to the possibility of changing its workplace. Then the process architect can help the organization to address, and often to reframe, its problems. Effective workplace practitioners, both outside consultants and inside managers, recognize workplace-making not only as a way of supporting improved work practices but as a powerful form of organizational intervention. This recognition contains two challenges: to see the organizational meaning of these interventions and to understand how work is or should be organized and accomplished within the workplaces practitioners program, design, and build.

Reiterating and expanding on the earlier definition, the workplace-making process is the way in which stakeholders in the creation or recreation of a workplace move through the stages of programming, design, building, and maintenance/management to bring a new workplace into being. In some organizations there are codified processes for dealing with these activities. These reference processes are rules and procedures intended to guide how a workplace-making process should unfold and how stakeholders should act. They specify, for example, criteria for design decisions and the forums within which such decisions will be made, or by what measures and methods building costs will be controlled. These reference processes incorporate, explicitly or implicitly, a set of principles, values, and frames that reflect an underlying approach.

Large organizations that undertake many workplace-making projects generally codify their reference processes. In organizations where workplace creation is a rare event, the rules specifying who gets involved, when, and in what capacity are generally informal. Organizations new to workplace-making tend to begin with no reference process of any kind.

Reference processes have life cycles. At a certain point in an organization's history, its reference process may become outdated and degenerate, incapable of producing beneficial outcomes. When there is a perceived mismatch between a given workplace and the evolving ways in which work is actually done, such a "canned" reference process tends to reinforce the old ways of workplace-making. Then the practitioners who follow the rules of the outdated process tend to forget to inquire; they hold onto fixed procedures, which produce yesterday's workplace, instead of engaging the urgent challenge of imagining the future.

The following activities are those we regard as central to the practice of process architecture. We view them as a menu for the creation of a strategy of intervention (Color plate 7).

1. *Situational awareness.* Entering the client system; mapping how work is currently done; diagnosing the problems of the workplace; mapping how the existing design process works; diagnosing its problems; setting specifications for the workplace, including its spatial arrangements and the objects within it; enabling all participants in the process to become similarly aware.

2. *Process design.* Building the client system and the professional team; creating alternate images of the design process; formulating and implementing strategies of change; learning from the experience of the design process; strategizing how to play the design game.

3. *Artifact design.* Designing the actual workplace; visualizing options; generating and perfecting ideas.

4. *Making Decisions.* Deciding on elements of workplace design; deciding on elements of the design process; securing approvals and continuously relegitimizing the approach.

5. *Evaluation.* Evaluating the existing workplace and work practices; evaluating the existing and the new or altered design
process; evaluating problems and practices and, if necessary,
reframing both; evaluating the new or altered workplace; when
appropriate, initiating a new cycle of workplace-making.

In practice we have found it useful to recognize that, while all of
these activities associated with workplace-making must occur, they
also must recur if triggered by circumstances or necessity. In more
traditional views of workplace-making, these (or similar activities)
are thought to happen once, sequentially in time, for each project.
But we believe their sequence is not rigid. On the contrary, all tend
to remain alive throughout the continuing life of workplace-making
and remaking. Leaps occur, both forward and backward. Activities
may be revisited as a consequence of learning. For example, the
client system may change, after a process architect's initial entry, as
the result of what is learned during the process of problem framing;
issues raised during the implementation process may provoke a rede-
finition of the problem, thereby generating new alternatives; and the
strategy of forcing preliminary decisions may serve to promote a
more adequate framing of the problem. The format of written text
requires us to present these challenges in the form of a list, even
though we would prefer to describe them more graphically in the
image of a game of soccer or pinball, whose moves are fluid but neither random nor uncontrolled.

Achieving situational awareness among participants cannot be a
one-shot event, but must continue over time to grow in depth and
breadth as they gather information and gain new insights. By-
products of this phase may include technical studies. The primary
product, however, is a growing understanding on the part of the
stakeholders of the workplace-making process, the circumstances
that compel it, the values held by key players, what is at stake, and
who will benefit and how.

Process design must be mindful of the existing design game. If the design game is changed substantially over the course of time, process design must be revisited and reworked. In some instances the intervenor must try to create a client system, knitting together fragmented organizations or previously uncoordinated fragments of a single organization in a larger field. Process design does not happen all at once, nor is it wholly rational. It happens repeatedly and is subject to renegotiation. Client systems are conservative in their attachment to existing ways of doing things. While it may be necessary to surprise or even shock the participants early in the process to shake them loose from favored ideas and beliefs, it may only be possible to design a more radical process later, when the project is under way. Finally, because workplace-making is strongly linked to organizational change, the design of the process for workplace-making must be guided by the norms and principles appropriate to change in that organization.

In artifact design, the process architect works with stakeholders in generating ideas for the workplace, illustrating suggestions, and testing propositions. For the work space, typical products of this task are principles for design of the work space, designs for specific parts of the work space, and more diagrammatic ideas for new types of work spaces or elements thereof. Equivalent artifacts for the other environments for work would be new management structure, new communications protocols, new meeting types and schedules, and plans for the incorporation of new groups into the information flow for the organizational environment; new incentive programs for teamwork, new product objectives, a project to explore a new market, or new levels of efficiency or speed in production mandated by management for the financial environment; and new communications software, new methods of data storage and sharing, and new computer-based display devices for assisting in face-to-face meetings for the technological environment.

As discussed earlier in this chapter, the design inquiry of process architecture is about two paths: One is searching for dynamic coherence between a changing work process and its workplace, and the other is achieving an understanding of how to benefit the organization as a whole through the workplace-making process. Making decisions occurs along each path throughout the process of workplace-making. To keep the process effectively on both paths requires that ideas about each path be revisited from time to time. If the organization's leadership does not do this, then the process architect—supporting or collaborating with stakeholders—needs to ensure that it is done. Process architecture needs to cultivate relations at enough levels of the organization to commit decision-makers and workplace stakeholders to the success of the process. These processes need to be shaped within the context of the organization's culture and against the context of the design game in play and the way in which it might be transformed. We do not find that there is a "best" model applicable for all groups. Just because decisions may be reached in a consensus-driven, inclusive manner doesn't guarantee that they can be achieved. As a corollary, a strong leader, like Manning, can push through good ideas because he or she has the power and resources to do so.

The process of evaluation and learning starts at the beginning of the project and continues as knowledge from previous projects is brought into the process and as the stakeholders are helped to understand the significance of their own knowledge and experience. Periodic evaluation can serve to tie the several phases of a project together in a learning cycle. An effective process architect will get the team to draw upon this accumulated learning as a platform for moving forward. The client group and other stakeholders, with the support of the process architect, continuously evaluate the existing environments for work, the design process, and the artifacts it produces, seeking to discover what works. Evaluation and learning are continuous and quite messy, because the very meaning of "what works" and the criteria to be used to make those judgments are open to question and determination as part the design inquiry. The uneven pattern in which the workplace develops means that each element of workplace-making (SOFT) impacts the effectiveness of the others, thereby requiring that evaluation criteria and processes must be shaped anew for each project and for each phase of each project (Color plate 8).

Tools

Process architects design and use tools in order to perform tasks of design inquiry. Tools are keyed to the first layer—the approach—and are answerable to its norms and purposes. They are deployed in accordance with the second layer—the strategy of intervention. Tools consist of structured events and instruments.

STRUCTURED EVENTS

Events are replicable social activities organized around a common core of procedures.[12] These activities help participants to develop a common language for sharing experiences that lead to greater mutual understanding and include walking through one's workplace (walk-throughs), floor meetings, and sessions during which participants render their ideas in graphic form. These events should have clear objectives—for example, that certain stakeholders will meet others, or that a particular group will be exposed to the work of another group. The theater provides a useful metaphor for workplace-making events. The stage must be carefully designed to support the desired situation; the actions, music, and costumes must be right. The director does things that make the presentation expressive and communicative and related to the contemporary world of theatergoers.

If, for example, on a walk-through, people are taken into a space that is intended for collaborative activity, but that has all of its desks bolted to the floor and electrical and computer connections locked into those desks, the conversation moves easily to the contradiction between the purposes associated with the work practice and the limitations of the spatial setting.

INSTRUMENTS

Instruments are tools specifically designed to survey workers, to gather or to display information, to facilitate meetings, or to surface ideas or preferences. Structured events are the settings within which instruments are utilized. Most events require the use of one or more instruments; others, such as monthly meetings, may use only one, like *Roberts' Rules of Order,* that is so familiar as to be barely recognizable as an instrument.

Consider a meeting (an event) of all the residents of a floor in a building, organized around a slide show of photos (an instrument) taken during a building walk-through (another event that occurred in the past). The slides act as screens onto which participants can project their thoughts and feelings about the workplace. The slides elicit information about how participants look at their environment: what they like or dislike about it, how they understand it, what they regard as important or unimportant, safe or dangerous, irritating or comforting. At the same time, the slide show stimulates the participants to communicate understandings and views of the environment that may not have been made public before.

Instruments like slide shows, used consistently within the framework of process architecture, contrast with instruments like the survey research methods used in more conventional ways. Slide shows and the like have greater potential for getting people out of themselves and facilitating group discussion that leads to comparing of perceptions and to surfacing of different views. Although survey research methods implicitly recognize building inhabitants as experts on their own work environment, they relegate aggregation and analysis of individual survey responses to a professional expert, who typically communicates results to a decision-maker. Nevertheless, surveys can give added weight to less powerful participants in a design game and can be combined with other instruments. For example, survey statistics can be combined with information derived from group discussions centered on a slide show. The selection of instruments, and the expectations held for them, should be integrated into the event in which the instruments are to be used, and the event must be carefully structured both to accommodate the instruments and to be in keeping with the intervention strategy.

In Chapter 3 we examine two cases that illustrate uneven development of a workplace and that demonstrate the inertia of stereotyped ideas about environments. In Chapter 4 we illustrate the design game in play in four cases, two of which reveal aspects of process architecture. In Chapter 5 we discuss the practice of process architecture and the tools practitioners employ.

3

From Stereotype
to Dynamic Coherence

Old images of the workplace tend to persist, even when they are mismatched to changing patterns of work and new technologies. Institutions as well as individuals tend to design space for old patterns of work: the way things have always been done. People have images in their heads about how their workplace can be improved, but these images are often outdated, reflecting the familiar world of the existing workplace—the office, the building, or the equipment to which workers have long since adapted. It is difficult for most people to visualize how work is changing, will change, or could change, and what attributes of physical and technological arrangements will support or interfere with that change. As the nature of work changes, triggered in some instances by the introduction of new technology, the work setting tends to lag behind, frozen in the mold of what we expect a workplace to look like, because we see it, in Marshall McLuhan's words, "through a rearview mirror."

Process architecture helps people break out of stereotypes and take a fresh look at their work environment. It does this by making the work through which the organization produces goods and services the prime focus of design inquiry. It explores the relationship between work and the physical spaces within which work is done. Movement toward new visions of dynamic coherence is uneven, as actual or potential changes in the workplace stimulate complementary changes in work process and vice versa.

This chapter uses two case studies to examine this uneven development that leads to a break from stereotypes. The first study examines a contemporary project: the redesign, after computers enter the workplace, of a traditional wet laboratory used for biological research. The second involves the design of nursing clusters in several health care institutions. This case took place several years ago, but it remains instructive today because of the way the architect collaborated with stakeholders to implement several concepts that were new and innovative in their day (though they may seem unremarkable now). This case is also of interest because it illustrates how the designer spent years learning from research and precedents while reflecting on his own practice and engaging health administrators and end users as his collaborators in design inquiry.

THE WET LABORATORY

The nature of work in the modern biological and chemical research laboratory has changed dramatically over the past ten years, but the spatial layout remains as it has been for decades. The concepts described here for a new prototypical laboratory were developed over a period of three years by a team led by Turid Horgen. These efforts took place in three organizations. The first (in 1993) evaluated a research building at the Massachusetts Institute of Technology; the second (in 1995) created a prototypical design for the European Center for Marine Microbiology Research at Bergen University in Norway; the third (in 1996) produced a plan for refurbishing laboratories for the Harvard-MIT Division of Health Sciences Technology.

The traditional wet lab used for biological or chemical research is based on a model developed long before the introduction of the computer into the researcher's everyday life. This laboratory is filled with rows of benches overhung with cabinets for glassware and other small equipment. Water, gas, vacuum, and compressed air spigots are conveniently at hand. Hoods and large equipment (freezers or gas containers) are set in the rear. The lab bench—where the chemist or biologist prepares and conducts experiments, observes results, and records results into a notebook—is the main workplace. It is also the place where the researcher is likely to discuss problems or puzzling results with colleagues, or teach an apprentice how to develop an experiment, even while keeping an eye on an experiment in progress.

Computers have significantly altered the nature of work in the wet lab. Some automate traditional laboratory work—monitoring experiments and processing experimental data; others replace certain experiments entirely through simulation. In addition, computers give the researcher access to large databases and provide real-time communication with remote laboratories.

Throughout the world, computer technology has generally been introduced into spaces designed before that technology became ubiquitous. Since computer equipment consumes a great deal of space—and old pieces of equipment are rarely retired—the work of the modern researcher must often be spread out among many different places. The researcher moves from one specialized room to another, or runs back and forth between experiments in the lab and a separate office where reports are written. ("Office" computers are often considered incompatible with the conditions of the wet lab.)

The 1993 study at MIT was occasioned when the senior vice president for administration took the initiative to look more closely at the efficiency of the existing laboratory buildings for biological research. Several senior research scientists—among them program group leaders such as the head of the Cancer Research Center—worked together with design consultants to help their groups understand how researchers could physically accommodate computers and also large, specialized, and expensive equipment in the work areas. The traditional layout in laboratories, developed for cost reasons to accommodate a clear division between dry and wet spaces and highly functional for its day, was no longer satisfactory when computers and other equipment filled up the spaces—but the faculty could not point to an obvious solution. The initial evaluation led to a better understanding of the problem by the group.

The design team involved the researchers in several exercises to help them open their thinking about how the labs might be used in the future. As a first step, the researchers were taken on a walk through the biology building. As they progressed, they periodically stopped to observe and discuss the work that was going on, noting how the physical space was designed and used. The facilitator-guide encouraged the researchers to comment specifically about what they saw in the labs they visited and to relate their observations to how they used their own laboratory space. Comments were recorded, photographs were taken, and sketches were made of the places and the physical arrangements that triggered each comment.

Several days after the building walk-through, the group met to review what it had observed and discovered. To provoke conversation, the designers presented a slide show of places seen and discussed during the walk-through. As the researchers viewed and discussed the slides and heard what they had said during the tour, they readily identified, for the first time, how the residues of old work practices were reflected in their laboratory spaces. Generations of equipment sat side by side with no apparent logic. The spaces had a Rube Goldberg look: Equipment was stuffed into every available area or placed atop other equipment.

Many of the researchers were surprised by the ubiquitousness of the computer in both wet and dry lab environments. Computers were embedded in all sorts of laboratory equipment, making even traditional instruments—pH meters, analytical balances, and spectrometers—smarter and faster. The researchers were also surprised to learn how much time they actually spent moving between the wet lab and the offices where they wrote their notes and met with co-workers.

As they compared the slides to their previously discussed wish lists for new space, the researchers noted a striking similarity. What they wanted was not much different than what they already had, or what they had already seen in another lab—just minor improvements to the existing work arrangements, such as larger space and faster computers. Mirroring the findings in most market research, what the researchers wanted was simply more of the same crowded space that had built up, somewhat willy-nilly, over the years (Figure 3.1). As is apparent in the photo, the costly, specially equipped lab bench still partially fulfills the old function, but partially becomes an expensive parking place for sophisticated lab computers and other instruments that could just as well sit in racks; in addition, the scientist might squeeze a desk computer onto the windowsill in order to use it for his or her logs.

While this initial evaluation session was important to the design team's understanding of the problem, their breakthrough concept design was conceived during a subsequent project involving researchers from the University of Bergen in Norway. In that instance, the assignment was to develop a prototype biochemical wet laboratory. The refurbishing of one floor of the Bergen Technology Center would house the European Center for Marine Microbiology Research and could function as a full-scale experiment for the new clinical research center at the university, already on the drawing board. Here, too, the design team engaged the researchers in design inquiry. Once again a walk-through of the work space was followed by discussion centered around a slide show. The results were similar to the MIT experience.

The next day, with the discussion fresh in their minds, the researchers were brought together and asked to draw their ideal work

Figure 3.1 The computer enters the laboratory work environment.

environment at whatever level of aggregation they wished—the workstation, the office, or the laboratory. They then explained their drawings to each other.

The third step for the Bergen group was playing the cardboard game, an activity that gave every participant an opportunity to explore the principles he or she thought should underpin the transformation of the traditional wet laboratory into a combined wet and dry laboratory (Figure 3.2). One alternative shows partial improvement of the existing prototype, developed in the drawing session; the other shows a breakthrough design developed in the cardboard game. The game consisted of a collection of cardboard pieces in different colors and sizes. The participants were free to decide what these represented in terms of laboratory space, equipment, or people. Working in groups of four, they used the pieces as building blocks to arrange the laboratory in terms of proximity of functions and desirable communication links. Periodically, the facilitator called temporary halts to the play during which each group explained its evolving ideas to the others.

These exercises provided the insights the designers needed to create a new vision for the laboratory. The drawings and the cardboard game indicated three types of change: slight improvement, partial change, and breakthrough designs. From this information, the designers identified and analyzed different concepts, took them apart, and rebuilt them into different patterns that integrated office, laboratory, and meeting spaces. As an alternative to the traditional configuration,

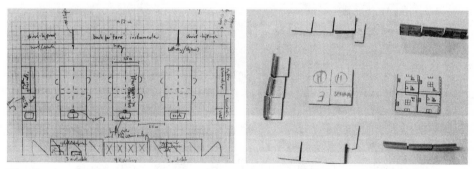

Figure 3.2   The two types of laboratory developed by the scientists in Bergen.

the lab bench was replaced by a rack of computers used exclusively to control and read experiments and print results. Benches and storage cabinets for glassware and other items were reduced in number and pushed to the sides. Computers for entering data, filing notes, and recording ideas were integrated into the lab. For example, laptop computers and light instruments were placed on a lower desk along the windows. Additional office space was created adjacent to the laboratory. Old and new design concepts for the wet lab are shown in Figure 3.3. In the alternative image of the lab, the computers influence the layout, which combines three traditional functions: office, dry lab, and wet lab.

The opportunity to verify the concepts developed in Bergen presented itself when the team was engaged in planning exercises with biology researchers at the Harvard-MIT Division for Health Science Technology. The designers started their work by listening to the laboratory's scientists as they described what they wanted in new labo-

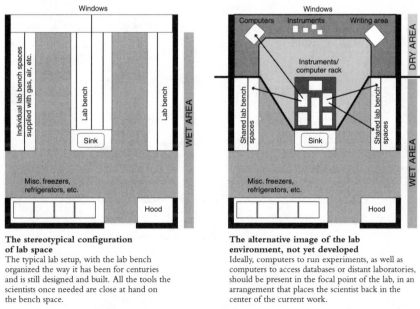

The stereotypical configuration of lab space
The typical lab setup, with the lab bench organized the way it has been for centuries and is still designed and built. All the tools the scientists once needed are close at hand on the bench space.

The alternative image of the lab environment, not yet developed
Ideally, computers to run experiments, as well as computers to access databases or distant laboratories, should be present in the focal point of the lab, in an arrangement that places the scientist back in the center of the current work.

Figure 3.3   Concepts of lab environment.

ratory spaces. Significantly, respondents generally took the conventional layout for granted. The ideal laboratory environment of one senior researcher illustrates this point:

> Up in New Hampshire, where I live, I drive by the evolving dream house of a family who lived in a trailer. It is set in the woods and made of logs. It has commanding views of the hill beyond. And it looks exactly like a very large trailer. So I hesitate to tell you that my dream lab looks like the lab I have now.

The next step was to engage the laboratory workers in an exercise consisting of describing one day of laboratory work. Each researcher explained to a colleague what he or she did on a typical day. As one scientist told his partner:

> Sophisticated computation is increasingly at the center of my research, not only for analyzing and displaying data, but for real-time control of experiments. For example, my transdermal drug delivery research involves pulsating skin samples with high voltage and measuring both the skin's passive electrical properties and the fluxes of two fluorescent molecules.

The scientist's next statement actually echoed the same need identified by the scientists in Bergen:

> This type of research requires both wet lab and dry lab environments close at hand. Increasingly, all sorts of laboratory instrumentation contains computers—smart instruments that do more things faster than the familiar pH meters, analytical balances, spectrometers, etc., of just a few years ago. My use of computers is rapidly expanding, and space that combines wet and dry environments is becoming essential.

These comments and those of other participants were summarized and distributed to all lab workers. A meeting was then held during which the paired members of each team took turns interviewing one another. The facilitator then consolidated all of the comments and displayed them on the wall. One conclusion drawn from this exercise was that the computers currently housed in a central resource room were very important to everyone. These computers, all concluded, should be integrated into the laboratory itself. As one researcher put it, "Laboratory space should be designed with the recognition that computers are an inseparable part of science."

At both MIT and Bergen University, the design of the wet laboratory continued to evolve and the scientists who participated in the design exercises pressed to have their laboratories developed on the model of the prototype designs they had created. The effort they had made helped free them of traditional visions of the laboratory. They no longer perceived their future needs by looking back at yesterday's practice, but by developing a better understanding of how work is done today.

The creation, over time, of a new workplace concept suited to evolving, more desirable work practice is also a theme of the case that follows. Again, new and superior design alternatives emerged from collaboration between workplace designers and the people who worked in the space under study.

Toward Cluster Design

By the 1970s, when this case began, Zack Rosenfield already had over twenty years of experience in the field of health care facility design. He and his colleagues had experimented with ways of bringing nurses closer to patients in order to make the nurses' work more efficient and to make patients feel more secure and in greater control of their treatment while in the hospital. As Rosenfield described it, his firm was "always trying to invent new nursing unit forms that would bring the nurse and her supplies and tools closer to the patient." He believed that optimal health care was linked to a nurse's ability to work so close to a patient that the nurse would see "the whites of the patient's eyes." Rosenfield's efforts were informed by inquiries on other fronts. During roughly the same period, John Thompson of Yale University had been evaluating hospital designs in terms of the time it took nurses to perform routine tasks; these measures were reflected in his Yale Index. Meanwhile, Gordon Friesen, a Canadian hospital administrator, had been working with many hospitals to implement *nurse servers,* a supply system of his invention that put important supplies close to patients. None of these separate efforts, however, had produced fully satisfactory results. Rosenfield's efforts did not change the way work was done; Thompson's ideas could not be readily translated into design; and Friesen's new logistical systems were expensive and caused a variety of new spatial problems.

But, as sometimes happens, separate lines of inquiry crossed, creating opportunities for remarkable insight and invention. Thus, work on these different fronts eventually bore fruit in the mid-1970s, when Rosenfield's partner Herbert Bienstock and Norm Girard, CEO of Somerville Hospital in Somerville, Massachusetts, collaborated in designing a hospital unit configuration that decentralized nurses and support services into five-bed clusters. The impetus for this development followed a trip Bienstock and Girard had taken to Canada to evaluate Friesen's nurse server units. Because Friesen's design virtually eliminated the time a nurse spent getting supplies, it scored very well on the Yale Index. However, it soon became apparent that the relative success or failure of this system was almost entirely dependent upon an organizational variable. If the hospital's materials management department was competent and efficient, the design worked well; if not, nurses capitulated and the nurse servers were abandoned. Even more troubling was the fact that nurse servers increased construction costs without reducing operating costs. Hence, there was little in the nurse server design to assure consistent improvement over traditional hospital systems.

On the return flight from Canada, Bienstock and Girard attempted to produce the rudiments of a new design—one that combined what they had just learned with earlier designs. As they reflected on their observations of Friesen's less-than-satisfactory nurse servers, they sketched on the back of a cocktail napkin a unit configuration that decentralized nurses and support services. Beginning with the premise that the nurses should be closer to the patients—with patient rooms grouped in clusters, each served by a single nurse—Bienstock and Girard considered how these rooms would be serviced. They asked themselves how many patients a single nurse could care for, and agreed that five was the most. They sketched out plans of fives with supply and utilities functions in the middle, forming a "double-corridor racetrack unit."[1] Upon examination, they decided that the opaque core of the racetrack was just in the way, and folded the napkin in a large pleat so that the core disappeared. Faced then with the problem of where to put the displaced core functions, they widened certain parts here and there, with the idea that many of the core's storage spaces could be replaced with carts that would service about five patients each.

Because the design took advantage of visual connections, it was important that nurses be where they could see their patients. As Rosenfield described their thinking, "They arranged that the nurse would not sit down. She is there to work. So at first they didn't give her a chair. After a while they gave her a stand-up desk, and then they gave her a fold-away stool under the desk, and it eventually became an ordinary desk with a chair."

Jumping back and forth between changes in spatial arrangements and work practices, Girard and Bienstock arrived at a new solution by the time their plane landed in Boston. Working together in the days and weeks that followed, they tuned and refined their idea, which eventually became the Somerville hospital design as well as the prototype for the Link Pavilion at Hackensack Hospital in Hackensack, New Jersey.

The new spatial expression for the relationship between the nurse and the patient came to be named the *cluster design*. Instead of the traditional central corridor that connected nursing stations but separated nurses from patients, there was a cluster of five rooms with line-of-sight contact between nurses and patients (Figure 3.4). This change could not be effected, however, until another problem was addressed and solved. The cluster design called for rethinking of the supply storage areas, which in their old form would have interrupted the nurses' visual contact with their patients. The solution was to return to concepts developed earlier by Friesen and eliminate storage areas in favor of frequent supply deliveries.

Clustering Patient Rooms around Nursing Stations

Rosenfield referred to the process of designing the nursing cluster units in terms of three inventions. The first he called *grouping:* enabling nurses to operate in a decentralized way while still being able to communicate with one another. The second was *folding* (as with the napkin), wherein physical obstacles such as the supply rooms were "folded out of existence." The third was *work-saving,* a mechanism to eliminate or redesign work, as when the materials management department agreed to deliver supplies in carts to the decentralized nurses.

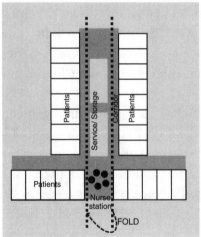

TRADITIONAL LAYOUT
Two Parallel Corridors
  – Rows of rooms are separated by
    zone of services
  – Nurses are stationed at a remote point

FOLDING THE PLAN
Eliminating the middle zone
  – More direct access to patients
  – Supplies are on mobile carts

Figure 3.4   Traditional layout versus new concept.

Defining Work and Generating Solutions

The inquiry process that led to the grouping and folding inventions generated a scenario that was presented at a series of user meetings and informal exchanges among hospital staff members. Those events created the third work-saving invention. The formal meetings set up by Rosenfield were attended by representatives of physicians, nurses, administrators, and service staff. The architects placed plans of their proposed designs on a table in the center of room, then sketched modifications of these designs as different ideas emerged from the conversation. Hospital personnel were questioned about the nature of their work—how they did things and what they needed. When conflicts arose, as in the case of supplies, appropriate personnel were brought into the discussion. The designers listened to the issues and problems that arose, then led participants through a collaborative effort aimed at shaping consensus on design solutions.

These collaborative exercises supplied information necessary for inventing new ways of doing things. For example, issues of supply were carefully worked over in detail in collaboration with nurses and the materials manager. Nurses were asked how many washcloths were needed, how many bottles of lotion, and so on. This process of inquiry determined that the delivery of one cartload of supplies three times per week would meet the needs of each cluster. Nurses were accustomed to keeping these supplies in storerooms and cubicles, but was this necessary for a single cart? They decided it was not: The cart could be rolled into an alcove. Materials managers concluded that this change would not result in increased cost or labor, and accepted the proposal. When these meetings ended, the architect would take the sketches back to the office to work out technical problems; he or she would not, however, invent new solutions. If a new idea did come up in the architect's office, it would be presented during the next meeting with hospital staff. For particularly critical features of the design, such as the patients' bathrooms and bedrooms, the architect produced full-scale mock-ups that people could view and rearrange.

This collaborative design process lasted between one and two months and involved approximately six meetings. Once core functions or facilities were folded out of the new design, an effort to find new places for them ensued. Some were clearly not needed in the new clusters; others were needed, but their numbers or sizes could be reduced.

In other cases, entire concepts were challenged. For example, some aspects of the current fire code were not necessary in light of the new design. The designers asked the fire marshal to rule on the acceptability of their proposed changes. In other instances, nurses and supply managers were asked to negotiate with the fire marshal to determine, for example, "Is a supply room necessary and, if so, does it need a door?" It was finally determined that no door or fire protection was needed for the alcoves off the corridor—a resolution essential to the adoption of the cluster design.

Organizational Conditions and Consequences

The process of learning and change continued even after the cluster unit was built and placed into operation. Existing relationships and responsibilities involving nurses and other hospital personnel were among the affected elements of the workplace. As the nurses got used to working with the new spatial and organizational arrangements, it became clear to them that the benefits of decentralized nursing stations could not be realized as long as patient records were kept in the central nursing office. In effect, the separation of nurses from their patients' records meant that key decisions about patient care remained out of the floor nurses' control and in the hands of doctors and supervisory nurses who had little contact with the patients. Relocating the records to the cluster-based nurses required a physical change, but this could be easily achieved. Less easily achieved was the organizational change that required supervisory personnel to trust floor nurses to take responsibility for a greater part of patient care. This represented a significant change in work practice.

If patient records were not where they were needed—with the nurse and her patient—two adverse consequences would follow. Either one, the designers felt, would cause the whole system to unravel. First, the caregiver would have to physically retrieve the records from the central records station, wasting time and disrupting the nurse-patient connection. This had been observed in another hospital where cluster units had been created but where records were kept centralized; there, nurses spent a great deal of time traveling between the central records station and patients' rooms, and the effect of the cluster design was less than optimal.

The second negative consequence of centralized records was organizational. The cluster design not only aimed for enhanced visual contact between nurses and patients, it was intended to foster greater responsibility among nurses for delivering care. As was discovered on investigation, nurses identified possession and control of patient medical records with authority and responsibility. Decentralizing records to the clusters, the designers reasoned, would encourage nurses to take greater responsibility and act as care managers, not as people who were simply taking orders.

THE CLUSTER DESIGN APPLIED
AT HACKENSACK HOSPITAL

After completing the Somerville Hospital project, Rosenfield and his colleagues had an opportunity to further develop the cluster concept, this time in a hospital in Hackensack, New Jersey. The decision of the Hackensack Hospital to adopt a cluster design was not made by an administrator, as had been the case at Somerville Hospital. Instead, it was selected from a pool of options by a group of doctors, nurses, and administrators.

At the outset of the project, before showing this client group any of his concepts for the cluster design, Bienstock took a representative group from the hospital on a two-day tour of other regional hospitals, where they were asked to keep an eye out for features that appeared particularly useful. In Rosenfield's view, it was important not to predispose his clients toward his earlier design: He wanted them to chose the model they thought would best serve their needs. Among the stops was Somerville Hospital, where an earlier version of cluster design was then operational. The hospital group agreed that the Somerville layout was the most functional of those visited, and decided on a cluster arrangement.

The Hackensack people developed their own variation of the cluster design: They decided to group four clusters together toward a common nurse area, a kind of decentralized pod containing four nurses. Three pods per floor were then positioned in a radiating array; this eliminated having to walk past one pod to reach another (Figure 3.5). The main features of the Hackensack version of the cluster design included the following: Patient rooms containing a total of twenty-four beds should be surrounded by a large rectangular open core containing the work area for four nurses; all charts, linen, and medical supplies should be kept within arm's reach of nurses at each nursing station; and nurses should be able to see each of their six patients and one another at all times, so that help would be at hand when needed.

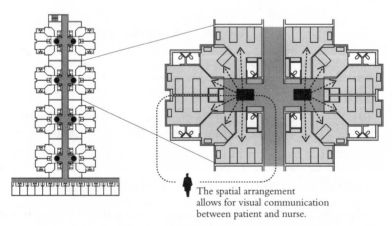

The spatial arrangement allows for visual communication between patient and nurse.

Figure 3.5   Cluster units at Hackensack Medical Center.

New concepts for the workplace also emerged from these working sessions (Figure 3.6). Nursing work areas were defined with half-height dividers. Patients could be monitored with a glance from the work area. These concepts also included new designs for service carts as well as guidelines for the proximity of one nurse to another, the treatment of medical records, and the placement of refreshment areas, sinks, light fixtures, and bulletin boards in patient rooms.

A post-occupancy evaluation of the Hackensack project indicated that the cluster design was highly successful, where *success* was defined as client satisfaction, a work environment more conducive than conventional ones to effective patient care, and positive reactions from nurses, patients, and physicians. Studies uncovered other positive benefits: Patients were perceived as more relaxed; supply thefts were reduced; nurse absenteeism and turnover declined; physicians felt more in contact with nurses; conflicts at the nursing station over possession of medical records and access to medication were eliminated; and nurses and patients felt in closer, more frequent contact. Nurses felt that the spatial arrangement of the cluster gave them direct access to patients and co-workers, utility and medication rooms, and supplies and equipment. This direct access, in their view, decreased fatigue,

Figure 3.6   Cluster units at Hackensack Medical Center.

improved performance, positively altered their attitudes about coming to work, and increased their willingness to work longer hours when necessary. Physicians, in turn, believed that the cluster arrangement had a positive impact on their patients, who felt more secure knowing that the nurse was immediately outside the room.

REFLECTION

The wet lab case and the nursing cluster case show people breaking free of old workplace images and discovering new ones that better support the way they work (Color plate 9). In each case, the designers focused on how the users of the workplace—researchers and nurses, respectively—actually went about their work, and how they wanted to improve that work. Exercises helped the laboratory researchers to step outside of their everyday work and examine what they did and how they did it. Walking through their work areas with facilitators, viewing slides that reflected their own observations and insights, playing design games, and exchanging visions with one another, the workers held a mirror to how they did their work and how spatial arrangements made that work easier or more difficult.

The processes of discovery and invention unfolded unevenly in both cases. Considerations about how to do work differently triggered insights about spatial needs, as when nurses and designers determined that the line of sight between nurse and patient was important. Insights about spatial arrangement triggered other insights about the organization of work, as happened when nurses recognized that record keeping needed to be decentralized. The physical layout of the cluster design provoked a change in supply logistics and how information was stored and controlled—and by whom. The new design would not have achieved its potential had patient information not been moved closer to the patient and had the cluster nurse not been made the keeper of that information.

The designers in both cases made use of the local knowledge of people who did the actual work. Doing so required the designers to be open to information and to listen carefully to criticism of their own work. Rosenfield exemplified this openness through his constant review of things he had already built and of questions for which he had yet to find an answer. This openness made it possible to seek rather than avoid problems, and to find solutions over time.

The nursing cluster design provides an example of a dynamically coherent workplace—one that attends to the spatial, organizational, financial, and technological aspects of the work process. Years of experimentation by Rosenfield, Thompson, Friesen, Bienstock, Girard, and others produced learning experiences from which each successive project could draw. For example, Thompson's work, which focused on the financial and organizational aspects of nursing care, informed the Rosenfield firm's thinking on the spatial dimension. Spatial solutions, in turn, created pressure for change elsewhere, as in the shifting responsibility for patient records—something entirely unanticipated by earlier design changes. Thus, the learning that occurred in one quadrant of the SOFT diagram informed learning in others, and helped all the practitioners to enlarge their understanding.

In both the cases cited in this chapter, reflection about work led to design innovation: Stereotypes were put aside, but only after considerable engagement with the problem. Breakthroughs were achieved over time, and the ownership of those breakthroughs belonged to many co-inventors.

4

The Design Game

The *design game* is what we call the game of interests, freedoms, and powers that is endemic to workplace-making. It is politically charged and carried out by people of unequal power who have interests in both the product of design and the process itself. Very often, those interests lead to conflict. This should surprise no one, since the spatial resources and physical accoutrements of the workplace are coveted resources. This competition inevitably provokes new antagonisms or provides new occasions for rekindling old ones. Thus, the organizational and physical settings within which the design game is played out become arenas of contention. People become players in a new and more focused game that we have found it useful to think of as draped over the existing organization with its ongoing game of interests and powers. An understanding of the game and its relationship to the organization in which it is played out is essential to guarantee the reliability of the design process and the quality and durability of the outcome.

If the metaphor of the game works, it is because a fundamental rationality, a gamelike logic, underlies both the conventional interactions of the players in games of amusement or sport and the real-life games of consequence in which human beings engage. In the complex, conflictual process of workplace-making, as in other fields of human activity, the metaphor of the game offers a powerful tool for both analysis and invention.

Those who influence the organization of work may not share a common vision or agenda. It is not surprising, then, that policy decisions about work patterns, resource allocation, or building management are made and debated (or avoided) even as the new workplace is taking shape. We use the design game as a way to help explain design outcomes or to invent strategies for managing or intervening in an ongoing design process so as to achieve better outcomes. Both of these uses require mapping of the players in the game and representation of their interrelationships and interactions.

Some design games are more complex than others. Complexity can be a function of the number and type of players, but more often it is a function of the problems being undertaken, the degree to which past practices are engrained in people's behavior, and the force and imagination of stakeholders. The images of the workplace and the agendas held by key players tend to be moving targets, further increasing complexity. In addition, players tend to move in and out of the workplace-making process, influencing it in unexpected ways. For example, senior managers may initially set themselves apart from the design process, believing they have empowered their staff people to work out the design issues for them. It is not unusual for these same managers to intervene late in the game if their staff's design solutions fall short of their expectations.

For all of the reasons just given, the design game is generally elusive, shifting, and unresolved. Nevertheless, effective workplace-making, like fascinating conversations and interesting games, combines order and disorder, constraint and freedom, predictability and uncertainty. Design games are neither inherently evil nor counterproductive to good workplace-making. They are simply among the givens of any design situation. As such, they should be understood by workplace professionals and by others who participate in the workplace-making process.

The technical-rational approach in which most professionals are schooled disdains the game and its intrusion into an otherwise orderly world. To the adherents of this approach, the politics of design is an unfortunate error—something to be avoided, minimized, or used to explain away the ineffectiveness of an otherwise professional job. "If it hadn't been for all the politics, we would have created a much better design," or "If only people had been rational about this, we could have met everyone's objectives." In contrast, process architecture sees value in design games and uses them to achieve responsible results for clients.

This chapter presents several examples of design games and uses them to explore how games affect—especially distort or undermine—the workplace-making process, how workplace professionals and managers are caught up in games that block effective workplace outcomes, the mechanisms by which design games yield different types of workplace outcomes, what is involved in mapping and diagnosing the design game in play, how individuals can use such understanding to perform more effectively in the workplace-making process, and how an existing game can be transformed to achieve the objective of dynamic coherence.

The role of the process architect is not given, but must be created. Workplace-making may play itself out in the hands of a single participant, or it may move from one person to another—or no single person may actually direct the process. Of the four cases included in this chapter, only in the last two do a process architect or even a hint of process architecture appear. The role of process architect may fall to an organizational insider, such as a space professional, an administrator, or a business unit leader. Or it may fall to an outside consultant—an organizational development specialist, an architect, or an interior space programmer. Any of these people can have significant effects on the play of the game. What they do and how and when they do it is affected by the roles they are given or assume, the authority they begin with or accumulate, and their own normative frameworks of action. In any case, the process architect enters the game with the aim of directing it toward greater collaboration and co-invention.

The analysis of the design game, like that of any game, asks the same fundamental questions:

- What are the rules?
- Who are the players? What roles are available to them? What constraints bind them? What freedoms do they enjoy?
- How is winning conventionally defined?

- What is the game's setting? How is that setting coordinated with the rules of play?

- What are the characteristic situations of the game? What constitutes advantage or disadvantage in these situations? What strategies are likely to be deployed in each?

- What styles of play do the actors adopt? How are these styles linked to the actors' identities and roles? How do they affect prospects for winning or losing?

Once the basic game is understood—even if imperfectly at first—the process architect can use that understanding to design a strategy for transforming the game. Over time, the game can be manipulated to take on a new and more effective style of play. Different perspectives can be made to confront, to inform, and to influence one another, sometimes leading to new paths for discovery and development. Suppressed or privately held images of the completed workplace and workplace-making can be surfaced before they erupt as unpleasant surprises. For example, though they might not admit it, powerful players may equate space with personal status. These images of status should be shared with and understood by other players while there is still time to assess and work through their implications for cost and building outcomes. The process architect can use a variety of tools to encourage open and reliable communication among the players in order to put conflicting values on the table in an atmosphere conducive to their discussion and resolution.

The possibility of creative change begins with reframing the situation. By reframing we mean seeing things in new ways, with new associations, perhaps within a new metaphor, but always with new organizing ideas. Almost any aspect of the situation may be subject to reframing:

- The focus of the change process
- The relationships among actors—from competition to cooperation

- Who should be included as participants and who should be included as instigators and managers of the change process
- The relationship between work practice and space; for example, introducing information technology as an important part of the solution rather than seeing it merely as infrastructure
- The role of the process architect in the design game

Organizations have many ways of avoiding or dealing covertly with conflict, but, as several of our cases demonstrate, the requirements of spatial programming and design bring conflict into the open, making it hard to ignore. Even though the co-invention of spatial and organizational arrangements may heighten conflict, this also presents an opportunity for productively surfacing and then resolving persistent organizational tensions.

We will explore these issues through several case studies. The first, the Ainsley case, describes the development of a university building. It shows how the design game contributed to cost overruns and an outcome that failed to satisfy the requirements of the users, and it suggests what makes the game resistant to change. The case of Robert Oliver explores a highly destructive design game woven around the development of an organization's headquarters building. It reveals how a limited concept of his role prevented a design professional from appreciating how that game had entrapped him. Oliver found himself embroiled in an organizational labyrinth he could neither understand nor influence.

The last two cases have more positive outcomes. The radiation therapy case involves the highly contentious siting of a new medical facility. Here, a team of consultants uncovers the design game and uses their understanding of it to invent a strategy for unlocking a stalemated workplace-making process. Finally, the Green Hills case shows how a consultant, step by step and often to his own surprise, transformed a dysfunctional design game into one that gave fuller expression to values held by the majority of stakeholders.

THE AINSLEY BUILDING:
A FRAGMENTED OUTCOME

The case of the Ainsley Building, a research and teaching facility in a professional school located in a major university, shows in a very dramatic way how a distorted design game can result in building outcomes that are both unfortunate and resistant to explanation. The Ainsley Building gave our team its first glimpse of a design game as we began to develop a shared conception of process architecture (Color plate 10). It was the analysis of this case that first led us to use the metaphor of the game as a way of understanding how the workplace-making process can distort design inquiry in such a way as to create unsatisfactory outcomes. To illustrate these ideas, we present a brief account of the Ainsley story. We begin with a set of paradoxical outcomes that seemed to us, as we looked back at the project, to require explanation.

How did it come about, for example, that in spite of a well-thought-out system of formal rules and procedures aimed, among other things, at keeping costs in line with budget projections, the actual costs of this building exceeded original estimates by a factor of 2? How was it that the researchers who occupied the building gave it a high score on seven dimensions of building comfort, yet found it utterly unsuited to their working needs? Why did a smart building, equipped with ergonomic chairs and sophisticated lighting, ventilation, and security control systems, nevertheless work poorly and prove expensive to maintain? Why did the look of the building seem inconsistent—luxurious in some areas and spare in others?

The research faculty and staff at the school had developed a substantial, prestigious, and well-funded program over a period of several decades. By the late 1980s, the school's research program had grown to the point where the practice of housing the staff in a number of rented buildings off campus was no longer satisfactory.

The faculty successfully argued to the university's administration that the visibility, quality, and size of the research program would significantly improve if the entire enterprise were housed in one building—a place where a community of faculty and student scholars could work together. The university authorized the building even before funds had been raised to supplement the university's investment from current endowment income.

Programming responsibility for the proposed new building was assigned to the university's office of planning, which engaged an architectural firm for programming and design. The design process would be guided by the planning office to keep initial and life cycle building costs within estimates. The university's real estate office was involved with the urban design and conference facilities planning aspects of the new building. The school's facilities managers were responsible for day-to-day contact with clients and architects and working out detailed aspects of the program and building. The research staff had clear needs in mind and pressed for excellent research space (individual offices that could accommodate both individual work and frequent interaction with student research assistants); office space for visiting scholars, researchers from sponsoring corporations, team rooms, and so on; and small conference rooms for academic exchange with colleagues from other colleges within the university. For the researchers, the building's architecture would have to be consistent with their vision of a community of scholars. The dean of the school supported the creation of a first-class research facility, but insisted that the building also be one that would welcome world-famous visitors who would attend conferences in the building's elite conference center.

Harris Ainsley, a successful businessman and an active alumnus of the university, expressed his desire to make a major gift to the school. But the gift would not be without conditions. In Ainsley's mind, the building would serve as a tribute to his career as a master builder, with public spaces that conveyed an elite, polished image. It would be a showcase for public programs that would put the school on the global map of world-class institutions. Ainsley shared the dean's idea of an impressive edifice and a place where world leaders and faculty from around the globe would gather. This was also in accord with the views of the real estate office, which wanted an architectural definition of entrance to the campus.

Ainsley entered into the design process at a relatively late date. Architectural plans had already been developed, as had construction schedules. Total building costs were estimated at $13 million, and the foundation was in process of being laid. Ainsley offered a gift of $15 million ($10 million dedicated to research programs, $5 million to the new research center), conditional on the school's compliance with his demands, which the dean of the school decided to accept. Ainsley wanted the building to have a strong business image and a spec office building format. He insisted on a conference center and a high-tech auditorium, and demanded that the rotunda, initially intended to be two stories high, be extended to five stories and be built without columns. These change orders were issued late in the game, and their direct and indirect costs led eventually to a construction budget that turned out to be twice the value of Ainsley's gift. Moreover, the new rotunda, like other add-ons, resulted in a much less efficient use of space and higher operation and maintenance costs.

The imbalance between Ainsley's polished public spaces and the more mundane design of the office space forced the process managers to focus on construction savings, which proved costly for the operating budget. The spec office building, which favored future income-producing uses, interfered with the image of the building as a home for academic research. As one of the researchers put it, "This looks more like an insurance company than a university." Ainsley's insistence on placing the main entrance on the square in front of the building reinforced the preexisting urban design agenda; it boosted the school's urban presence, along with Ainsley's self-image. But again, it weakened the academic agenda, siphoning off funds that would have been used to serve academic purposes.

As the consequences of Ainsley's demands became apparent, the university's facilities management staff, supposedly in charge of developing the building within previously approved guidelines, brought these matters to the attention of both the dean and senior faculty members who had been active in the programming. Having received no satisfactory response, the facilities management staff turned to senior university administrators, who deferred the choice of complying with the guidelines or waiving them to the dean of the school.

The politics of the Ainsley building pitted the donor and the dean against the researchers and the university's planners. But these actors, with their conflicting images of both the building and the building design process, exercised unequal degrees of power. As one of the university planners ruefully observed, "Those of us who are in the thick of this all the time can't always influence the people who make the decisions. Who are they going to listen to: a big-time executive who gives 15 million bucks to the school, or us?"

Although he was by far the most powerful player, Ainsley's image of the building did not wholly carry the day. Rather, his image of the building was superimposed on the preexisting building plan through design changes made while construction was under way. Conflicts between the old and the new images of the building were not resolved by rethinking the initial program and design, but were managed by making suboptimal adjustments such as compartmentalizing polished from working spaces and absorbing costly change orders through greatly increased operating costs.

Beyond these immediate building outcomes, the Ainsley case illustrates several long-term negative effects of a win/lose design game. The research staffers in the building have given the office environment high scores in their evaluation of the building, but they feel uncomfortable with the polished appearance of the public amenities. The cost of maintenance is very high, and the professional staff, responsible for operating costs and facilities management, has lost control over areas that are formally under its authority.

Thus we explain the main building outcomes by reference to a design game of stakeholders who held conflicting agendas and exercised different degrees of power over key decisions. Because the key actors failed to reconcile their conflicting agendas within the process of design inquiry, their unresolved conflicts became embedded in its outcomes: the doubling of actual over estimated costs; the high-technology features that no one knew how to use; the absence of effective linkages between building design and maintenance; the unfortunate urban design interventions, and, architecturally, a dual, compartmentalized structure caught between the images of a spec office building and an academic workplace.

The design process itself is recalled as a frustrating and confusing experience that resulted in exacerbated tensions among key staff groups. Those who were formally responsible for decision-making in programming, design, and construction were not the ones who actually made decisions. And those who did make decisions—the major donor, Ainsley, and the dean of the school, who complied with Ainsley's wishes—held a different image of the building than the workplace professionals who were ostensibly in charge of the process.

Carefully designed planning procedures were repeatedly short-circuited by actors who insisted on taking the fast track. Some participants claimed they could not get what they wanted "because the architect wants to have his building published in an architectural magazine." The outside consultant, hired to keep the project under budget, refused to address operational issues raised by other participants. The planning group, less powerful than other actors in the administration, was able to act on the problems it saw only to the extent, as members put it, that they were "willing to be witches." The building turned out to be really two buildings in one: elite, high-cost spaces (the atrium, auditorium, and conference center) that reflected the donor's views, coupled with low-cost spaces for researchers and faculty. The architecture of the Ainsley Building expressed the unresolved conflict of agendas and the dominance of certain individuals who played principal roles in the building's development. Thus the Ainsley case represents many of the worst features of the design game.

We can take the story of the Ainsley Building one step further by asking how its unfortunate outcomes might have been prevented. How might the actors have better played their roles within the actual design game? Could they have productively changed the game? Despite the multiplicity of players, introducing new formal procedures and organizational structures for planning and cost control would have been unlikely to solve the problem, since there was no lack of such procedures and structures already in place. There was a great deal of discontinuity among the key players in the game, and a more stable cast of players might have helped to guard against certain bad outcomes. On the other hand, those high-level actors in the university planning system who did remain in place throughout the whole design process were no more willing to confront the central issues than were those who moved in and out of the process. One could argue that, as early as possible, Ainsley and the dean should have been made aware of the tangible and intangible costs of their alliance. But neither of the two signaled their readiness to listen to such information, and none of the workplace professionals in nominal charge of the design process were prepared to bell the cat.

Fear on the part of the less powerful players coupled with arrogance and blindness on the part of the more powerful ones kept the key issues undiscussable, preventing them from surfacing soon enough to be productively dealt with. Had the planners been readier to risk raising the issues, and more skillful in doing so, they might have engaged the two powerful players in a more productive synthesis of the conflicting agendas—or at least made them aware of the costs of failing to achieve such a synthesis. Had the two most powerful players shown themselves readier to listen to unwelcome information, they might have avoided the worst of the building outcomes—or at least had the opportunity to make a more informed choice concerning the strategies they were pursuing.

OLIVER IN WONDERLAND

Robert Oliver was an environmental psychologist who had built a consulting business around a specialized approach to post-occupancy evaluation (POE). Developed in the United States over the last several decades, POE is a formal way of finding out whether a recently occupied, remodeled, or built environment is performing as intended in its programming and design and whether it conforms to certain standards of comfort, amenity, and efficiency. In POE methodology, data are collected through comprehensive surveys in which a building's occupants are asked to give feedback on their experience of the built environment.

Robert Oliver had been trained in POE methodology and had long functioned as an expert consultant in its use. He had evolved a firm and explicit view of his professional role: He was a scientist who expertly gathered survey research data and analyzed it according to a framework that enabled him to evaluate a building's performance for its occupants. In his view, his role as an expert consultant was to engage the occupants in providing the relevant data and then to present the data and an analysis to the manager who had authority over the building. Oliver's technical-rational view of his professional role provided no room for involvement in the politics of the design process. The phenomena of the design game, as we have described them, lay outside Oliver's understanding of professionalism—both undermining the effective use of scientific data about building occupancy and entrapping him in a political dynamic he had defined as irrelevant to his professional role. This is the focus of the present case.

When we first met Robert Oliver, he had just completed an assignment for InterCorp, a large international organization whose headquarters buildings were located in a major American city. This consulting experience had proved exceptionally frustrating. Oliver had been hired to study the performance of headquarters building 1 so that the lessons from this experience could be incorporated in headquarters building 2, then on the drawing boards. But, after many months of effort, Oliver walked away from this assignment feeling that he had had little impact on the management of the existing building or the design of the new one. His studies had been rebuffed by InterCorp's architectural and construction staffs, and there had been little or no follow-up to his efforts. All of this puzzled Oliver and frustrated him in the extreme.

Oliver's assignment for InterCorp had four elements:

1. Conduct presurvey meetings with occupants from each of the eight floors of building 1 to assess their satisfaction with the work space.

2. Administer a building satisfaction survey to all the occupants of building 1.

3. Analyze the survey results and write reports based on the analysis for those responsible for the management of building 1 and the programming of building 2.

4. Develop methods for postsurvey focus groups with selected employees and managers from each business unit within building 1, and train InterCorp facilities management staff to carry out those focus group surveys.

Oliver's assignment came under the authority of the Facilities Management Division and his principal client, Bender, the head of the newly created Integrated Technology and Facilities Task Force. Also involved in the project as members of the POE committee were the heads of two other groups within facilities management— Applethorpe, the architect responsible for spatial design, planning, and project management, and Whitlock, the engineer responsible for HVAC, construction, and management. Both Applethorpe and Whitlock expressed strong support for the study. All of these individuals reported to Prem, an InterCorp vice president (Color plate 11).

Oliver proceeded to conduct his presurvey meetings and then to adjust and administer the survey itself. He produced several findings of interest. On one floor of building 1, for example, he found that the staff complained bitterly about hot air and insufficient privacy. Yet ventilation, temperature settings, and work area layout were the same as on other floors where there were no such complaints. Oliver believed he had discovered the solution to this puzzle in postsurvey focus groups. Occupants of the floor were frustrated for other reasons. To promote better communication across groups, management had arranged these employees in a cross-functional fashion, which hindered efficient work flow. Staff had to spend extra time running around. In addition, cross-functional seating may have made the staff feel a loss of privacy. Oliver noted these findings in a memo to the business unit's manager, with copies to Bender, Applethorpe, and Whitlock.

In the space occupied by InterCorp's international division, Oliver also discovered what he believed to be an important source of employee dissatisfaction, which he partly misattributed to work space arrangements. In this division, professional economists from many different countries worked in constantly shifting relationships with their colleagues, variously functioning in task forces, project teams, and one-to-one interactions with returning field-workers. Their spatial arrangements shifted accordingly. Oliver believed that this instability undermined the group's cultural identity, which depended in part on the stability of its spatial boundaries. Again, he wrote up these findings, as well as more detailed results, and sent them to the manager of the international division as well as to the members of the POE committee.

Contrary to his expectations, Oliver found that none of the members of his client group took his work seriously. The training sessions he organized for space professionals in the organization were sparsely attended. No one appeared to use any of the training received. And when Oliver questioned Applethorpe and Whitlock about these matters, he began to discover a disturbing picture. Applethorpe said that his already overworked staff had no need to take on the new tasks of POE; and although he gave Oliver no direct criticism, he was reported to have downplayed the survey results behind Oliver's back. Whitlock distanced himself from the study and followed up on none of Oliver's recommendations. Bender, to whom Oliver reported these reactions, held informal discussions with the architect and engineer, but gave them no directives about their responsibilities, which remained unchanged.

At first, Oliver responded to these puzzling and increasingly disturbing outcomes by limiting his reports to survey data and refraining from giving any more advice. Later, when Prem left the organization and was replaced by a new vice president, Oliver had his assistants conduct a series of interviews with staff in the architectural and engineering divisions to explore the reasons behind the nonuse of his POE data. What emerged, apart from some complimentary references to Oliver's professionalism, was a pattern of fragmentary organization and poor communication in the Facilities Management Division. The two main groups headed by Whitlock and Applethorpe were run as little fiefdoms and had little interaction with each other. Neither group seemed to have much decision-making power with respect to work space within InterCorp. Workplace professionals within the facilities division communicated directly with the managers of business units, bypassing their own superiors. Bender, to whom Oliver reported these findings, acknowledged the problems and sympathized with Oliver's predicament, but appeared to take no action to involve the new vice president in these issues. Moreover, Bender told Oliver that he would soon be taking early retirement.

Oliver strove to understand these disturbing outcomes. He had, in his view, behaved with the highest professionalism. Yet, the results were uniformly disastrous: Few if any of his findings had been put to use, the POE methodology introduced to the organization had been largely ignored, he had been treated with hostility or indifference by the heads of the architecture and construction groups, and staff members who had participated early in the project felt they had wasted their time because there had been no follow-up. And when

Oliver had tried to involve his main client in dealing with these issues, he had been disappointed.

Oliver initially attributed these outcomes to the fragmented and dysfunctional organization of the Facilities Management Division. Later, he came to see that he might have made some contribution to the problems. He learned, for example, that when he had given the business unit manager and senior facilities managers information and advice about the sources of dissatisfactions in building 1, the business manager saw him as "telling people what to do in their own building." The facilities managers resented unsolicited advice from someone "who was not even an engineer." Nevertheless, Oliver saw himself as a victim of InterCorp's dysfunctional organization. This traditional hierarchical organization, he believed, faced an insuperable dilemma: It was an authoritarian system trying to mount a participatory dialogue with building occupants about the uses of their work space. As Oliver wrote in one of his memoranda on the project, "The facilities division dispatched me the way a serial killer dispatches his victims. It dismembered my reputation and buried it. Getting rid of me helped it to protect itself and the status quo." Oliver's anger was perhaps understandable, but it did not help him gain a deeper understanding of the organizational morass into which he had fallen.

Our review of Oliver's experience revealed that the POE exercise had been trapped from the beginning in a political arena that was not of Oliver's making. Hostility and distrust among the major players—the employees, Bender and the facilities division, the architectural and engineering groups within the facilities division—had preceded Oliver's entry onto the scene. In the ongoing contest between Bender and other groups within the facilities division, the heads of these groups saw Oliver as Bender's man, read Oliver's professional reports as "setting them up," and did not want Oliver or Bender to get credit for making things better. Prem, the vice president, worried that Oliver's meetings with employees would rock the boat, which he wanted to keep on an even keel. As Whitlock and Applethorpe saw Prem distance himself from the study, they allowed their hostility more open expression, dropping the mask of professional collegiality and cooperation. Within a month, Bender called Oliver to thank him for his work to date, saying, "Our facilities management staff will be taking over the remaining evaluation studies."

Oliver began his assignment in the belief that rigorous data gathering and analysis would inform users and managers about the effects of building 1's characteristics on employees' satisfaction and productivity; and he was convinced that his analyses would inform decision-making about the programming and designing of building 2. He was largely unaware of the design game that swirled around his work. He had fallen into the game like Alice falling down the rabbit hole. Even if he had been aware of the game, he would have lacked a method for dealing intelligently with what he viewed as organizational politics. His conception of technical-rational expertise left no room for politics as a topic of professional attention; it led him to assume, on the contrary, that facts and data would be sufficient to lead to insight and then to action. But Oliver had as little control of the use of his facts and data as Alice had over the wickets that moved about in the Queen of Hearts' game of croquet (Color plate 12).

Could Oliver, or, for that matter, any professional brought into InterCorp, have figured out how the organization might make better use of the data that were produced? We can only speculate about the answer. That person would have had to approach the assignment with two questions: (1) "How should I understand the organization's version of the design game and my place in it?" and (2) "What is the organizational meaning of the data produced by the surveys?"

THE CENTER FOR RADIATION THERAPY: SURFACING AND MANAGING COMPETING INTERESTS

If Robert Oliver found himself trapped in a design game about which he had little understanding and over which he had no control, the radiation therapy case presents the opposite. Here, consultants functioned as skillful detectives, sizing up the design game as it was played within the organizational arena of their consulting project. They used their understanding to facilitate an effective negotiation among key players.

In the early 1970s, when this case began, the medical regimen and technology for treating illness amenable to radiation therapy had changed dramatically. So, too, had the qualifications for health care providers: State-of-the-art thinking required that radiation therapy be administered by board-certified radiation therapists, not by board-certified radiologists. In view of these trends, Dr. James Boser, executive director of the region's medical health planning program, worked with medical leaders in a midwestern American city to come to an important agreement: The city's four medical institutions then engaged in radiation therapy needed to merge their resources into a single facility capable of providing economical, state-of-the-art service. This was seen as the best way to improve the quality of care offered in the region and to remain competitive with adjacent regions.

In the wake of that decision, a steering committee representing the four institutions engaged consultants to determine the best location for the new facility and to develop a space program for the facility. Michael James and Mitchell Lawrence were chosen because they had experience planning several radiation therapy centers in other parts of the country. The location of the new center was a question of potentially explosive conflict among the participating institutions, and it is likely that Dr. Boser brought in the consultants for the classic reason: delegate the job to someone seen as a neutral and expendable expert. As the consultants later concluded: "We came to believe that Boser brought us into the situation to push and cajole. If the process left scars on the medical community (no matter how necessary), they would be attributed to us. If the process was successful, he would be recognized as the one who inspired it; if it failed, we would get the blame and he could move on to other projects." The two consultants engaged the medical director of one of the nation's leading radiation therapy centers, Dr. Frederick Bell, as the third member of their team. At their first meeting with the steering committee, James and Lawrence were introduced to the eleven key players in the city's medical community: the director of the region's medical planning agency (Dr. Boser); the dean of medicine and head of radiation therapy at the state medical school; the administrators and chiefs of radiology of the city's two private hospitals and the university hospital; and the president of the city's private practice radiation center.

The consultants described their experience with a number of leading radiation therapy centers in other cities. These were represented by three models: university-based, hospital-based, and freestanding. The consultants anticipated that these models would stimulate discussion on the criteria for the new center's location; instead they were greeted by stony silence. They concluded (correctly, as they were later to find out) that the group faced deep and troubling issues concerning the location of the new center and that the participants were not prepared to talk publicly about these issues with one another. Figuring that the medical leaders might say in private what they would not say in the presence of others, the consultants arranged to meet privately with representatives of each of the participating institutions.

Over the next several months, the consultants visited each of the participating institutions, seeking to understand what really mattered to each and what each might be willing to trade in a process of negotiation. These contacts surfaced a number of issues involved in the siting decision:

- The role of the university teaching program and its implications for nonfaculty members

- How issues related to service quality control would impact the ability of certified radiologists to practice in the therapy center

- How decisions involving a central radiation therapy facility would affect relationships between participating hospitals and subsequent decisions about potential centers for burn and cardiac care

- How to coordinate or merge different organizational cultures
- The space, staffing, and financial obligations of the host center, and the consequences these might have for existing programs

Some participants hoped that moving ahead with the relatively easy facilities issue would cause the more difficult issues to resolve themselves. To the consultants, the challenge was to invent a new organization as they thought through the spatial program for the new facility.

Though Dr. Boser had instigated the idea of a "Center of Excellence," he carefully avoided committing his agency as to its location. Instead he presented the consultants with a slate of principles and performance standards and put them in front of the effort to site the center. As the consultants saw it, Boser was deliberately remaining in the background, nudging the process forward, but relying on them to take the heat for whatever conflicts his brainchild spawned among the city's health care institutions.

Each of the participating medical facilities had, to varying degrees, an interest in hosting the center. But each was ambivalent about the commitments the center would require. For instance, Dr. Clinton, the director of the Baptist Medical Center, was eager for his institution to proceed with the new center, having just completed fund-raising for a cardiac care facility wing. Clinton was supported by his chief of radiology, but his medical director urged caution, arguing that the new center would be too much for the hospital to absorb for at least five years. Likewise, Phil Crandall, the administrator of St. Mary's Hospital, agreed that the region needed the center, but he thought the university would be the best host, given its strong research program and associated specialty practice. Dr. Ambrose Kasten, the vice president of academic affairs of the state university, also wanted the center in University Hospital, seeing its acquisition as a potential coup for his institution. The dean of the medical school, Dr. Jack Harmen, a close friend of Boser and chairman of the regional medical planning agency's board, had often told Boser how much the center would contribute to community care and to improving the quality of medical practitioners in the region. Those two issues, Harmen told the consultants, were his primary concerns. The head of the radiation therapy department at University Hospital, Dr. Sheila Crestan, likewise supported a university-based center. Her support was both personal and professional: She had accepted her current appointment with the understanding that she would direct the new center, and moreover claimed that few of the region's practicing radiologists had the credentials to teach or practice in the new center.

Not everyone associated with the university, however, favored playing host to the new center. University Hospital's administrator, David Britt, argued that the school lacked the resources to do this. Any new funds, in Britt's opinion, would be more productively allocated toward upgrading physical facilities and the nursing program. "And since Dr. Crestan is the only board-certified radiation therapist in the region," Britt pointed out, "the issue of quality control in the new center would be a serious stumbling block." Robert Foden, the president of Radiology Associates Center, a private facility, extolled the region's private medical practitioners. Two of his senior radiologists, he told the consultants, already looked forward to associating with the proposed new center, which, in his opinion, "will make us competitive with neighboring cities." However, he echoed his staff's fear that siting the center in the university would create credentialing problems for his people. He and they favored a freestanding facility for research and teaching, to which any local board-certified radiologist would contribute.

Once James and Lawrence had a sense of the key stakeholders' initial positions and of their shared interests and differences, they set out to test the organizations' willingness to accept the costs and other responsibilities of hosting the new center, their receptivity to different solutions, and the conditions under which they would accept one or another solution.

Their first stop was at University Hospital, at the offices of Dr. Ambrose Kasten. If you accepted the center, Kasten was asked, what would the university be required to give up: salary increases for nurses? affirmative action programs? new links to neighborhood health centers? Kasten deflected the line of inquiry. There was no need for trade-offs, he told the consultants. The state legislature would come up with the necessary funds.

Seeking greater assurance that the university would be able to fund the new venture, the consultants asked Kasten if he would schedule a meeting with the university's chief financial officer. Kasten promised to arrange this meeting, but failed to do so. The consultants took this to mean that Kasten wanted to avoid a firmer commitment. They then turned to David Britt, the administrator of University Hospital, who blanched at the estimated dollars and square footage required to host the new center.

Despite a lack of assurances, and Britt's outright negativity, the two consultants were not willing to count out University Hospital as possible host for the proposed center. But unless someone in authority offered some clear sign of commitment, University Hospital would have to be scratched from the list. So, at their next meeting with Kasten, the consultants proposed that he commit the university *in writing* to the projected financial requirements and submit a sketch showing how the university would provide the required space. Kasten produced neither, but he did bring Dr. Crestan to the next meeting.

The consultants had established their bona fides with Dr. Crestan through their interview with her friend and medical colleague, Dr. Foden, who had also sounded out Crestan about her bottom-line position. James and Lawrence knew that Crestan was prepared to give up the university's claim to host the center and to begin negotiations about the university's more basic interests. Crestan, in fact, turned the discussion to the issue of quality of care and the need to upgrade the community's practitioners in the field.

A second meeting with Phil Crandall, the administrator of St. Mary's Hospital, produced a new piece of information that changed the siting puzzle in an important way. Crandall took the two consultants on a walking tour of his hospital. As they paced through the nursing school building, Crandall commented that St. Mary's was considering a plan to close the school for financial reasons. If that plan went forward, his board was thinking of offering the space to the university on a long-term lease. Expansion plans for University Hospital and the medical school were public knowledge, but so was the fact that building space in the University Hospital area was scarce and expensive. Crandall seemed to be signaling that he had space to accommodate the new center and might have something to trade— the nursing school.

Several weeks later, when they had a better sense of the strain that housing the new center would put on both University Hospital and the Baptist Medical Center, the consultants approached Crandall again. They presented their floor plans and sketches for the radiation therapy center, along with pro forma financial statements and staffing charts. Crandall studied these for almost an hour, asking periodically for clarification. "You've done your homework," he said approvingly. "Could I share these with our board chairman and medical director?"

James and Lawrence were glad to oblige, and later that day found themselves in a hastily called meeting with Crandall and the board chairman and medical director of St. Mary's. Using the same materials they had shown Crandall, the consultants indicated how the new center could fit into the current nursing school facility. The St. Mary's officials liked what they saw. "You understand, of course," the board chairman apologized, "that we still have to make a decision about whether to continue operation of our nursing school." James nodded his agreement. "But, you have brought us something that we here would like to think about."

As the search for the right location continued, the issue of who would be qualified to practice in the new location continued to be addressed. The consultants talked with practitioners to map the therapy practices of radiologists in the region. They met with a group of practitioners identified by Dr. Crestan, all of whom affirmed the need for a center open to all practitioners and the fear that a center controlled by the university would be more closely aligned with research than with patient care.

Dr. Foden, president of Radiology Associates, asked how other radiation therapy centers dealt with credentialing practitioners to participate in patient care, research, and teaching. How, the consultants asked Foden, would he reconcile the professional's right to practice, which he advocated, with the need for high-quality care? His answer was, "Recognize the professional's right to practice, then press on to achieve quality." Foden's statement seemed to contain the basis for a deal.

At their next meeting with Foden, Lawrence and James were joined by Drs. Bell and Crestan. The two consultants presented the physicians with a document they had prepared, called "Profiles of Quality." This document summarized the staffing patterns of several leading radiation therapy centers. At the core of each center were board-certified radiation therapists, with board-certified radiologists participating on a select basis. At the urging of the consultants, the three physicians agreed to visit several of these radiation therapy centers jointly. Doing so, they believed, would help them to work out difficult quality issues in a neutral environment.

Over the course of many subsequent meetings, the consultants were able to hammer out a siting agreement with the leaders in the medical community. The directors of St. Mary's Hospital made the decision to close their nursing program and offer the vacated space to the new center. The university's radiation therapy department agreed to run the facility as a regional care center with a strong teaching and research program. The newly named Batten Center for Radiation Therapy would accept all board-certified radiologists in the region, but Dr. Crestan, the center's medical director, would set standards for future qualifications with the advice of directors of radiation therapy centers located elsewhere in the country. Radiology Associates agreed to refer all therapy patients to the new center. Several of its senior partners expressed their interest in maintaining their practices in radiology but not therapy, and one announced his pending retirement.

Shortly after these agreements were in place, they were confirmed at a meeting (only the second such meeting) of the full group of institutional players.

In the Batten Center for Radiology Therapy case, the team of James and Lawrence saw the problem from the beginning in terms of competing interests and jockeying for ascendancy. But the motivation for the game remained a mystery. The two intervenors used a number of instruments and events to surface and then negotiate highly complex and volatile issues among subgroups within the decision-making group, slowly bringing the key stakeholders to see their initial interests in a different light. The spatial/institutional solution was always seen as something that would follow from the resolution of the puzzle. The consultants had used spatial and financial concept design to intervene into the existing organizational dilemma (Color plate 13).

Following their "meeting of silence," as they became aware of deep chasms among the stakeholders, James and Lawrence sought to understand the positions and needs of the players. They engaged each player in framing institution-specific problems, negotiated the broad outlines of an agreement, and crafted the eventual solution. In a series of investigative rounds, the two consultants built up the process, learning as they progressed. They shared their learning with the stakeholders so that each could better understand his or her relative position and potential points for bargaining. They structured the situation for success, bringing people together with care and a clear agenda.

The process evolved collaboratively because each step was customized in response to stakeholder positions, interests, and needs.

GREEN HILLS: DESIGNING THE CLIENT

In this case we observe a consultant in the process of discovering a design game in which he might easily be trapped, learning to navigate within its confines, and changing it in fundamental ways. Here, organizational and interorganizational politics becomes a medium for the professional's rebuilding of the client team and redesign of the space planning process. The consultant, Stanley Nobel, was drawn into the project when the Green Hills Hospital's proposal for land development met with determined and effective resistance.

Green Hills Hospital was a prestigious institution located on 235 acres of hills, woodlands, and developed space on the edge of a growing metropolitan area. The psychiatric hospital was regarded as being on the cutting edge of its field in several areas, among them eating and sleep disorders, and had the largest psychiatric internship program in the country.

From its origins as a psychiatric hospital in the late nineteenth century until the 1930s, Green Hills' bucolic setting was central to patient therapy, isolating patients from the surrounding communities and providing them with green space for healthful walks and useful agricultural work. In the 1930s, however, as psychiatric practice began to turn to clinical and drug-based treatment, the patients abandoned the fields. After that, the hospital was no longer used for long-term residential care. At the time of Stanley Nobel's study, it housed a psychiatric community that provided extensive outpatient service, school programs for children from the neighboring town, and other types of outreach.

Of the 235 acres on the Green Hills campus, 55 were used intensively for the purposes of the psychiatric hospital and were encircled by an oval road (Color plate 14). About thirty more acres were used for staff housing and for other buildings that served hospital functions. The remaining acreage was open space. Recent growth had brought the metropolitan area to the doorstep of this once-rural location, creating an opportunity for commercial development of the hospital's open spaces.

In the early 1980s, Justin Raymond, an aggressive local real estate developer, formed a joint venture between his company (Rayco) and the Green Hills board of directors. The goal of the venture was to develop the outer part of the hospital's sprawling campus. The hospital's long-time board chairman, Myles Alper, a retired corporate executive, was the driving force behind the joint venture. Alper expected that the development would provide significant returns to the hospital, which in recent years had found itself under increasing financial pressure.

Alper had become an aggressive advocate of development in the past five years. As he saw it, the board's role was to ensure a sound financial and business footing for the hospital: This vision, however, ran counter to the medical staff's view that quality care—at any price—was the true mission. Alper viewed this countervision as laudatory but inappropriate in an environment of regulated cost control and shrinking resources.

In May of 1992, Rayco presented a concept plan for the Green Hills development. The plan included 2,300 housing units, 2 million square feet of office space, 36,000 square feet of medical office space, a 500-room hotel, and a new 325,000-square-foot shopping mall linked to an existing mall that occupied land leased from the hospital. Further, during one of the meetings with the medical staff, the development planners proposed a high-rise office building in the middle of Green Hills' oval.

Some city officials and local businessmen praised the plan, which they viewed as having the potential to generate new jobs and substantial property tax revenue. The general reception, however, was negative—if not angry. Criticisms fell into four categories. The most vocal came from city residents and a large number of hospital staff members who lamented the potential destruction of one of the metropolitan area's most significant open spaces. There were also concerns about the historic nature of some of the buildings and of the landscaping, which was the work of the renowned landscape architect Frederick Law Olmsted.

Another group focused its criticism on the scale of the proposed development, arguing that it would change the character of that part of the city and would generate unacceptable levels of traffic, noise, and pollution. A faction composed mostly of hospital physicians and administrators questioned the radical change of the character of the property and the scale of the proposed development. These people also challenged the appropriateness of the uses identified by Rayco. Why, they asked, weren't more medically related uses, such as a retirement community or ancillary health care services, included? The proposed high-rise tower—"in our front lawn" as hospital staffers complained—became a symbol of the animosity that quickly developed between the hospital group and the developer.

A fourth body—again within the hospital community, with considerable overlap with the group just mentioned—expressed its dissatisfaction with the process through which the plan had been developed and put forward by the joint venture partner. The plan had indeed been developed without input from the hospital administration and staff, which had for months been developing its own long-term vision for the institution.

The citizens, hospital personnel, and local business community were vociferous in their views and in their criticism of the plan and the process through which it had been hatched. The city likewise joined the opposition and refused to hear the developer's rezoning petition.

Leaders of the joint venture were stunned by the intensity and breadth of the opposition to their plan. It was clear to Justin Raymond and the hospital board that their plan would not get off the ground in the face of this resistance. They would need help in getting it accepted.

Stanley Nobel—architect, planner, and educator—was contacted by Jonathan Cross and Howard Mann, the coordinators of the development project. Cross was the hospital's legal counsel; Mann, an historian, worked on the issue of whether preservation requirements might block new development on the site. Nobel was hired in April 1985 to do a number of things: review the concept plan, provide contact with top design professionals who could be hired later to implement the plan, deal with any preservation issues, and establish liaisons with the faculty and administrative staff, who were regarded as the main impediment to the project.

Nobel's hiring first had to be approved by the developer, Justin Raymond, the hospital president, Peter Eustis, and the rest of the joint venture leadership. Nobel met with these individuals over the next few weeks to work out his role as design consultant. The leaders of the venture were particularly eager to determine whether Nobel would buy into the basic land use principles of the concept plan. To their great discomfort, Nobel's informal critique of the concept plan was devastating: "Design: awful and limiting; illustrations: appalling; too much office; design principles: missing; open space concepts: too limiting; numerical targets: too precise; oval: too isolated; sight lines: blocked . . ." Despite Nobel's criticisms of the concept plan, his meeting with the developer's planner, Tom Baxter, produced what Nobel viewed as general agreement on the shortcomings and strengths of the plan—the strengths being principally the position and types of land uses. By October Nobel was able to work out a clear set of tasks:

- Establish a liaison with the hospital staff and obtain its acceptance of a revised development proposal.

- Assist the joint venture in revising the concept plan and in defining and monitoring professional services for carrying it out.

- Block listing of the site on the town's Register of Historic Places.

At this point, Nobel saw himself as working with a collection of stakeholders whose views of him and his role were sharply divided (Color plate 15). The joint venture wanted him to be a salesman for their plan, whereas the hospital staff saw him as someone who would help them to develop their interests in the project. Nobel was the man in the middle. At the same time, he defined his role as one of translating into physical terms what he understood to be the site's inherent values. Clearly, he was in danger of falling into the cracks between the members of his client system. To make his roles clearer, in January 1986 Nobel entered into three distinct, though related, subcontracts:

1. With the hospital alone, for services related to bringing along the faculty and staff
2. With the joint venture, for plan-related services
3. With the joint venture and the hospital, for preservation-related services

To minimize potential confusion about his role, Nobel decided to put his different responsibilities in writing. And because there were so many issues on the table and so many conflicting views, he also decided to follow up each delineation of his role with a written summary, which he sent to the different parties. (This was a practice Nobel continued throughout the project. It helped to cement his central role in communication within the hospital and to maintain mobility among the many individuals to whom memos were sent.)

Nobel spent the first month of his assignment talking with people in the hospital community, seeking to understand the range and depth of their concerns. Although relatively few of these people were publicly outspoken, many had strongly held views. Nobel also discovered that the majority of those actively involved on one side or another of the controversy viewed him with suspicion; they were unclear as to his alignment within the opposing camps. At the same time he defined his role as one of translating into physical terms what he understood to be the values inherent in the site. Clearly, Nobel was in danger of falling between the cracks that separated members of his client coalition; this was better, in his view, than being seen as a creature of any one client in particular.

Nobel was also at risk of becoming a scapegoat for existing conflicts, something that did happen but that he was, in the end, able to use to advantage.

Nobel continued meeting with people during August to get the lay of the land. Sometimes he met with individuals. When he saw a chance either to build consensus or to get people to confront divisive issues, he brought together small groups. In each case, Nobel used the concept plan as a lightning rod for eliciting information about the different visions people had for the hospital. He would put the original drawing of the plan on the table, cover it with a piece of yellow tracing paper, and ask: "What do you like or dislike about the plan? How do you see the hospital's future influencing or being influenced by it?" As people started drawing on the plan—or just doodling— they started talking. When they were finished, Nobel summarized their points of difference or agreement.

Meetings held with Adam Piper, the head of the Psychiatry Department, and Joshua Sims, the chairman of the Division of Psychiatry, were typical of those initiated by Nobel. Sims was outspoken in his opposition to the plan. He was "personally outraged" by the proposal to site a high-rise office building in the middle of the oval. That site, in Sims's view, was an esthetic legacy. Piper, too, disliked the plan, but reserved the greater measure of his distaste for the developer, Justin Raymond, whom he viewed as an avaricious individual who was simply using the hospital for personal gain. Piper attributed the same self-serving motives to Mann and Cross.

Following these two informal meetings with the doctors, Nobel shared his notes with Mann and Cross—whom Piper and Sims viewed as the enemy. The two physicians saw this action as a breach of confidentiality, though Nobel had assumed there was enough community of interest to warrant the disclosure. Nobel received cordial letters of complaint from both men, but when he met with them individually, he learned how seriously upset they were and was roundly chastised in a meeting with them.

The effects of this episode were surprising and worked to the consultant's benefit. One of the aggrieved doctors was known to be difficult, and Nobel's problems with this individual earned him the sympathy of the hospital community. Eustis, the hospital president, actually called Nobel to his office and told him, "I'm sorry you had to go through that." This meeting gave Nobel an opportunity to tell

Eustis that the hospital had a problem of communication, that it lacked a functional project team, and that it needed to put together a new team that would allow it to participate in forming substantive ideas underlying plans and designs.

Meetings with hospital personnel, administrators, and other interested parties over the next several months provided Nobel with further insights into the controversies surrounding the concept plan. He observed, for example, that organizational issues seemed to have as much to do with resistance to the plan as did the particulars of the plan itself. One of these organizational issues was a schism between Eustis, who had been appointed hospital president just three years earlier, and the trustees. The trustees had micromanaged the hospital's finances and nonmedical development plans for twenty years; Eustis, however, had been struggling to wrest more control of these duties into his own hands. He had, for instance, established a hospital development committee to look at the hospital's future in terms of growth and sources of support. Although several board members served on that committee, the committee had not been directly involved in preparing the joint venture's concept plan, nor had the two plans been reconciled.

In addition, the relationship between Alper and Eustis was highly competitive. As Sims confided to Nobel during a lunch meeting, "How the development plan is settled will determine who's top man around here."

About six months later Nobel had developed a sense of where people stood and of the controversial concept plan. He met with Chairman Alper, Eustis, and the leadership of the Green Hills division and conveyed his sense that the current concept plan did not reflect the hospital's interests as embodied in the hopes of the staff and the hospital's own long-range plan. The plan, Nobel argued, failed to embody forward-looking ideas for the Green Hills division, failed to provide for preservation of the best architectural and landscape features of the site, and failed to furnish a basis for relating functional and visual aspects of new development to the existing site.

These views were developed in subsequent meetings and articulated in a "White Paper" crafted by Nobel. This document recommended that the hospital gear up to full partnership in the joint venture, an act that would shift control away from the joint venture leadership and toward the hospital, where a new and powerful coalition was forming. The importance of trust and straightforward communications in that coalition became more evident to Nobel as he met with each of its major players. The key to maximizing the contribution of each, he realized, would be to create a forum through which hospital staff members could involve themselves with the development plan and communicate with one another. Toward this end Nobel proposed that Eustis and Alper put together a functioning project team. "The team," he suggested, "will be the vehicle for getting the hospital involved in forming substantive ideas around plans and designs."

Both men liked the idea and gave Nobel the go-ahead. Working with Alper, Eustis, and Sims, Nobel compiled a list of people to be included on the new project team; each of these people received a letter of invitation stating that the role of the project team would be "to craft the relationship between the hospital's plans and commercially viable possibilities that the developer and others might suggest. This will require a planning process that guarantees skilled consideration of all interests relevant to this project."

Nobel worked to strengthen the new client group he had helped create. He did this through a series of technical studies aimed at helping team members to understand key issues, and also organized a number of internal workshops with hospital medical and administrative personnel. At the same time, he sought to rebuild the client's trust in him. Some of those most strongly in favor of preserving the campus had wondered, for example, "how someone not on the faculty, who has opposed the faculty on the preservation plan, could be seen as working for them on the new plan." Nobel suggested that the newly formed project team should undertake new studies of the site, of the values people held toward it, and the programming the hospital wished to include in a new concept plan. To deflect any suspicions of conflicting interests, he proposed that a reputable design firm be brought into these activities. The developer grudgingly agreed to this suggestion.

At a press conference held in September the original concept plan was declared off the table and it was affirmed that Nobel had been hired to review the plan and lead a new planning effort. At that conference, the joint venture was represented only by Nobel. The diversity of the hospital's real interests was now being demonstrated, and there was greater energy behind the assertion of its right to control the process. Moreover, the new planning effort became a vehicle for getting people around the table, helping them make up their minds about what the future would be like. As an example of this effect, in December 1987 Nobel conducted a workshop with thirty-two faculty and staff members of the Green Hills division. These individuals had been selected by Sims to represent the full spectrum of opinion. The goal was to draw out their values for the property and what they felt were its important elements. Nobel prepared a base map of the site (Color plate 13) divided into zones. People were asked to comment on each zone with respect to opportunities, problems, and suggestions. This exercise forced people to think about particular places, hear other views, and consider the interests of the outside community. Initial ideas were improved and alternatives were introduced as team members were moved between groups to cross-fertilize thinking. The one rule for the workshop was that no one criticize the concept plan; rather, everyone was to focus on what he or she would like to see in the future.

Nevertheless, the workshop did reveal the widespread opposition to the concept plan. By day's end, it became apparent to all that this plan would have to be shelved in favor of one developed through a new and collaborative planning effort. The workshop also helped to isolate the "radical greens," who would accept no development at all, and to identify "moderate builders" who were willing to adopt a wait-and-see attitude—a group whose voice had not yet been heard.

Meanwhile, Nobel and Sims met with community associations, listened to residents' concerns about development, and informed them of the much less threatening plans for new development.

Before long, the hospital-client team had overshadowed the joint venture's team. Mann and Cross were removed, as was the developer's planner. The developer himself was the next to go. This displacement of the "old boys" coincided with the installation of a new hospital president/CEO and a new general counsel. Nobel considered both these people a breath of fresh air—people who would take a brand-new approach that would be more pragmatic and political than ideological.

In September 1988 the hospital's board took advantage of a provision in the joint venture agreement that gave it the right to withdraw if reasonable progress had not been made. This cut the hospital's ties to the developer. The project team proved to be a powerful instrument for bringing together people with different views. Over a period of six months, the diversity of interests among people associated with the hospital was revealed, and those interests began to coalesce around a few basic beliefs about the future of the Green Hills site. Based on this work, the project team and Nobel formulated a new concept plan for the property's development, containing guidelines that linked to the hospital's long-term development plan. These guidelines included a much lower-density treatment of the oval, preservation of strategic open space, a buffer around the oval to block the encroachment of new development, buildings scaled and placed in ways that allowed unimpeded vistas from the campus, and a landscape plan within the oval that maintained the most important features of the site's historic landscaping.

The new plan was generally well received by the project team, hospital officials, and the hospital board. A few days after the plan was submitted, Alper and Piper expressed their appreciation to Nobel for the steady course he had held throughout the confusion and acrimony of the previous months. In their eyes, he had been an effective broker, giving honest opinions, helping opposing parties to understand different views, and acting as a reconciler of conflicting interests.

The Green Hills development situation had been messy, fragmented, and conflicted. Nobel could have observed, analyzed, and reported on this situation from a safe distance, but doing so would have failed to engage the warring parties around the critical issues or to reconcile their differences. Instead, Nobel waded into the currents of distrust and disagreement. He learned to play the design game as it unfolded—inventing his role and transforming the game as he moved forward. Step by step, he reframed the design problem at hand and his own role as designer; and through a series of events he helped to build a collaborative client group capable of addressing the salient issues.

The Green Hills case reveals a design game in play that is messy, fragmented, and conflictual—a game within which process managers or consultants are in danger of being trapped. As in the radiation therapy case, the consultant gradually discovered the nature of the game and tracked its evolution. Unlike the consultants in the radiation therapy case, however, Nobel did not simply play the game as he found it; instead, he actively reshaped it (Color plate 16). Nobel treated the game, the framing of the design problem at its heart, and the framing of his own role as lying squarely within the scope of his inquiry. He treated his own role, the makeup of his client system, and even the rules of the game as amenable to influence by his own professional thought and action. This influence was achieved by creatively extending the methods and approaches of an architect and spatial planner, not by starting with the language of traditional organizational consulting.

By fostering a new coalition of actors within the hospital, thereby helping that institution to establish itself as lead player, Nobel helped engineer a shift away from a development plan that he had come to see as deeply flawed. In the process, he transformed his own role from concept plan salesman to critical reviewer of the concept plan to custodian of the values inherent in the site. In this process, he took advantage of the insights brought to the surface by his mistakes, creating and building on relationships that enabled him to move flexibly among competing interest groups and eventually helping the new client team to play an active role in the development process.

❀

THE CASES IN PERSPECTIVE

The four cases in this chapter display variations of the design game, but also reveal critically important common features.

In part, the design game reflects situational factors specifically related to the design process and not otherwise associated with the political dynamics of the organization in question. For example, there is the faculty's growing hostility to the developer in Green Hills, or the engineers' defensiveness triggered by the post-occupancy evaluation data gathered by Robert Oliver. In this case the evidence suggests that the defensiveness was exacerbated (and possibly caused) by Oliver's treatment of the engineers as nonexperts and by his belief that knowing all there was to know about the place could be accomplished by assembling a few data about dysfunctional services rather than by addressing long-standing controversies within the organization. On the other hand, in the radiation therapy case, the question of where to locate the center swirled around long-standing controversy over which organization would have prominence and who in the community would be the arbiters of quality of care. Therefore the design game also becomes in part an extension of the organizational process. As such, the advent of workplace-making can reveal what conditions already exist within the organization or between organizations.

- There is a configuration of different institutional players represented by individuals who hold different, and often conflicting, interests in workplace outcomes: These different interests sometimes carry over into conflicting attitudes toward the process of workplace-making. Differences and conflicts are played out within and across organizations. For example, we have the competition between radiologic institutions in the therapy case, but we also see conflict among people within the same institutions (the president and the financial officer, for example).

- The configuration of the stakeholders exhibits the full range of phenomena associated with win/lose social games: alliances, exchanges, bargains, negotiations, and various mixtures of cooperation and antagonism.

- The configuration of interests and powers is not static. To greater or lesser degrees, it evolves throughout the workplace-making process—something best revealed by Green Hills, but also, for example, in the Ainsley case when a new player— Ainsley—enters the project in midstream and completely changes the ongoing process.

The design game also displays itself in the attitudes of the parties toward one another as they are playing the game.

- The parties may believe in the honesty and reliability of their adversaries and partners, or they may distrust one another. For example, InterCorp employee representatives distrusted their managers; the hospital staff distrusted the developer and, for a time, Nobel.

- Players may be more or less unwilling to talk publicly about the game and the sensitive issues it raises. Undiscussability appears most dramatically in the radiation therapy case (the meeting of silence): The first major challenge to the consultants is to figure out through private meetings and guesswork what is going on behind the public arena. In the cases of Robert Oliver and Green Hills, we also see the importance of undiscussability: It takes a "mistake" to reveal underlying patterns of animosity, distrust, and defensiveness.

- The hiddenness of the design game forces the process architect—whether a member of the staff of the organization or a consultant—to do two things at once: invent how to operate within the game, or change it as he or she is playing it and by entering the game figure out its nature.

- By entering the situation, and simply by asking questions, while at the same time presenting alternative options, the process architect helps the players to reframe their interests, see those interests in a different light, and shift their perspective on what would be a reasonable solution to the problem. Showing the client system the consequences of what might happen if what the client wants is achieved opens up new options and creates the opportunity for collaboration.

Workplace-making processes conditioned by the design game are neither wholly rational nor wholly irrational. The Ainsley case shows how a framework of technical rationality built into the university's reference design process—a set of carefully articulated procedures to achieve high-quality building outcomes and at the same time keep costs under control—is abandoned when these procedures stand in the way of the design goals the two most powerful players have set for themselves. The case of Robert Oliver shows how the technical-rational approach of a post-occupancy evaluation was subverted by the key actors' turf protection, defensiveness, and distrust. The potential for this subversion of agreed-upon processes—or the hindrance to the development of successful processes—is increased when distrust and undiscussability build up through the competition among different interests and when ideas cannot be tested, evaluated, and negotiated in a manner that engages stakeholders.

Collective purposes, institutional goals, and the instrumental means for achieving them are subverted by the play of interests and powers that revolves around the disparate, and often unstated, purposes of the institutional players. This subversion is raised a power when a layer of distrust, undiscussability, and untestability builds up around design games, increasing the likelihood that no one's purposes will be effectively realized. Nevertheless, technical rationality does not wholly disappear. In the Ainsley case, for example, some design decisions are still made in accordance with the institution's reference process. At InterCorp, some of the findings of the post-occupancy evaluation are put to use in designing the next headquarters building.

Our cases reveal some of the critical features common to the game of interests and also show the various ways in which managers and consultants are affected by these features or try to deal with them. In two instances—those of Ainsley and Oliver—the cases mainly show individuals being victimized by the game. The planners and the facility managers in the Ainsley case are overridden, and the project manager is scapegoated and almost fired. Oliver emerges battered and bruised from his encounter with the organization, which he learns to see as a serial killer of its consultants. In instances like these, staff members of an organization, or its consultants, suffer the effects of a design game while remaining largely ignorant of the causes. Their understandings of the game are insufficient to inform effective action on their part, and they do not take the game as a serious topic of professional inquiry—in contrast to the cases of the radiation therapy center and Green Hills, whose protagonists actively inquired into the nature of the game. In the case of Green Hills the protagonist walked into the game and began to work with it; in the course of transforming the game, he gradually understood it and could more effectively play it.

Two main variations on the theme of active inquiry into the game are represented, respectively, by the radiation therapy and Green Hills cases. In the radiation therapy case, the meeting of silence revealed how the specific form of the game of interests and powers, triggered by the prospect of locating a new radiation therapy center in the region, was clouded over. The general structure of such a design game was undoubtedly known to the consultants, although its specific form was not. Following the meeting, the consultants embarked on a process of inquiry in which they combined action and discovery, trying to learn the nuances of the game in play while at the same time educating the participants about criteria and costs for the new center and working out the shape of an eventually acceptable deal on which everybody could agree. In this process, the consultants worked at deciphering underlying agendas, patiently stripping away layers of verbal camouflage, and gently probing the real self-interests of their informants. The consultants did not transform the relationship between the players, but opened it up for redesign, which set the stage for the consensus meeting at the end of the intervention.

In the Green Hills case, Nobel began by discovering where he was and what was happening—who the players were, what coalition sponsored the developer's concept plan, what the important issues were (e.g., preservation of the land) around which the game was being played. At the same time, he formed his own judgments about which values were important at the site and became a stakeholder in the game. On this basis, Nobel sensed the need for a client group he could work with, and perhaps also the need to see how he was being used (by Piper) to effect a shift that established a new client. The change in the makeup of the dominant coalition that Nobel instigated, or abetted, is important to the planning and architectural values he believed he was serving. The Green Hills case shows how the interests of the intervenor created a focus around which to coalesce the interests of the parties in the game, and how these interests shaped the new course the game took as well as the new rules of play.

The change in the game that Nobel effects brings a range of new hospital players into active and collaborative engagement in the development process. An old set of players—the developer, the developer's staff, and the old coordinators of the planning process—drops away. One could say that Nobel helps to substitute one design coalition for another and influences how people in his client system behave toward one another—especially how they deal with animosity, distrust, defensiveness, and undiscussability.

5

The Practice and Tools of Process Architecture

W e have described process architecture as an approach to workplace-making that seeks dynamic coherence in the relationship between the work process and the work environment—integrating spatial, organizational, financial, and technological features of the workplace through uneven development. We have advanced the idea that workplace-making is a design game played by actors holding different (and often conflicting and unequal) interests, freedoms, and powers. Process architecture brings these players into active collaboration. The selection, design, and use of tools in process architecture relate to all the layers of the framework for professional practice introduced in Chapter 2: the approach, with its normative and philosophical aspects; intervention strategies, including strategies for transforming the game; and tools, including the design and structuring of events and the specific instruments to be utilized within them. This chapter presents tools utilized in the practice of process architecture.

The word *tool* tends to be used loosely to refer to many insufficiently differentiated kinds of things. Moreover, tools are often treated as objects in themselves, wrenched out of the context in which their application makes sense. The process architect, however, uses tools with fine-tuned sensitivity and timeliness, guided by the principles and values inherent in this approach. William Coaldrake's *The Way of the Carpenter* is a study of the tools used by master carpenters in Japan and of the spirit in which those tools are used.[1] It is a study of the way of a craft that is also an art. In Japan, an underpinning of religious ritual underlies the building process and craft, as well as the master carpenter's special way with his tools that is embedded in a deep understanding of the materials he uses. We have a similar appreciation for how tools can be used to achieve the purposes of process architecture.

Like any craftsman, a master of process architecture selects and uses tools in very special ways; these are strongly related to the people and circumstances of each particular situation, and blend their effects so as to contribute value to the organization beyond the creation of the workplace itself. In process architecture, tools are used as much to move the design game toward a successful outcome as to develop or convey information and insight. The blow of a hammer by a journeyman carpenter drives a nail, connecting pieces of wood. The blow of a hammer by a master craftsman is a step toward the creation of a temple. The execution of a post-occupancy survey by a skilled social scientist provides information about how people react to their space. In the hands of a process architect, such an analysis is accomplished and used in ways that help clarify what a high-performance workplace means and that integrate this new insight into a process of workplace-making that advances the development of the organization as a whole.

In Chapter 2 we suggest that as process architects seek to make such co-invention of the new workplace a reality, they must cope with five challenging tasks: creating situational awareness, process design, artifact design, decision-making, and evaluation of the existing and the altered workplace. For each of these professional activities there are tools that lend themselves to collaborative approaches through design inquiry.

Process architects also focus on how work in their client organizations is actually done and how the structure of the work is or ought to be changing. Collaborative engagement of stakeholders in the process of inquiry is essential for this learning to occur. This is difficult to achieve with the typical tools available to workplace professionals, such as survey research and other tools drawn from applied social science. However, these tools may also be used within the framework of process architecture.

We have chosen to describe two types of tools that are particularly useful in surfacing latent views and values of the participants in the workplace-making process and in discovering how work is actually done and how it might be improved. The first approach, illustrated by the DEC/Monsanto case in the first section of this chapter, uses the methods of ethnography to uncover actual patterns of work, especially the social networks of interaction or *communities of practice* through which workers cooperatively tackle emergent issues. These methods include the empirical study of work in process by field researchers skilled at both the unobtrusive observation of work practices and the conducting of interviews to elicit stories from which underlying patterns of practice can be inferred.

A second approach to the analysis of actual or desirable work practice depends on collaboration between outside consultants and insider-practitioners. A collaborative process of design inquiry seeks to surface and test the players' objectives, agendas, and preconceptions. Concrete design games are one form of interactive tools used for surfacing values, evaluating the existing workplace, and framing its problems and opportunities, and are important ingredients in this process. Two examples of such concrete design games will be discussed in the second part of this chapter.

THE ETHNOGRAPHIC APPROACH TO PRODUCT DEVELOPMENT

The story of the DEC/Monsanto case[2] tells how an ethnographic approach to the study of work evolved. Unlike post-occupancy evaluation, which relies on social survey research methods and other techniques of applied social science, the ethnographic approach employs the methodology of the anthropological visitor. The ethnographer focuses not on workers' satisfaction or dissatisfaction with the current workplace, but on how work is actually done, especially the social interactions essential to organizational performance. This approach also considers the organizational culture of work—that is, the systems of beliefs, values, and underlying assumptions built into the performance of work in a particular organizational setting. The ethnographer observes who does what and with whom, noting how materials and information are used. Observations are supplemented by open-ended interviews with workers and managers. Ethnographic inquiry is conducted over relatively long periods of time (months or years). The insights gained make it possible to define patterns of interaction among the various dimensions of the work environment—spatial, technological, and organizational—and the actual processes of work.

The DEC/Monsanto case offered here helps us understand how ethnographic methods can be used for the study of work, which influences workplace-making and, particularly in this case, the development of technological products to support the work practice. It describes a project carried out between 1988 and 1993 by Charles Kukla of the Product Development Organization at the Digital Equipment Corporation (DEC) and Anne Clemens, formerly a DEC staff member and now a principal of the Da Vinci Group, a human factors consulting firm. The project was undertaken in collaboration with the Monsanto Company, first at its nylon production unit in Pensacola, Florida, and later at its Saflex (car window adhesive) plant at Indian Orchard, Massachusetts. At both of these facilities, DEC researchers focused on the process control function with the aim of designing and testing software systems. The design of the resulting software product occurred at Pensacola, and the testing mainly at Indian Orchard.

The DEC ethnographers organized their data collection around key business processes. For example, they studied responses to production breakdowns and the handling of customer complaints. They emphasized the discovery of communities of practice—the informal networks of practitioners through which key functions are actually carried out, regardless of how formal organization charts may indicate they are carried out. The field techniques employed were mainly ethnographic. The researchers collected information in the form of individual stories about the performance of work. They gave special attention to collective stories of the workplace, that is, stories frequently told—though seen in different ways—by different practitioners. The researchers used these multiperspective stories in the design of new technological or spatial arrangements; the quantitative data collected from observation or survey research were, in contrast, minimally useful for these purposes.

Kukla, Clemens, and their colleagues evolved their ethnographic methodology over the course of a four-year collaboration with Monsanto. Thus, we present this story as a developmental account of their work, showing how they invented tools for study and design in response to problems encountered and discoveries made.

The Pensacola Project

In 1988, DEC's Integrated Manufacturing and Product Development Group began a project at Monsanto's nylon production plant at Pensacola, Florida. The purpose was to study the use of existing process control equipment, how control room operators worked, and how DEC's workstations could be introduced into the environment. Initially, the DEC group visualized the Monsanto study as a large-scale project involving the automation of nylon production operations; they saw their task as figuring out what people in the plant actually did, so that DEC could better introduce its ready-made package for production control.

Anne Clemens began her investigation of work practices with traditional task analysis, using standardized questionnaires and interviews. She soon discovered, however, that these techniques did not yield information useful for the design of workstations. Her methods and models described a static list of activities, showing who did what, but they could not capture how groups of engineers interacted with one another, especially when their work was not routine. The survey methodology was selective in that it excluded certain types of data, notably those relating to change and interaction, it presupposed a stable and routine practice, and it did not capture the dynamics of the work environment (Figure 5.1). Although the photograph portrays a

Figure 5.1   The control room.

controlled, ordered environment where problems apparently receive ample consideration and thorough analysis, Clemens described a different picture: "alarms buzzing, and people talking, people jumping up and down, walking around . . . [the models] don't reflect what the workplace is like."

Clemens discovered that process control engineers spend most of their time talking with one another about problems, but she was puzzled about what made it crucial for them to spend their time in this way, for what purposes they did so, or in what combinations. Nor could the engineers give her a clear picture of the kinds of problems they encountered or how they tried to solve them. When asked what they did, they would simply say, "We make nylon."

The most confusing aspect for Clemens and Kukla was that their observation of what was going on did not match what the statistical data told them. To their surprise, they also discovered that once they had made a list of recommendations to consider, they couldn't implement any without implementing all. Their methodology and the data they harvested based on that methodology did not help them to see the interdependence between the different activities in the production process, between the work and the technology, or between the space and the technology. The key insight in their discovery of this was that their data showed that communication tasks represented 10 percent of the total workload, but their interpretations of what they observed showed that communication was the predominant task.

The confusion led Clemens and Kukla to adopt a new research approach. They realized that in order to design new work-related software products for Monsanto's process engineers, they would have to develop tools within the ethnographic approach in order to make sense of a rapidly fluctuating work environment—one in which, for example, operators called in sick, pumps broke down, and customers complained: a series of unanticipated, independent events. In the light of this realization, in 1989 the researchers began a second study of control room operations at Pensacola, but based this time on the ethnographic methods of detailed, long-term observations of collaborative work and open-ended interviews with workers. Using her new tools, Clemens asked her informants, "What types of events trigger the need for talking together?" and, "With this type of event, who talks with whom?" Questions were framed to elicit stories in which engineers would reveal what *they* saw as important about their ways of working together.

In her new approach to interviewing, Clemens treated control room engineers as experts on their own work environment, while she and her partner functioned as experts on work analysis, collaborating with the operators to uncover how unanticipated production problems arose and how they were solved. Different engineers told similar stories, but from different points of view. These stories, generated by the engineers, were thought of by each group as its own. The stories revealed the existence of informal problem-solving groups—a revelation confirmed by subsequent observation of work practice. By drawing circles around individuals who were actors in the same problem-centered story, and noting overlapping circles of actors involved in different stories, the researchers were able to identify informal work teams that did not exist in formal organization charts. The DEC researchers called these groups *communities of practice*[3] (Figure 5.2). The organization's official hierarchical structure at any given time was shaped by the current ideas held by management. In contrast, the membership and structure of the problem-solving teams were shaped by events and by the competence associated with solving various problems. These teams were event-driven—convening intermittently—and autonomous, and outlived the multiple reengineering efforts during the time Clemens and Kukla studied.

Just prior to the study, the Monsanto facility had reorganized from a system based on hierarchical decision-making and reporting to one based on decentralized, relatively autonomous multifunctional teams. Each team had responsibility for a production area. In 1988, when Clemens and Kukla were working at Pensacola, the new teams were in the process of learning how to establish communication routines among themselves. This reengineering process and design of new work practices did not recognize the informal communication pattern represented by the problem-solving teams (Figure 5.3). Hierarchical organizational structures are treelike and assume that work is routine, stable, and predictable. The working organizational structure

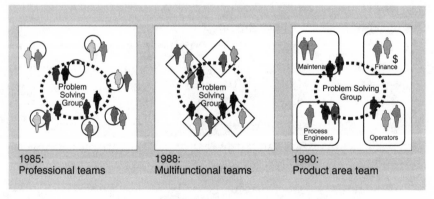

| 1985: | 1988: | 1990: |
| Professional teams | Multifunctional teams | Product area team |

Figure 5.2   Identifying communities of practice.

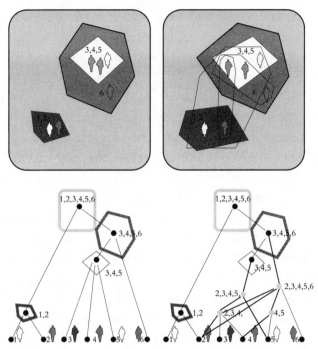

Figure 5.3 Detecting the communities of practice.

in the Pensacola facility looked more like a semilattice than a tree. This structure was the basis for Clemens and Kukla's tool design. Working from the narratives Clemens collected from the operators, she and Kukla used graphic analysis as a tool to map the problem-solving groups.

The problem-solving teams uncovered by Clemens and her colleagues did not exist on any of the organizational charts. They reflected the informal rather than the formal structure of the organization. Membership on these teams was shaped by events and by the competencies required to solve various problems. The teams formed communities of practice, and, since these communities of practice were critical to the task of keeping production flowing smoothly despite nonroutine disruptions, they were even more important to day-to-day work than were the newly organized production area groups or the functional teams that had existed prior to Monsanto's reorganization of the Pensacola facility. Indeed, it turned out that the informal problem-solving teams had both preceded and survived the Pensacola reorganization.

Based on the stories and observations they had collected, the researchers constructed four descriptive work scenarios. From these detailed accounts they developed eleven product mock-ups. Initially, DEC's strategy had been to automate existing work patterns, replacing individual workers with machines. Now, however, the emphasis shifted to the development of products aimed at supporting the collaborative operations of individuals in informal work teams. The researchers also constructed prescriptive scenarios, which described what it would be like to work under new circumstances with the new products in ways that seemed real to the workers. By using these scenarios, the operators, engineers, and managers could then describe their own work and experience and could see how the new tools might be built and used in their own unique situation. The prescriptive scenario is still useful today, several years after its creation.

The main result of Clemens and Kukla's new research methodology was a product called DEC@aGlance, which was introduced to the market in 1992. DEC@aGlance was a tool-building product created to improve communication for the process engineers. The researchers believe the strategy they used to develop DEC@aGlance was influenced by the tools they developed for inquiry. "We were faced with trying to describe and represent a dynamic and ever changing work environment in the same fashion that the engineers and operators were faced with solving problems in a dynamic and ever changing environment."[4]

Large chemical plants often control major operations through computerized systems, storing data in a real-time database. The Pensacola plant had eleven large control systems, each with its own database. Process engineers working in the plant's control rooms accessed data by means of PCs and spreadsheets. When they needed a particular data set, they had to write a program to access the data and deliver it to the spreadsheet in the form of prescribed rows and columns. But writing programs was time consuming, and the moment for solving a hot problem often passed before the program could be completed.

The established system called for process engineers to predefine their programming requirements, when in reality they were usually unable to predict the problems they would have to solve on any given day. DEC@aGlance was designed to provide process engineers with online access to the data they needed when they needed it. The product consisted of pieces of software overlaid on the databases and the spreadsheets, so that a process engineer could, as Kukla explained:

> . . . ask the system to give him the temperature of this unit over the last three hours and put the data into rows and columns on the spreadsheet. The system goes out and gets the data and delivers it to his spreadsheet. The engineer talks in the language he works in—for example, tag names, process temperatures, and process pressure. He does not have to know what computer the information is on, what network the information goes over, or anything about the computer technology.

DEC@aGlance allowed operators and process engineers to use familiar spreadsheets or statistical packages such as Excel or Lotus 1-2-3. The system made it possible to communicate across databases without having to shift software. For example, an engineer whose spreadsheet showed the effect of temperature on nylon production could communicate with someone else whose spreadsheet related nylon productivity to pressure, calling up that spreadsheet on his or her own machine without having to worry about the software or the network. In the process, the engineer could substitute certain operations in cyberspace for the same operations in physical space.

Applying the New Tools at Indian Orchard

Having developed DEC@aGlance at Pensacola, the DEC researchers initiated a new project at a Monsanto facility in Indian Orchard, Massachusetts, to test the software further and to introduce it at that facility. The Indian Orchard plant manufactured Saflex, an energy-absorbing adhesive placed between two layers of glass to make a shatterproof automobile windshield.

Initially, the researchers saw the Indian Orchard project as an opportunity to test DEC@aGlance as a new tool in the control room. Kukla and Clemens also wanted to continue to develop their methods for studying informal work groups. Their new client, on the other hand, wanted them to take a problem-centered approach and design new products in response to the work problems encountered at Indian Orchard. With these combined objectives, the researchers took several steps toward the further development of their methodology. In accordance with their clients' wishes, they focused on the business issues Monsanto was trying to resolve. To do this, they set up a program to study the work of process engineers, zeroing in on the task of solving problems signaled by customer complaints. Clemens' group began to study customer complaints, and Kukla undertook the design of products to support the process engineers.

Clemens and her group began collecting voluminous background information. Though they were not chemists, they learned to trace the flow of chemicals required for the fabrication of the end product and the ways in which production functions were organized. Their interviewing techniques were, again, open-ended searches for stories centered on problems: in this case, the problem of responding to customer complaints. They sought out collective stories shared by communities of practice but seen in different ways by different informants. They were searching, again, for common threads that would suggest the design of tools useful for a variety of activities.

The researchers soon discovered the need to understand two key dimensions of any work process: (1) the properties of information

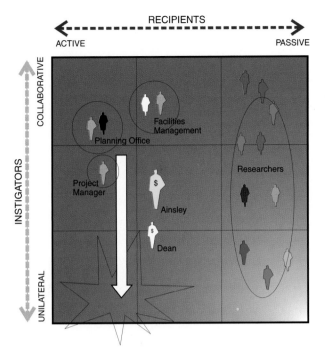

Color Plate 10 *The Ainsley design game.* The project started out as a process of collaborative and engaged design inquiry. Despite the many actors involved, it became an example of active but isolated decision-making as soon as the powerful donor entered the scene.

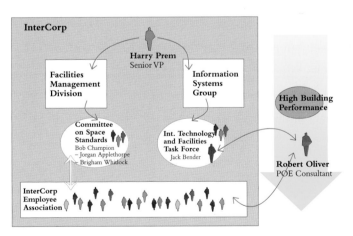

Color Plate 11 *InterCorp: a client system in conflict.* Oliver's principal client was Bender, the head of the Integrated Technology and Facilities Task Force. However, Bender had neither authority nor influence over the other key stakeholders in the project. This included the architect responsible for the spatial design, planning, and project management (Applethorpe) and the engineer responsible for HVAC, construction, and management (Whitlock), and the InterCorp Employee Association.

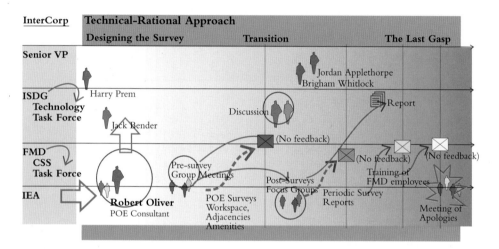

Color Plate 12 *Oliver's journey.* Robert Oliver found himself in a destructive design game woven around the development of an organizational headquarters building. He became embroiled in an organizational labyrinth he could neither understand nor influence.

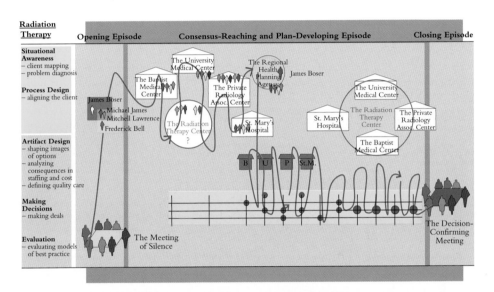

Color Plate 13 *Radiation therapy center: aligning interests.* The siting for a new medical facility raises contentious organizational issues. The consultants uncovered the design game and used their understanding of it to invent a strategy for unlocking a stalemated workplace-making process.

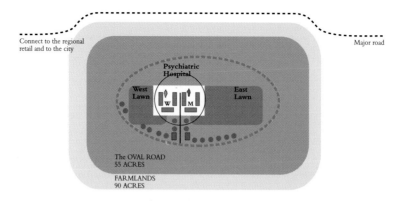

Color Plate 14 *The Green Hills site.* Growth in land use had brought the metropolitan area to the doorstep of this once-rural location. Of the 235 acres on the Green Hills campus, 55 were used intensively for the purposes of the psychiatric hospital and were encompassed by an oval road. About 30 more acres were used for staff housing and for other buildings that served hospital functions. The remaining acreage was open for possible development.

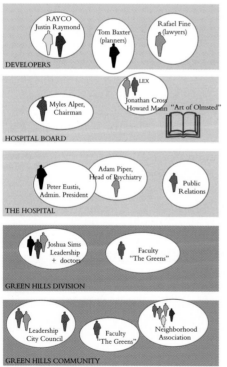

The developer team
1. The developer: Justin Raymond and his firm, Rayco
2. The lawyer: Rafael Fine, Rayco's counsel
3. The planning firm: Tom Baxter, planner for Rayco

The hospital board team
1. Hospital board: Myles Alper, chairman
2. LEX: Hospital's legal counsel; Jonathan Cross, representative; Howard Mann, historian, working with Cross

The hospital (the city)
1. Hospital administration: Peter Eustis, president; Adam Piper, head of psychiatry (both the city and Green Hills divisions)
2. Hospital public relations

The hospital (Green Hills division)
1. Leadership: Joshua Sims and his steering committee, about a dozen doctors
2. Faculty and staff of Green Hills division, including a small, determined "not a single blade of grass" group, dubbed the Radical Greens

The town of Green Hills
1. The Green Hills leadership, including the city council
2. The Greens
3. Citizens, especially the neighborhood associations

Color Plate 15 *Green Hills stakeholders.*

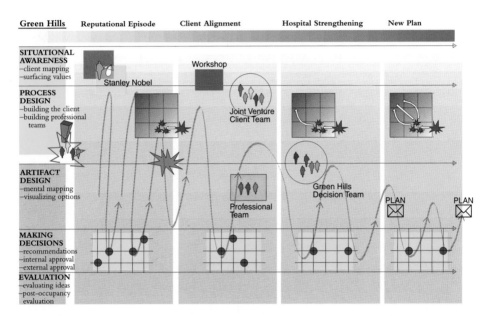

| Green Hills | Reputational Episode | Client Alignment | Hospital Strengthening | New Plan |

SITUATIONAL AWARENESS
–client mapping
–surfacing values

Stanley Nobel

Workshop

PROCESS DESIGN
–building the client
–building professional teams

Joint Venture Client Team

ARTIFACT DESIGN
–mental mapping
–visualizing options

Professional Team

Green Hills Decision Team

PLAN

PLAN

MAKING DECISIONS
–recommendations
–internal approval
–external approval

EVALUATION
–evaluating ideas
–post-occupancy evaluation

Color Plate 16 *Green Hills process development.* A process architect, step by step, but often to his own surprise, transformed a dysfunctional design game into one that gave fuller expression to values held by the majority of stakeholders.

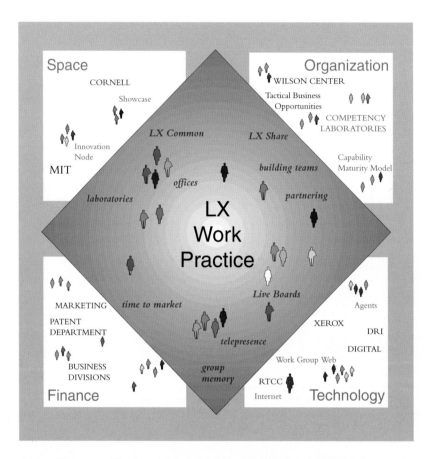

Color Plate 17 *The key players in the LX workplace experiment.*

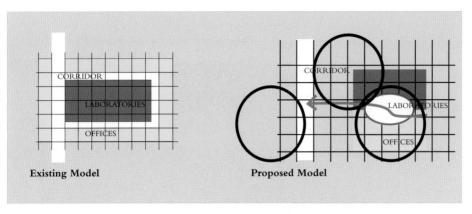

Existing Model

Proposed Model

The traditional layout of research building
Laboratories are located in the center of the building, with offices along the perimeter.

Virtual co-location
The focus of the research is located in an innovative node that is networked with related laboratories in other buildings. The corridor is transformed into a common, an interactive workplace and news center.

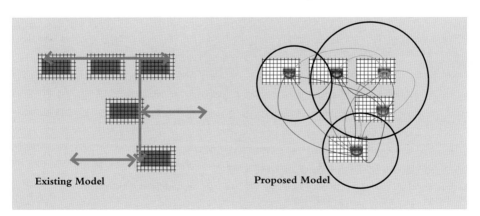

Existing Model

Proposed Model

The campus model
Buildings linked by the infrastructure—a city grid of roads, utilities, and services, isolation of various processes, segregation by function.

The New England town model
Multiple linkages, integration of various processes, sharing of information and services. Overlapping towns and location of commons within the existing grid, creating virtual co-location of project centers.

Color Plate 18 *Traditional and innovative organization of research activities.*

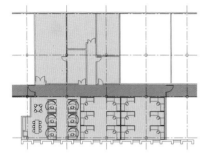

The original plan for the LX labs: The narrow corridor lined by office compartments, some closed offices, and cubicles. The footprint of the old wall was still dominant in the layout.

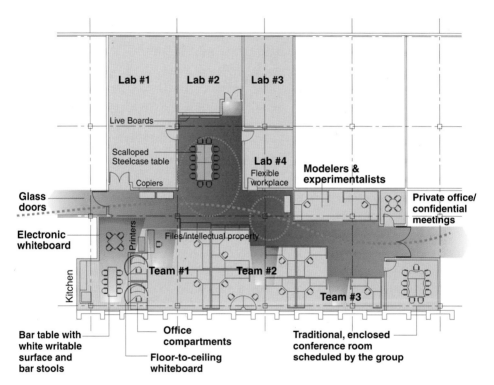

The new plan of what became the core of the LX work area: The traditional double-loaded corridor widens and allows for constant spill-over from the adjacent laboratories, meeting rooms, and service areas. Boundaries are blurred; individual offices are replaced by cubicles feeding energy into the Common, fostering collaboration and communication.

Color Plate 19 *The marketplace for research.* As contrasted with the traditional corridor layout shown at the top, the LX Common has a very open feel. It is partly open to the main path of circulation and has windows and a door leading off to adjacent LX work areas. The Common is an open window, giving the lab members contact with the outside world.

that engineers use in their collaborative work (for example, the type of information used, together with its quality, location, mobility, and mode of representation) and (2) how work practices of engineers and operators are structured by spatial location, the design of physical space, the use of paper or electronic media, and such organizational factors as systems for policy-making and exercise of authority.

In their study of engineers' responses to customer complaints, for example, the researchers found that when process engineers try to identify the root causes of a production problem, they must recreate the operation in question. The engineers generally did this through simulations, the effectiveness of which depended, in turn, on the properties of information, media, and spatial and organizational arrangements.

The physical layout of the Indian Orchard facility was not particularly conducive to the process control work effort (Figure 5.4). The

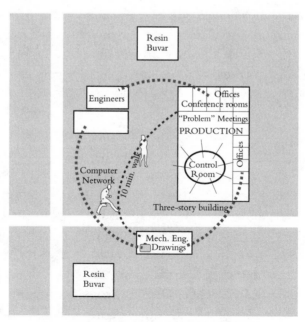

Figure 5.4 The Saflex facility.

entire process engineering operation, consisting of engineering support, mechanical support, and storage, was contained in a single building adjacent to the production facility. This building housed two groups of engineers: one assigned to the plant as a whole, and the other responsible solely for the smooth operation of Saflex production. Saflex's principal raw materials were produced in another adjacent building. The corporate research building was located at the opposite end of the Indian Orchard facility, far from the production buildings, and engineering drawings, often needed for day-to-day work, were produced and stored in yet another building, a five- or ten-minute walk from the production and engineering buildings.

The Saflex building also housed process engineers close to the production activity. Control rooms and offices were located at different levels and on different sides of the building. The laboratory where samples were analyzed and tested was in the same area as the control room, adjacent to the production facility. Engineering offices and conference rooms were grouped together at one end. Design or problem-solving meetings were often held in offices, application meetings in conference rooms, and routine production meetings in a variety of places.

The focal point for information was the control room, which, in Anne Clemens's words, was ". . . very small, very noisy, with temperatures that may vary from 70 to 45 degrees. You can't go there and have a conversation, because it's either freezing or hot. [The engineers] are just not there. They go other places to meet."

DEC set up a joint client-researcher design team at Indian Orchard. That team met every two weeks over the seventeen-month project period to review progress, form a shared understanding of design issues, and decide how best to attack particular problems—by designing new tools, modifying existing ones, or changing business processes. The DEC researchers discovered that there were serious problems with the plant's spatial and technological infrastructure. Some people had PCs, while others had regular computer terminals, without any connection to each other or any ability to read information in a common format. The control room operators and the engineers did not have access to the same information. Some information was recorded only on sheets of paper (called hand logs), which meant that to get it people had to go up to the control room from their offices, write the information down, and come back down again. The scheduling was done in a location distant from Indian Orchard and did not take into account breakdowns in the production line. The downtime reporting was important for adjusting the production flow, but that information was available only to a handful of people. Based on these and a number of similar issues they detected early in their work, Clemens and Kukla became convinced, as they said, that "these problems had to be fixed before we could do anything else." Of the problems encountered, those relating to scheduling and downtime reporting appeared to offer the greatest opportunities for technical solutions. The scheduling and the downtime reporting were interdependent and were closely related to customers' complaints. Therefore these issues quickly became the key problems the team grappled with understanding and trying to design solutions for. In detail, the difficulties in these two areas (scheduling and downtime reporting) were as follows.

SCHEDULING

The schedule (the critical document of production control) specified how many rolls of Saflex had to be produced in a given hour, and in what customer-specific combinations. The master scheduler was located in St. Louis, as was the computer for worldwide Saflex operations (a batch processing system—so, as Clemens said, "communication stopped in the middle of the night."). Each computer system had been created independently to solve different problems: in St. Louis, tasks at the corporate level; at Indian Orchard, problems of reporting. Every morning, the master scheduler phoned the Indian Orchard scheduler, who kept her own version of the master schedule on a PC. The Indian Orchard scheduler had to create customized schedules each day, always looking one week ahead. Communication between Indian Orchard and St. Louis was either by phone or handwritten on paper, even though both systems had data on computers. Therefore the transfer of information was highly prone to error, and it did not even contain such information as whether rolls had been returned because of defects or whether a production line was down.

At any point in time in a complex and highly dependent system a unique combination of breakdown events can occur. Resources are limited and usually committed to resolving the current set of breakdowns. Automation strategies can anticipate a limited number of breakdown situations, but not all. Since any combination of breakdown events can occur at any point in time, the work situation is dynamic even in highly automated systems (Figure 5.5).

DOWNTIME REPORTING

This was another problem. When, for example, a pump failed, the process controller had to leave the control room, collect the shift logs, and bring them back to his or her office for analysis and adjustment. In some cases these logs could not be removed from the production line—the controller had to hand-copy the data. The information in the downtime report was available to only a few people, few of whom understood how to use the data.

The DEC researchers envisioned a product that would enable the shift foreman to scan his shift logs into the computer, thereby making

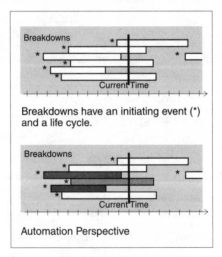

Figure 5.5 Detecting combinations of breakdown events.

them available to everyone in the work group. What the researchers found most interesting, however, was that downtime reporting was closely related to scheduling and to customer complaints. From the master schedule (required number of lots of a certain type by a certain date) a daily production schedule was produced. A plan for the shift (three shifts per day) was produced based on the daily production schedule and the previous shifts' performance. At the end of the day, a summary indicated what was produced and identified the cause of any variance from planned production (e.g., breakdown). Downtime told the scheduler what the current capacity of the production line could be, as well as the discrepancy against what the plan was and against what was needed as stated in the master schedule. The downtime report was the link between the master schedule, the shift plans, what was actually produced, and the current line capability and capacity.

This report had a dramatic influence on the scheduling of the line. Downtime reporting was, in fact, part of a much larger issue concerning the number, consistency, and utility of reports. The researchers found that some thirty-seven people generated eighty-five different types of reports—shift logs, schedules, equipment reports, and so forth. One possible strategy of improvement, they thought, might focus on redundancy and inefficiency. In gathering production data for use in management control, for example, a piece of data such as a shift log had to be transcribed by seven different people (including operator, foreman, and operations manager), each of whom had to copy it as it passed up the chain. The entire shift report was not necessarily transcribed seven different times, but each person had to extract information out of the report for his or her own purposes. On the surface this might seem acceptable, but the shift report no longer served to coordinate work or provide a record of actions taken. This led to difficulty in recreating the situation, and, therefore, in reflecting on what actually occurred in a given day. Since the reports were not connected, nor were actions tied to the reports, it was difficult to analyze problems, and corrective actions taken were apt to be counterproductive. This document did not serve to coordinate work or to provide a record of actions taken.

But the researchers also saw a potential for using reports to show how information entered into the performance and control of work—what people chose to count, how categories were established, how information was collected—especially for purposes of quality control. The reports, taken together, presented a picture of how the plant operated or how it ran at a given point in time. These two potential uses of reports matched the two kinds of problems the process controllers had to solve.

The DEC researchers chose the problem of downtime reporting as a first step into the more general area of reporting. They designed a space with computer support in which it was possible to scan in shift reports so as to make them generally accessible to the engineers, thereby providing what Kukla called "a blueprint for the bigger picture." The aim of this intervention was to simplify and consolidate the reporting process, making reports more transparent and widely accessible, so that engineers in different parts of the world could bring their multiple perspectives to bear on the same problems. For instance, a change in line speed with a change in material was producing a quality problem. In the existing system the discovery of the cause occurred only inadvertently when an engineer who was working on the problem was present during the event and was able to create a causal path. However, "The idea was not just to simplify and consolidate. First we wanted to reduce the overlap and redundancy, then map the reports together to form the big picture. The other strategy was to link the reports to actions so that actions could be better coordinated and so that situations could be recreated for later analysis." The computer-supported room was not going to fix all these problems but was viewed as a step along the way.

Afterword

The primary significance of the DEC/Monsanto case is its illustration of an ethnographic, design-oriented approach to the study of work and of how the understanding thus obtained can be used to develop a new technology product that can both improve and trans-form existing practice. The DEC researchers learned to adopt an open-ended, event- and problem-centered approach to interviewing and observation. Their new methods produced stories that revealed which problems were perceived as important and how informal work groups—communities of practice—mobilized themselves to under-stand and overcome obstacles to the smooth flow of production.

One of the remarkable things in this project was that, because of the nature of their conclusions, Kukla and Clemens had to convince not only the client but also the technology developers themselves to rethink the types of products that should be built. From the view-point of the workplace professional, the DEC/Monsanto case illus-trates a critical advance. The new professional must learn how work is really done, and, drawing upon the expertise of those who do the work, help them collectively articulate requirements for the future workplace. The process is basically the same whether one deals with information technology or spatial arrangements. Ethnographic methods can help the researcher to enter new substantive realms of work and to observe and listen to workers as experts, learning to make productive use of his or her own ignorance. In this process, the ethnographic researcher can develop a feel for the common patterns that show up across different worlds of work.

Because of their understandable focus on computers, the DEC researchers initially tried to solve spatial problems—for example, the distance between the process control room and the building that housed engineering drawings—through computer technology. In effect, the researchers wanted to use the computer to make relations of spatial proximity irrelevant, a strategy with major implications for workplace design. But in their study of production control, the researchers discovered situations where spatial proximity seemed to be unavoidably important. Their findings suggest certain limitations to a strategy that relies exclusively on the computer, and point to the benefits of an integrated spatial-technological approach to the work-place.

Using the new understandings gained through ethnographic methods, the DEC researchers changed their objectives. Having begun with the goal of automating the production control process, they shifted to the goal of enhancing the collaborative work carried out by informal problem-solving teams. They changed course, as Shoshana Zuboff has put it, from *automating* to *informating*.[5] In this process, the researchers learned to focus on the infrastructure of space, technology, and organization through which information is generated, processed, represented, distributed, and used to set and solve problems.

❖

CONCRETE DESIGN GAMES

The workplace professional can also surface and test the values, objectives, agendas, and preconceptions of all the stakeholders in the workplace as players within the context of a concrete design game— an actual game in which the players experience a situation that feels authentic and that helps them to be more effective in playing out the larger design game of which they are a part. Concrete design games are real games that require interaction among stakeholders in a workplace-making process and that are used by process architects for collaborative design inquiry. Success in utilizing these concrete design games usually depends on collaboration between outside consultants and insider-practitioners.

These tools may be used for many purposes: to diagnose existing design processes; to imagine design products and processes that synthesize the conflicting interests and images of a variety of stakeholders; to invent strategies for change in product and process; and to enact strategies of change. They can also be used in such contexts to build teams of professionals, clients, and users, and to train participants in methods and attitudes conducive to collaborative design and redesign of workplaces or work processes.

Two concrete design games are illustrated in this section: the sailboat game used by the Coopers & Lybrand team in the Bank of Boston case, and the envelope game used by Julia Voysey in the case of University Research Laboratories for the purposes of clarifying how space was, and might be, arranged. In both instances, the game was used to help the participants gain new awareness, involve them in an inquiry into the relationships between work processes and work environments, and prepare them to engage in further rounds of collaborative design inquiry.

The Sailboat Game

The sailboat game, developed by Eliza O'Donnell of the firm of Coopers & Lybrand, was first used in setting up the redesigned paper processing operations (stock transfer and stock custody) at the Bank of Boston's Canton facility. In that application, the game served several purposes: (1) critiquing existing work processes; (2) inventing alternative work processes; (3) teaching the just-in-time approach; (4) improving work processes; and (5) building teams for the new workplace.

In a more fundamental sense, however, the sailboat game is about learning to redesign and improve business processes. It aims at communicating to players a certain mind-set and associated techniques for the continual improvement of such processes.

HOW THE GAME WORKS

The sailboat game is designed to represent a typical manufacturing situation. Here, the customer has ordered a toy sailboat. The customer's marketing and engineering departments have worked with the manufacturer's operating people who will produce the sailboat. The customer has said what he or she wants the product to look like, and the marketing and engineering people have come up with a design (Figure 5.6). The sailboat consists of four layers of Lego-like plastic "stickle bricks." These can have double or triple rows of interlockable

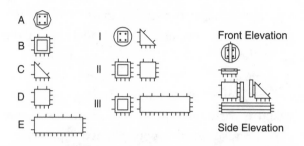

Figure 5.6   The sailboat and its subassemblies.

pegs, and have different colors. The engineers have divided the sailboat into four subassemblies and have come up with a set of instructions—words and drawings—for producing each one. The customer has never seen the instructions, which are very cryptic. Marketing has said, "This is what we want," and manufacturing and engineering have said, "Okay, this is how we've designed it." The engineers have never worked with the people out on the floor, though they may have worked with the highest level of people in manufacturing.

THE SETUP FOR THE GAME

Participants, who play the role of operators in the manufacturing group, are to put the sailboat together. They are divided into four groups, corresponding to each of four subassemblies. Each group has a workstation (a table). In addition, a material handler provides materials for the operators. There is also a station for the customer.

Each workstation gets a model of the complete sailboat it is to produce, plus written instructions for assembly as prepared by engineering. Workstation 1 gets red and white bricks. Workstation 2 gets only yellow bricks, and must wait for inputs from workstation 1. At workstation 3, which receives inputs from workstation 2, there are only blue bricks. At workstation 4, the operators have only green bricks, plus instructions for the final assembly. The work flow is initially set up so that each department gets its supplies from the material handler. The semifinished parts then flow from one workstation to the next.

The game requires twelve players. There are four operators, one per table. In addition, there are three quality control inspectors, assistants who move the material, suppliers, and a supervisor who maintains order. Game instructors play several roles: the customer, calling out orders; the accountant, providing information on plays of the game; and the consultant, making suggestions during caucuses that take place between rounds of play.[6]

When the sailboat game is applied to a paper processing function, such as opening up an account in a financial service organization (the Bank of Boston was the first such application), the different-colored pieces represent different tasks: Red signifies filling out paperwork, blue signifies looking up account numbers, and green signifies typing account cards. In the end, a completed account is produced.

PLAYING THE GAME

The customer yells out one order for sailboats every minute for ten minutes; thus, there are ten cycles per round. The number of sailboats ordered can vary from one to twenty-five. After each round, the operators receive data from the accountant, conduct root cause and value-added analyses of operations during that round, and try to make improvements, subject to the following constraints:

1. The manufacturing group must respond exactly to the customer's order—for example, delivering eight completed boats if the customer asks for eight.

2. The group can't redesign the product.

3. The group is limited to two improvements per round, so it has to weigh the value of any proposed improvement, which may involve redesign of jobs, work flow, or spatial arrangements.

Stress levels in the game rise with the number of improvements attempted, so there has to be a balance of improvements and stress associated with them.

Customers have clear expectations in the game. The customer expects to pay a fair price for a sailboat. The customer also expects a quality product and timely delivery. If the customer calls out "Eight sailboats," he or she should have eight in hand at the end of one minute.

In the first minute of the first round, the customer orders eight sailboats. The operators can usually deliver eight, because each group will utilize the four already completed samples. Thus, with only four more to make, the groups can easily supply eight sailboats with zero defects. In the second round, however, the customer boosts the order to ten. There are no more samples available, and the operators are trying to work from the cryptic directions supplied to them. It is not unusual for them to get nine wrong. So when the client orders six in the next round, the players have to deliver fifteen—the new six and the backorder of nine.

In ten minutes, the customer asks for a total of sixty-six sailboats, creating a great deal of stress for the players. At each step, the three inspectors struggle to determine, "Is this sailboat (or subassembly) put together correctly?" The probability of not producing sixty-six acceptable sailboats in the first round is high.

Worksheets kept by the accountants show deliveries, returns for defects, backorders, costs per boat, and prices paid by the customer (Figure 5.7). The worksheet indicates how learning through repeated

Round	# Ordered	# Made	Labor Cost Per Unit	Space Cost Per Unit	Reject Rate	$/Unit	Profit
	66	50	$ 85	$ 15	0.9	$ 100	$(80)
2	66	57	$ 25	$ 15	0.5	$ 40	$(20)
3	66	66	$ 10	$ 8	0.2	$ 18	$ 2
4	66	66	$ 9	$ 8	0.12	$ 17	$ 3
5	66	66	$ 8	$ 8	0.08	$ 16	$ 4
6	66	66	$ 8	$ 7	0.05	$ 15	$ 5
7	66	66	$ 7	$ 7	0.05	$ 14	$ 6
8	66	66	$ 6	$ 5	0.01	$ 11	$ 9
9	66	66	$ 4	$ 5	0.01	$ 9	$ 11

Figure 5.7   Sample worksheet.

rounds of the game and adjustments in work processes lead to reductions in space requirements, unit cost, and product rejection rate. The game provides for a twenty- to thirty-minute caucus between rounds, during which costs are tallied and performance is assessed. Players find that they are losing money and draw lessons that can be applied to real-life work.

Some quotes from the participants indicate the degree to which this game concretizes the larger design game of which they are all a part:

> At the end of a round, there is a caucus, lasting twenty or thirty minutes. The costs are tallied up. You show them the price they sold each widget for, and how much it cost to produce. And you find out they're losing loads of money. They draw lessons learned, and see which ones can be applied to the real-life situation in their offices.
>
> For any given layout and number of people, these are the cost drivers: assembly, training, inspection, rejects, misdeliveries, inventory, space (for which a certain cost is allocated), all feeding into total costs and unit costs. Labor costs include inspectors and non-inspectors. Costs are associated with rejects, and with misdeliveries, because the customer has put a dollar value on timely deliveries. In

designing the game, you can adjust each of these factors, making space, people, or work in process more or less expensive.

If you have work in process on the floor, and not in the storage room, then you have to have more space in the work location. They're going to have partially completed assemblies—not like the JIT environment where it's "complete, move it on; complete, move it on."

Analysis during the caucuses identifies the cost drivers of boat-making: assembly, training, labor, inspection, rejects, inventory, and space (for which a certain cost is allocated). Even the failure to deliver on time bears a cost, as the customer puts a dollar value on timely delivery. Each of these factors can be adjusted in the design of the game, making space, people, or work in process more or less expensive.

LEARNING FROM THE GAME

Players quickly discover that they have too many people, bad quality, or inefficient use of space. They can only make two improvements, which they must prioritize: people costs and the cost of fixing quality. In most cases, the players want to get rid of some operators and move the tables. Or they say, "We want training." The accountant provides information on specific cost drivers if asked, but people often fail to ask. This is part of the learning: The workers may not empower themselves to learn the impacts of their improvements.

Sometimes, especially after several rounds, people get all sixty-six sailboats delivered. They may even get their costs down to the point of producing a 50 percent profit margin. They can do this with only three people at a table, but only if they understand the most efficient means of putting the pieces together.

Some subassembly operations require greater dexterity than others. As one player put it: "The hard part is getting this little green part in there. It has fewer prongs on one side than the other, and can be centered using the side with fewer prongs." If people use their intra-round caucuses to master processes and procedures, they can provide effective assembly with two assemblers and one final inspector. They continue to need the accountant, but can eliminate the supervisor once they feel empowered to supervise themselves. They can also eliminate the supply room, putting their supply bags next to them. They have the option to downsize from twelve people to four, with dramatic space- and labor-saving implications.

Successful players adopt the mind-set of business process redesign and quickly focus on the factors that increase effectiveness—for example, quality assurance through training and inspection. Investments made in assembling sailboats right the first time, and in preventing defective subassemblies and finished sailboats from reaching upstream customers, pay off handsomely in terms of total cost reductions and, hence, profits. Players also learn the 20/80 rule—that 20 percent of errors usually cause 80 percent of the cost. One training session can eliminate many of these errors. As one participant observed, "There are 'break points' at which you make a quantum leap in process improvement. For example, in the process of claim adjudication, you can do your best to see that the flow of paper, the number of people touching the paper, the space the paper travels, are all reduced. But you still have the paper. Then the day comes when there's no more paper. The claim comes up on a person's computer screen, and is in a queue for that person to work on. That's a technological break point. It could require different people entirely, and a different work setup."

THE USE OF THE SAILBOAT GAME IN DESIGNING
AND IMPROVING WORK PROCESSES

The Bank of Boston team that developed the Canton Service Center (see Chapter 1) utilized the sailboat game in its effort to establish the mind-set, language, and techniques of continuous process redesign; these were central to its new business strategy and the projected use of its new facility, and they carried over from the game to actual bank operations. For example, during the game, workers became aware of problems within their work processes without having to rely on supervisors or outside consultants. They did the same when they returned to their regular jobs—and with notable effect. The bank's operations managers testified to being overwhelmed by the insights contributed by rank-and-file personnel to work process improvement. Peer pressure and a shared understanding of the whole process resulted in dramatic improvements. Previously, these same employees had put their heads down when a problem arose; now they identified problems and offered solutions. In some paper processing operations, for example, departments learned to scan papers at the beginning of the process, minimizing the number of hand-offs and reducing the amount of space normally allocated to paper storage.

The prevailing model was to first straighten out work flows, then go to new technology—for example, bar-coding documents to indicate what had to be done with the document, thereby eliminating the operations of "open, read, interpret, sort." For the most part, these improvements were undertaken within the global work flow design developed by Coopers & Lybrand in parallel with the software systems analysis of Bank of Boston staff member Gail King. Improvements were adapted to the facility rather than moving back and forth between work process and facilities. But it would have been possible to tie business process improvement to redesign of workstations and to changes in the footprints of these workstations.

Customers were intimately involved in business process redesign and kept the bank moving with their demands for new services. The bank's operations managers negotiated with customers about their demands to some extent, but felt that, on the whole, "they pushed us in good directions." For example, customers made the bank see the opportunity of developing a new printing and mailing operation. So many clients demanded dedicated areas for their own production needs that the bank created a floater unit capable of moving across dedicated areas to deal with special customer problems or fluctuations in demand. The customer became a co-producer, making aggressive demands on the bank, and the bank learned to behave in like manner with its vendors.

The Envelope Game

The envelope game offers another opportunity to explore the use of a concrete design game. This game was first piloted in a case we call the University Research Laboratories case, and it involved researchers, administrators, and heads of research groups in a process of spatial programming and design. The case dealt with allocating space to work groups within an institution—the research university—and several of its biological and biomedical laboratories. In the spring of 1993, consultants Julia Voysey and Elizabeth Browning were asked by the university's space planning department to undertake a space evaluation and planning project for three buildings that housed important programs, including cancer research, brain and cognitive science, clinical research, environmental health, toxicology, and biotechnology. The consultants were assigned three main tasks: to demonstrate tools for evaluating the work environment of the research laboratories housed in the three interconnected buildings; to develop a master plan for these buildings and, in doing so, produce short-term solutions to certain "burning issues"; and, within the framework of making the master plan, to help the university develop an improved policy and system for space allocation.

BUILDING THE CLIENT TEAM

The first step taken by the two consultants was to establish a project team. This included a steering committee made up of administrators formally responsible for allocating space and space users—research workers and heads of research groups. By involving these actors as co-inquirers, the consultants hoped their involvement would help in the development of an alternative to the existing system for space allocation and demonstrate a way of resolving the "space wars" endemic to the university.

The university's formal space allocation system was centralized and vertically organized. Operating beneath this seemingly rational system, however, was an informal system through which most criti-

Step 1

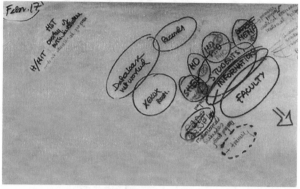

Step 2

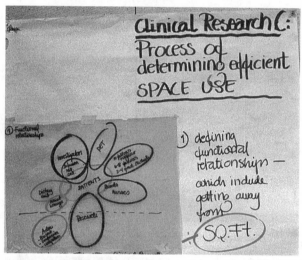

Step 3

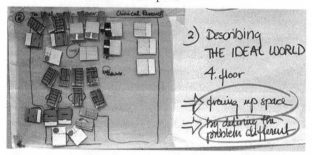

Figure 5.8   Playing the envelope game, phase one.

cal space decisions were actually made; it was a highly politicized design game dominated by the most powerful researchers. The consultants hoped that collaboration in data gathering and interpretation, and in co-inventing practical solutions, would help the contending parties learn to work out lateral resolutions of their space wars and develop the embryo of a new reference process capable of guiding workplace change in the future.

To carry out their three main assignments, the consultants used a variety of events and instruments. One of these was the envelope game, a concrete design game through which a master plan would be constructed and agreed upon. This game became the means of implementing a design and decision-making process that Voysey and Browning envisioned as an alternative to the university's current counterproductive process. The game was played in two main phases.

PHASE ONE: FRAMING THE DESIGN PROBLEM

The first phase of the envelope game involved an event, carefully structured by Voysey and Browning, with three steps (Figure 5.8). It was played in three of the research units where space disputes were most heated: Health Sciences and Technology, the Clinical Research Center, and the Department of Brain and Cognitive Science.

Step 1: Defining the core business. The first step required members of each group to identify the focus of their work. This provoked them to reflect on their work agenda and to redefine their work environment in these terms. One member of the Health Science Technology group jokingly said: "The copy room is our core business." From this opening wisecrack a discussion grew, highlighting that information really was central to their services and to their workplace. This led them to rethink the location of the administrative function—from the fifth floor with its magnificent view to the first floor with its busy "street." Information was, in fact, central to their services and to their workplace.

Step 2: Defining spatial relationships. In this step, participants were asked to work with a particular instrument, *relationship diagrams,* to explore and rethink their functional relationships with other groups, depending on their respective definitions of their core activities. The Clinical Research Center, which considered visiting patients as its focus, defined its workplace as a hospital, laboratory, or day hotel, depending on whether the people the staff worked with were patients, subjects, or guests. For example, the Health Sciences and Technology Group defined its core as information—covering questions about programs or combinations of programs for students, dealing with financial aid matters, and handling the production and distribution of reports—which led the group to reformulate its internal spatial relationships and reconfigure its spatial agenda. Each notion would generate a different spatial relationship diagram.

Step 3: Ideal world scenarios within building constraints.   In the final step, users described their ideal world scenarios and developed their functional relationships within a given building envelope. They were given a game board representing the footprint of the actual floor they occupied, but with only the entrances and the outer walls defined. They had to explore principles for spatial and organizational layout within the boundaries of this space. Various work areas were identified, along with allocation of people and necessary pieces of equipment. Movable cards freed participants from the tendency to perceive space in terms of square feet or to focus on costs associated with moving and refurnishing offices and laboratories. Freed from the constraints of actual internal spatial arrangements, the participants used 25% less space in a possible master plan.

Each three-step session took an hour and a half. Some sessions were played with more than one group. In the case of the Clinical Research Center, the consultants conducted sessions with the dietary unit, the nurses, and the investigators. They combined the game with a walk-through of the workplace to make it easier for people to imagine and discuss the consequences of proposed space changes. In the course of these sessions, the researchers were likely to shift their perception of the problem and look for ways to open up new possible solutions.

In centers that were to move out of the building, or centers with clearly defined or straightforward space problems, the game was not introduced. The previous evaluation meetings and interviews of administrative officers and research center heads gave the consultants enough information to construct consolidated scenarios that included these groups.

PHASE TWO: THE GAME UNFOLDS

The second phase of the envelope game began with the consultants' evaluation of the spatial scenarios created in the initial phase. Each floor plan was taped to the wall, using sectional drawings to aid in visualizing the possibilities for consolidating space and in constructing scenarios in which space was allocated to all groups. The consultants also analyzed transcripts of earlier sessions in order to determine how everybody could have his or her core activities spatially defined and at the same time move toward consolidation within each of the research centers.

The consultants then developed ideal world scenarios for the three buildings taken together. They illustrated space use consolidation for the immediate future and for the next five to ten years. They found that user preferences boiled down to variations on two main, contradictory principles, which they represented with equal attention in drawings and models against the backdrop of existing space use.

The information the consultants had gathered about the core work, functional relationships, and ideal worlds was based on using a particular spatial envelope as a constraint. This was intended to make people set priorities within the limits of particular buildings. But the information gathered in that way was then used to figure out what other envelopes would satisfy the same needs for each research center and department within the three buildings. The consultants used the main principles they had developed as guidelines for working out alternate spatial scenarios with reference to which the boundaries of the envelopes might be redefined.

This approach was applied at all levels of decision-making, with greater detail at the lower level and greater concern for principles at the higher level of the different university schools. The idea was to afford the maximum degree of freedom in decision-making at each level and to minimize the need for higher levels to intervene at lower levels. The aim was to shorten the decision process currently used to deal with the ebb and flow of research activity. As things stood, if one research area were particularly successful, it would ask the administration to enlarge its total allocated space at one time rather than to respond to each small incremental need. Enabling multiple levels of decision-making about space, from the lower level of the laboratory to the upper levels of the school and the university, would afford a quicker response to a changing research agenda and would minimize the administrative overhead involved in making such decisions.

The consultants developed three scenarios for alternate uses and space distributions within the envelopes of the several research groups. These scenarios served as inputs to the project's pivotal event, the final round of the envelope game. In that round, all the research heads met with the consultants to try to reach consensus on a single space plan.

In February of 1994, the consultants convened a working session of all the research heads and their respective administrative officers. The purposes of this session were to communicate the ideal worlds the several research clusters had developed, to test the idea of consolidation as well as critique the consolidated space scenarios the consultants had constructed, and to work through a process of invention and negotiation that would—it was hoped—reduce the multiple suggested variations to two principles for the use of the available space. Starting with these two principles, the participants could either converge on a single space plan for their three buildings or leave the final decision to the university's space allocation committee.

Inputs to this session included a final set of proposals, alternative long- and short-term scenarios for space allocation, and evaluations of each alternative with listings of its advantages and disadvantages. In addition to space consolidation, the scenarios included another design principle: the establishment of gray zones between the schools that would allow for cross-disciplinary collaboration and accommodate the ebb and flow in research activity.

The meeting began with Voysey explaining how she and Browning had arrived at the scenarios. "We are trying to get off the traditional focus on square footage," Voysey explained, "because numbers do not define the function of space." She then gave participants a briefing on costs for different types of spaces, again warning that a fixed cost number could inhibit thinking about how the use of space could be optimized in producing, in the end, a least-cost solution.

Voysey had prepared a diagram of interconnected activities within the schools, showing how research activities would cut across institutional boundaries. The diagram explained how faculty were borrowing space from other schools or departments. These cross-school spaces, small in square footage but highly prized, were real blockages to the flexible rearrangement of work spaces. As soon as space changes involved more than one school, decision-making became so complicated that inefficient use of space was likely to result. The proposed solution was to consolidate space within envelopes, together with the provost's establishment of gray zones between schools. Voysey added, however, that space consolidation ran counter to the university space planners' philosophy of creating a spatially distributed population of diverse disciplines. In the space planners' view, "it doesn't matter if people are spread out all over the place."

Each research head was active in the ensuing discussion, with the head of the biology department taking the lead. Administrative officers, in contrast, remained quiet, even though they knew a lot about relevant particulars. People were used to a hierarchical and deferential etiquette with restrictions, for example, on who was privileged to talk. The consultants, on the other hand, wanted to open the discussion to everyone. However, the unspoken rules of organizational life dictated that administrative officers were there to give information, not to offer opinions (Figure 5.9). Short-term and long-term scenar-

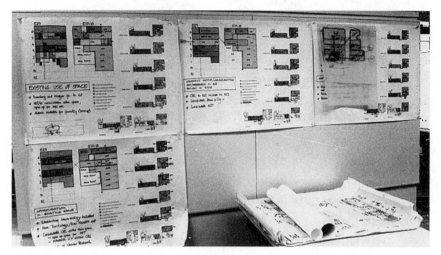

Figure 5.9   Playing the envelope game.

ios were presented in the head administrators' meeting. The participants themselves used yellow trace to explain their points and to
develop the consensual ideal world scenario that was later presented
to the provost.

The head of the biology department opened the discussion,
pointing out that "Consolidation of people who have physical proximity, and of people who have common interests, is a valuable thing
in making organizations work." Another research head seconded the
idea of consolidation, arguing that "Consolidation within departments is probably more important than mixing them up, because
interactions rarely come from mixing people who have different
interests." This person thought it was more important to get the people likely to interact to make use of shared facilities. A third research
head agreed: "If you own a block of space, you can move boundaries
fairly independently and easily. But if you're trapped between other
people's boundaries, you're really stuck." The head of the biology
department nailed this point home:

And . . . if you've got space mixed between the deans of Research, Science, and Engineering, that is paralysis beyond belief. You can build a new institute faster than you can move that. So from an administrative point of view, "This is your square footage, board space, and you can take care of it; but don't come and ask me again for any more."—it's just the only way to run a world . . . If you have intermingled space in which three different reporting lines to the provost all have authority, then the only person who can do a deal is the provost—the person who has least amount of time for such things.

The participants decided to pursue the principle of consolidating space. Only one research head dissented, believing that his group would be a loser under that arrangement. However, on a direct question, at the end of the scenario discussion, the head of the biology department, in whose department the research head worked, said he would endorse presenting to the provost the final short- and long-term scenarios that had been worked out in the meeting.

While participants came to near unanimity on the short- and long-term scenarios for this particular building, they failed to agree on the lateral process that led up to the scenarios, including the principle of space envelopes for each school. They preferred the university's existing reference process. Browning suggested the idea of envelopes within envelopes, where each school would be given an overall quantity of space. Departments and research centers could then negotiate laterally for spaces within the overall school allotment. The envelopes would allow for entrepreneurial initiatives, and gray zones could be introduced between the schools, allowing programs to grow or shrink.

The research heads, however, opposed these proposals. One defended the "messiness" in the university's current use of space as in its departmental structure. "Messiness," he said, "reflects flexibility in dealing with new kinds of problems, and the new kinds of individuals who will work on them." He doubted that a more rigorous and forward-looking space and decision structure would give the university the responsiveness it needed. "The best you can hope to do," he said, "is to catch it at a moment in time, and rationalize the existing situation. Imposing a five-year plan implies that nothing intellectually important will happen during the next five years that would change the plan."

Another research head suggested identifying the spaces that do work well, changing them as little as possible. He emphasized that "the present space situation accurately reflects the confusion that surrounds the intended uses for the building."

Browning asked if there should be a mechanism for resolving conflict without the dean's intervention. One research head, who had been quiet to that point, said, "Well, they've tried and they've failed." Another pointed out that while lateral negotiations were needed for interdepartmental space planning, the dean would still need to have the final say.

When Browning asked whether the meeting would "endorse the way things are done now," the answer was characteristically ambivalent. One researcher replied that although it would be nice to seek a more rational process, "Given the dynamic nature of this place, we're skeptical about whether a more rational process can be found. When new opportunities appear, somebody has to end up carving out space for them." Nevertheless, this individual suggested that when trade-offs could be made within the boundaries of a department or laboratory, a more efficient administrative process would result, and therefore the idea of the gray zones was well worth exploring.

Voysey and Browning shelved their own proposal for lateral space allocation and took the consensual space scenarios favored by the research heads to the university's space administration. The aftermath of this process is discussed in Chapter 8.

Reflections

The sailboat game demonstrated multiple functions. At one level, it functioned as a training exercise in just-in-time production. At another, it helped the participants to grasp certain operating principles that the game masters had already formulated as things to be learned— for example, the relationship between quality and profitability and the emphasis on the cost-effectiveness of forward-looking measures such as production training. At a third level, the game helped participants cultivate a mind-set of continuous business improvement, and could demonstrate the benefits of conditions that would foster such improvements, such as motivated and responsive employees, reliance on local knowledge, and understanding of the entire work process.

The envelope game offered a framework that allowed contending groups to work out a consensual solution to their space allocation problems, converting space wars into a collaborative process. The rules of the envelope game were different from the current rules for space decision-making in the university. Thus, unlike the real world, the game became an arena in which alternative processes for decision-making about space could be considered. By use of a concrete design game, the process architect created a situation in which each research group could look afresh at its own work and derive new implications for space and technology. When the game asked participants to envision an ideal work setting, it freed them from constraints that bounded their thinking about the problem. By framing one of the tasks of the game as envisioning an ideal work setting, Voysey had freed the participants from constraints that bounded their normal ways of thinking about the problem; she also defused their fears that they might be forced to give up something of great importance to them.

The envelope game was a collaborative design game in the more specific sense of the term. Participating groups engaged in broadbrush designing of their idealized work spaces. Using this as raw material, the professional designers synthesized a limited range of design options. The participants rejoined the process by critiquing and choosing among those options. Thus the game afforded consideration of both spatial and organizational alternatives to the present (or reference) processes.

Concrete design games give operational teeth to the metaphor of the game; process architects can invent concrete design games—both structured events and the instruments employed within them—and adapt them to the contexts of client organizations. The fundamental themes of the games are the same: collaborative involvement of participants in process design and artifact design, and the freeing of people from constraints imposed either by the organizational culture they live in or by the limits of conventional thinking and workplace stereotypes. Concrete design games educate in that they expose participants to the experience of active collaboration in the design process; and, finally, concrete design games help workers to build design inquiry skills, internalize the values of collaboration, and bring these abilities to their daily practice of work.

In Chapter 6 the reader will encounter a case that more fully develops the idea of process architecture and that utilizes the full range of the process architecture framework in an integrated way: from approach to strategy of intervention to tools.

6

A Synthesis of Ideas and Practices: The LX Workplace Experiment

This chapter synthesizes much of what we believe to be important about process architecture—both the key ideas and the practice challenges—through an extended case study. In particular, the case underscores the relationship between workplace development and organizational transformation, suggesting how a change in one creates a pressure for change in the other. It also reveals how an existing design game can be transformed so as to achieve collaborative design inquiry. Each of the key players in this case entered the game with different views. Over time, however, these views changed as people learned more. Gradually the problem was reframed, and new work practices and arrangements of the workplace presented themselves. The case demonstrates the existential nature of process architecture—how sense-making and invention occur on the spot, rather than through mechanical delivery of preestablished procedures.

This case reinforces our conviction that transforming the workplace supports the transformation of work itself. Mobilizing people around workplace intervention entails developing the organizational capability for design inquiry and facilitates shifts in the fundamental culture, enabling collaboration across competencies, which in turn may result in a more innovative work practice. Finally, if established in one part of the organization, process architecture may create lessons that can be strategically applied to new situations elsewhere in the same organization.

SEEKING PROCESS IMPROVEMENT AT XEROX

The financial rewards for being first in technology-related markets are impressive, and every high-tech company tries to capture these markets by improving the pace and productivity of R&D work. The Xerox Corporation is probably more aware than others of the need to develop and move innovation to market quickly. Indeed, the company learned this lesson the hard way in the late 1970s, when new Asian competitors shattered its apparent invincibility in the photocopier business by releasing a stream of inexpensive but high-quality new machines. Soon after, Xerox-inspired innovations like the graphic user interface for personal computers (forerunner of the Apple Macintosh), laser printing, and computer networking lingered in its Palo Alto Research Center while other firms took the same concepts to market, making billions and establishing leadership in the process.

It is no surprise, then, that Xerox is today constantly seeking to speed the process of technology and product development. That urge to move more quickly has produced process improvement initiatives in many parts of the company. This chapter examines the formation of the LX laboratory that began in August 1994 within Xerox's Wilson Center for Research and Technology, focusing on the LX workplace experiment. The events of this case were set in motion by the management imperative of reducing the time to market for new product development.

Reshaping the Work Processes of the Wilson Center

In the summer of 1994, just as this experiment started, The Wilson Center, located in Webster, New York, had been formed out of the combination of two centers: one of research and the other of advanced technology development. The Center's mission was to position Xerox as the leading supplier of color marking systems. It consisted both of competency laboratories that aimed to create innovative marking technologies and platform teams that attempted to integrate those technologies into new product prototypes. The intent was for the new center to break free of traditional linear models: Instead of following sequential processes of technology development, product design, and engineering, it would use cross-functional teams working in parallel to create new products. There would be no more over-the-wall handoffs of projects from one stage of the process to another. Management expected that this more contemporary model for research and technology development, combining organizational change with corresponding changes in work processes, would create new business value for Xerox and improve overall performance in quality, cost, development cycle time, and productivity. Integrating these two centers would enhance the corporation's ability to pursue new opportunities, further the progress of its technical architecture, and create new technologies capable of penetrating emerging markets.

The Wilson Center's emphasis on interdisciplinary work exacerbated long-standing needs for new forms of information exchange and new places for collaboration among professional employees who were geographically dispersed but who had to keep in close communication and coordinate their activities. It was hoped that virtual co-location through the application of information technology would solve this problem. Xerox Vice President for Research Mark Myers was enthusiastic about the prospects of virtual co-location and was willing to engage the resources and outside expertise capable of developing it with the Wilson Center.

At about the same time, a consultant group had recommended to the administration of the research center that actual physical co-location of project groups would speed innovation and reduce time to market. However, consolidating work teams by relocating people was not easy. People might serve two or three research teams at once, or move downstream with the flow of technology. The relationship between volatile organizational boundaries and team collaboration, with the focus continually shifting geographically with the changes in product cycle, created a situation in which it seemed infeasible to have stable team space for the groups within the Wilson Center. Moreover, from a hardware perspective, moving established laboratories and research equipment, and getting the equipment and its instrumentation properly readjusted, would be expensive and time consuming and might actually slow the innovation process.[1]

These two seemingly contrasting proposals—one of physical co-location and the other of virtual co-location—represented the two leading ideas present in the Wilson Center at the time of the LX experiment. The new LX workplace evolved as a design that merged these two ideas into a synthesis in which the technology solution became intertwined with the spatial solution.

The LX Workplace Experiment

Among the leading laboratories in its field, the LX laboratory, formed at the outset of the Wilson Center, has become a benchmark for Xerox research centers. Research in the technology area on which LX was working had roughly ten years of history at Xerox before the LX lab was created. The LX workplace experiment started Monday morning, August 1, 1994, only days after the Wilson Center was formally organized. During the period we describe, the laboratory has undergone a dramatic change in its work process, which can be attributed to collaborative design inquiry that occurred in all areas of the space, organization, finance, and technology (SOFT) diagram through a living experiment. The resulting changes have had profound impacts on work process and team behavior that include achievement of a new team identity and a shared commitment to generate the knowledge base for the company's twenty-first-century marking technology. The LX workplace experiment is still evolving as this book is being written.

The LX laboratory was one of nine competency laboratories within the Wilson Center. Unlike other labs within the Center, which were highly specialized, LX uniquely brought together people with a wide variety of backgrounds and disciplines: xerographers, chemists, process experts, materials experts, computer modelers, and experimentalists. The LX lab had the particular charge of developing Xerox's next generation of color marking technology, which would challenge its existing technologies, its knowledge base, and its conceptions of its products. In this endeavor, the LX lab would need not only to rely on conventional xerography technology but also to find new approaches.

The membership of the LX lab included some of Xerox's top scientists. Among them was John Knapp, one of the company's most senior scientists and the holder of numerous important patents. Individuals like John Knapp and Jim Larson, senior scientist and lab manager, would play key roles in the LX workplace experiment as designers of new work processes, workplace improvement, and their own internal organizational culture. Knapp and Larson used insights gained from their experience as technological innovators and research team leaders to guide the evolving experiment and provide leadership. Both were capable of recognizing the new work practices that emerged and ensuring that these practices became part of the social fabric and formal rules of the organization. Today Knapp and Larson are engaged in taking the lessons from LX into a larger segment of the Wilson Center in their new research initiatives.

John Knapp, in his capacity as the technology advisor in the Wilson Center and the leader of the day-to-day work in the LX lab, became one of the foremost champions of the experiment early on, and it would probably not have taken the course it did without his active involvement. Knapp was a man with a vision for how to produce the twenty-first-century marking technology and how to mobilize a group of scientists around that mission. He was also a leader who understood the pressure from a fast-changing internal as well as external market. He believed that collaborative design across competencies and professional experience would enhance the problem-solving activities that permeate normal life in any lab. For years he had been brewing ideas on how to do things differently, but had not seen any practical way of organizing a lab environment conducive to work process experiments, even though he was quite familiar with developing experiments in xerography.

He also knew that the LX lab was challenged to improve productivity in order to survive. The diverse group of people assigned to the LX lab were given the mandate of coming up with something promising within color marking technology—a type of technology in which other competitors already held numerous patents—within a few years, or else facing the possibility that management might close them down. The LX members knew from the outset that they were facing fierce competition. Product research and development was painfully expensive, and unless output could be improved, Xerox business units were likely to prefer to either shift the lab's resources to the company's other research centers or acquire new product technology elsewhere—for example, from its Asian partner, Fuji-Xerox.

Intervention in the LX Environment

One initiative to speed the process of technology and product development at Xerox was the Laboratory for Remote Collaboration (LARC) project.[2] Its mission was to develop computer technologies, systems, and applications to enable highly effective cross-functional teamwork among people scattered across different locations. The LARC project foresaw the application of several of the following technical solutions, including groupware, LiveBoard™, networked personal computers, and video systems.

To test and validate its collaborative technologies, LARC created a pilot project known as the LX workplace experiment, to be located in one of the Wilson Center's laboratories. Although its goal was to apply communications technology, this pilot had an unexpected result: It made people aware of the importance of physical work space and work processes in the effectiveness of teams. This awareness caused the LARC mission to be expanded to include these factors.

DIFFERENT PLAYERS, DIFFERENT PERSPECTIVES

The LX workplace experiment involved players with different interests, powers, and freedoms of action. Each of the key players entered the design game with a different view of the problem and a different perception of the challenge of improving the LX lab's productivity.

The decision to create a LARC pilot project was made at the Wilson Center's management level, but the choice of LX as the target organization was not a part of that decision. The LX lab was invited to participate and decided to do so. The decision to join was largely motivated by the opportunity to acquire a new PC infrastructure and 4000 square feet of newly renovated lab and office space. But once lab manager Jim Larson had taken the plunge, the interest of many of the lab members in the project was initially to defend their individual offices, each sized in relation to the occupant's rank and service within the Xerox Corporation. Office space was a hard-earned prize not to be traded away.

Bob Lechner, head of facilities services for the Wilson Center, had already introduced some innovation into the provision of facilities. He was, in fact, charged with co-locating teams of engineers and lab researchers in ways that would improve their productivity.

Lab members and their managers represented yet another set of participants in the LX project. Their views on the problem of R&D productivity and how to improve it varied greatly. Yet all shared the outlook of innovators and scientists—that no condition or solution should be viewed as final or perfect. For this group, current technology, current work space, and existing working relationships were simply components amenable to incremental improvement, reconfiguration, or replacement by something new and better. Unlike most corporate employees, for these people change, uncertainty, and surprise were neither foreign nor threatening. In this sense, they operated with the attitude of the process architect.

The LARC team—the intervenors in this case—included insiders (from Xerox) and outsiders. It was composed of people from three other organizations in addition to the Wilson Center itself (Color plate 17). Each person had an agenda for change, and these agendas overlapped.[3]

The Design Research Institute (DRI). This was a group of Xerox scientists and engineers located on the Cornell University campus in

Ithaca, New York. DRI had been established in 1990 to take advantage of the research and teaching environment at Cornell, giving Xerox scientists an opportunity to work together closely with faculty, students, and other companies on information, collaboration, and computation research related to engineering design.

Digital Equipment Corporation (DEC) and its Product Development Group in Littleton, Massachusetts. The aim for a company like DEC was to develop marketable hardware and software solutions to problems like the ones faced by the LX lab. DEC saw two opportunities in the LARC project that induced it to participate: (1) The pilot project would illuminate appropriate product directions in several key areas, including mobile computing. (2) Digital would be able to implement some of the project findings in its own development environment.

MIT's Space Planning and Organization Research Group (SPORG). SPORG's mandate was to engage the LX personnel in the process of analysis and design of their new work setting and help them evaluate the results of the change process. SPORG would structure the workshops to maximize the occupants' involvement in designing the new workplace. Within this task, in order to figure out where it was realistic to expect that collaboration could operate remotely using information technology, SPORG initially framed its role as that of identifying which work situations required face-to-face contact or would benefit from spatial proximity.

The initial core players in the LX intervention—Greg Zack from DRI, Chuck Kukla from DEC, and Turid Horgen from MIT SPORG—represented each of the three collaborating organizations. Neither they nor others who gradually became members of the LARC team had previously worked together. Though they had some preliminary ideas of each other's interests and approaches to workplace-making, they came from different disciplines (computer science, engineering, and architecture), and throughout the project they would continue to develop their mutual understanding of a workplace intervention.

Greg Zack was a computer scientist and manager of DRI. His goal was to build a partnership with Digital and Cornell in LARC that would benefit all parties. Zack was the project's principal initiator and consultant and its most vocal champion. He coordinated planning, development, and deployment of the information technology components of the pilot.

Chuck Kukla was a systems analyst with a previous career as a chemical engineer and designer of chemical plants. Both Kukla and Zack viewed the project as a test bed for remote collaboration—a real-time experiment with people working on technologies central to Xerox's business. Kukla, one of the protagonists in the DEC/Monsanto case in Chapter 5, advised that the experiment look more closely at the relationship between space and technology. Earlier experience had taught him that technology was an imperfect substitute for spatial proximity; he also knew that there was more to learn about the close interdependencies between space, technology, and problem-solving. Computer-based tools had conventionally been developed either to automate a work process or to inform a problem. Kukla, however, was trying to understand a third category of computer-based tools: the kind that bring people back to the situation where the problem occurred. He was convinced that the spatial setting was crucial to triggering the thinking necessary to understanding the problem and advancing possible solutions.[4]

Turid Horgen, one of the authors of this book, represented SPORG on the project. She had been hired because of her skill at designing and running workshops in which new concepts for work setting could be shaped in relation to the organization's work practice. Horgen had been told that she was to work with a group of engineers who were trying to develop a machine with more parts and more complexity than a small airplane, but little else. She recalls: "Chuck Kukla and I had discussed my way of working with organizations in the initial stage of a design process. When he asked me to run the workshops and develop the spatial concepts for the experiment, I thought it would be quite interesting to refine my tools for intervention, since my approach seemed to overlap with the ethnographic approach he was attuned to." Since Horgen's initial mission was rather limited, she took it for granted that somebody had a grasp of the overall process, that all parties involved understood the purpose and the goals of the project, and that someone would pick up on the findings and reflect them in new software, hardware, or spatial solutions.

We mention this incident because it is typical for the LARC team: The understanding of the problem developed only gradually, and the project shaped itself through a rather bumpy process. As the process evolved, new members would enter the LARC team. Champions for new parts of the project emerged as the LX experiment matured. The interplay between inside leaders, like Knapp, and outside intervenors, like Horgen, created some interesting synergies in which the inside managers and the outside consultants built on each other's strengths to make the experiment work.

At the outset, ambiguity among these many agendas and lack of collective understanding about the nature of the work and the intervention process resulted in frustration, resistance to change, and dimmed prospects for success. Nevertheless, these parties were persistent, they shared a commitment to the workplace experiment, and they were in positions to exercise the necessary leadership to drive the project forward.

PHYSICAL FACTORS RESISTANT TO CHANGE

The Xerox Webster site, where the Wilson Center was located, had been developed in the 1960s in a traditional campus plan, segregated by function: manufacturing, research, services, supplies, administration. A town grid of roads and indoor walkways linked its many buildings. The buildings themselves were two- and three-story steel grid structures enclosed with brick curtain walls. There was also an infrastructure of heating, plumbing, and wiring that ran throughout the grid, with the expectation that the resulting framework would be highly adaptable. The typical layout of activities at the Wilson Center positioned laboratories in the centers of the buildings and offices on their perimeters, as shown in Color plate 18. Inside, the place had the look and feel of a dreary industrial facility, with rabbit-warren offices on one side of the corridors and closed laboratories on the other. The slit windows that allowed one to peer into these laboratories were almost always pasted over, shutting the labs off from the outside world and from observation by passers-by. Social and intellectual interaction at the Wilson Center mirrored the physical environment within which people worked. Researchers gravitated around their scientific specialties, with little interaction or cross-pollination of ideas.

The original concept behind the physical layout of the Wilson Center was to allow for change; in reality, however, change proved cumbersome and expensive. Over time, the research laboratories had accumulated large fixtures and test machines with delicate attached instruments that had to be painstakingly calibrated and adjusted. It was simply not feasible to move these fixtures every time someone wanted to redesign a research program. The Center's open, flexible town grid had become rigid, with immovable laboratories, each developed and fine-tuned to one or another specialized form of research.

Members of the LX lab were nevertheless slated for co-location. Lechner, within the constraints of the existing Wilson Center facilities, had provided the lab with a space originally planned for a group that had been dissolved—sufficient for only about one-third of LX personnel and their laboratory space. He had purchased a number of small prebuilt individual alcove-shaped office units to be used by that same group. These units were relatively efficient in terms of general space planning, because minimizing private space by making it more efficient enabled team spaces to be created without increasing the total square footage devoted to a group. Lechner hoped that these units could be recycled in the new LX area, and engaged an architect to do the design work. Facilities services viewed these office units as the key to a co-location strategy and appropriate for individual lab members. Prospective occupants were less kind, calling them "phone booths." There was adverse reaction to their general use by the LX members, who did not see how they could collaborate with their colleagues if they were housed in these "containers." One researcher threatened to quit rather than move into one of the units. This explosion of the underlying irritant that the office compartments represented was a critical incident in that it provided some of the creative energy to frame the problem more accurately, building an awareness that would help define a new type of research environment.

LARC WORKSHOPS

The intervention began with a series of workshops set up by the LARC team for members of the LX group and two of the Center's platform teams. These took place in August and September of 1994. The workshops, each spanning four days, aimed to give participants a grip on how work was done. The first part of each set of workshops was devoted to discovering what each team did and what environmental problems team members encountered in their work. The second part encouraged the teams to describe an idealized environment that would best facilitate their work. The purpose of this was to develop generic diagrams for ideal work arrangements; these would be the basis for the redesign of the workplace and its tools.

The LARC workshop structure and techniques introduced by Horgen had been developed over a number of years in Norwegian and U.S. settings. The workshops were composed of a series of structured events and instruments designed to help participants understand the lab's work practice and discover important elements in the existing work environment that could be used as generative ideas for the new lab environment.

The approach assumed that the expertise about the problem at hand belonged to the user group, not the consulting professional. It required the professional to be facilitator and coach as well as guide and teacher. Meetings were conducted in an open and informal style, with participation expected from all who attended, regardless of their place in the institutional hierarchy. The matters discussed typically were generated by the participants, not by the consultants or by management. Meetings were held where anyone could stop in and listen; those who had to leave could drift away without disrupting the atmosphere.

On each of the four days the workshop took a different form. The lab members met for 1½ hours every morning, received homework, and discussed the results of the homework the next day. Through documenting and examining each event carefully, the LARC team and LX lab members gradually built a set of potential images of the new lab. Table 6.1 lists the events and illustrates some of the documents produced day by day using various different instruments. After four days the concept for the new workplace was conceived. There were still controversies to be resolved: for example, whether valuable lab space should be given over to open conference areas and how many office compartments should be used. The design would go through several iterations over the next couple of months before the LX lab agreed to build what the group had invented: the LX Common and the LX work area.

The LARC workshops exhibited on-the-spot invention rather than the use of preestablished procedures. The four core events were planned, but each day was full of surprises and improvisation. The walk-through had to be extended into the late evening to include other labs that all of a sudden wanted to be involved. The workbook session on the second day did not work: The LARC consultants were met with complete silence. The LX lab members refused to have their intimate lab environment be the subject of collective inquiry and evaluation. The LARC team quickly changed the agenda, introducing another exercise instead—the drawing of the ideal laboratory—and asked people to do the worksheets as individual rather than group homework. The cardboard game was initially designed to discover how to furnish the LX work area, so the game boards showed floor plans. Just as the game was to start, Horgen turned the boards over, blank side up, and made up a different way of using the same pieces in order to encourage development of a new organizational structure for the entire lab. Lab members were grouped initially in twos, then gradually into larger groups, in order to facilitate exploration of principles for lab organization and to simulate both remote and face-to-face communication.

Changes like these—in event structure, practice strategies, and use of tools—were made for various reasons: in some cases to deal with tensions or difficult situations that evolved; in others to build on what came out through the discussions and use those results as ingredients of the new design. Thus the intervention itself was a game in play, where the process architect made adaptive use of the repertoire of available design tools and displayed the necessary mobility to deal with unexpected situations.

The confusion that marked the initial stages of the project was indispensable. It signified a willingness on the part of the client to proceed on the basis of a sense of something important to be done and a dimly seen image of the goals to be achieved—business contribution, decreased time to market, increased research productivity—but no clear sense of how those goals could be crystallized in the situation at hand. On the consultants' part, the confusion signified a willingness to let go of a preconceived picture of the consulting mission and the procedures by which it would be carried out.

The content and effect of these workshops is summarized in Table 6.1.

REVEALING THE NATURE OF THE WORK AND ARTICULATING LEADING IDEAS

The LARC workshops identified a number of characteristics of the nature of the work at the LX lab. Most importantly, the workshops revealed certain limits to work at a distance and described situations in which face-to-face contact between individuals, or between individuals and mechanical artifacts, was of critical importance. The

Table 6.1 Workshop Activities

Day 1: The Lab Walk-Through

One observation of the walk-through was that the corridor was where communal interactions took place.

A place-specific inquiry into each occupant's work experience

The project team visited ten laboratories in three different buildings and met with a host in each lab who introduced the lab occupants. The host described briefly how the work of the lab was performed.

Day 2: Spatial and Organizational Diagnosis

Worksheets were assembled to evoke further response and discussion.

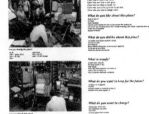

Evaluation of a collection of graphic images—photographs, floor plans, and so on—acquired during the previous day's walk-through

Lab members, working in groups of two to three, were asked to mark aspects of images they found important, either positively or negatively, with respect to four fundamental workplace issues: appreciation (like/dislike), change (wish to keep/abolish), safety, and efficiency. They were then asked to evaluate their own work environments in terms of these photographs.

(continued)

TABLE 6.1   *(continued)*

Day 3: Drawing the Ideal Work Environment

From these drawings workshop participants could analyze the different concepts, take them apart, and rebuild them into different types of office space, lab space, and meeting areas.

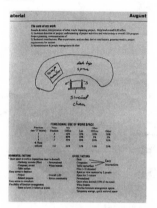

A set of drawings of an ideal workplace, based on what each lab member found important in his or her own work environment

Drawings could address any level of scale from a single work space to the whole company. Participants were asked to amplify their drawings with suggestions and explanatory notes, and to explain the drawings to each other. Drawings created in such an exercise are usually of three types: a slight improvement of existing places, partial changes, and occasionally break-through designs.

Day 4: Interactive Organizational Design Game

This interactive design game laid out a possible organizational structure for the new lab.

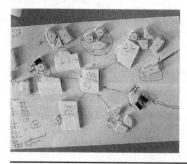

A cardboard game to play out different options for the organization of work and the communication process

Participants were given an assortment of cardboard pieces in various colors and sizes, then invited to let the pieces represent any chosen objects or functions and arrange them in different relationships to help understand the implications of proximity of functions and of the communication links between people.

understanding and the awareness of the nature of the work grew out of a series of evaluation meetings, design sessions, and debriefing meetings (the workshops we have just described being the first ones) among the lab members and the LARC team. Certain propositions about the future work processes emerged that could be publicly shared and endorsed, like the distinction between being outside and inside the situation, which differentiates between those working directly with the mechanical fixtures and those reflecting on the work by means of computer modeling or talking with others.

There were also sessions held at MIT to debrief the LARC consultants, to evaluate progress, and to discuss the strategy for further work. These sessions included individuals not intimately associated with the project—faculty, students, and visiting scholars—all of whom brought related experience and a wish to find ideas and principles that extended across project boundaries. It was in these sessions that some of the leading ideas emerged that formed the basis for the next round of inquiry and action, some of the diagrams of the process were drawn, and certain guiding criteria for evaluation were instituted. There was synergy between the inquiry in the work setting and its counterpart in the academic setting. The passing back and forth between fine-grained discussion of particulars by those immediately involved in the workplace and the abstracting of general principles in a broader context by more detached parties turned out to be a fruitful way to develop an understanding of what was going on.

Some of the leading ideas that emerged were:

1. *The work is not routine:* Workshop participants could not identify anyone whose work stayed the same. For lab workers, every day was different. "You come in, and you figure out a problem, you design a way to test it, and you run the test." Each problem, design, and approach to testing might be unique. The only stable elements in the lab setting were the resources and the tools.

The question then became, "What do the different types of work done at the Wilson Center and in the LX group have in common?" Both theoretical and experimental work was being done. Investigation of the literature and discussions of strategy were also important elements of the work. Experimentation was a common practice; this involved planning, developing suitable controls, running experiments, measuring and analyzing results, and interpreting and documenting the results. Given the complexity of the interactions in the systems being investigated, changes in one subsystem might require that experiments on another subsystem be done again.

In addition to the technical core of work, other activities associated with the LX lab included demonstrating the technology to investors and to technical personnel in the downstream processes of development, manufacturing, and marketing; transferring the technology to personnel at the next link in the development chain; scanning for possible new markets and for competitors' products and ideas; strategic business planning; and discussion of critical nontechnical issues such as intellectual property, patents, and the like. These activities required communication with a diverse collection of personnel, cutting across organizational boundaries in ways different from activities associated with the technical aspects of the laboratory.

2. *The fixture is the centerpiece of lab work:* Xerographic research was the LX lab's fundamental work. Xerography entails the integration of specific subsystems—a paper path, a photoreceptor, the transfer of ink pigment to paper, and supporting electronics and software. Photocopying has six major steps: charging, exposing, developing, transferring, fusing, and cleaning. Several very different technologies involving principles of chemistry, physics, and both chemical and electrical engineering must be integrated for these steps to take place. Someone must put all of these technologies and scientific principles together in order to conceive of new machines. Lab personnel use a *fixture,* an outsize, one-of-a-kind machine, for testing the various elements and visualizing their complex interactions. The fixture's parts are substitutable, so that new ideas can be tried out quickly; measuring and monitoring instruments can be attached to the fixture in order to provide the basis for evaluation along many different dimen-

sions of performance. Contact with a materialized version of a potentially new machine, even though dissimilar in appearance, is a key part of the creative process.

3. *People are either inside or outside the research situation at different times:* Being inside the situation means being at the fixture, working on the experiment, and observing the data as events happen. Being outside the situation means reflecting on the data and talking with other people about it. People collaborate in quite different ways in these two settings. The challenge to the LARC team became the development of space and technology that supported both.

4. *People need to get around the data:* As they observed lab members discussing technical problems, the LARC team found intensive sharing of visual information. When a researcher goes into a colleague's office to discuss a problem, or perhaps to look at the computer screen where the researcher has outlined a theory, one of the two will say, "I need the whiteboard to scribble on, because I think as well with my hand as I think with my head." All the lab workers interviewed emphasized the need for a "spread-out place," where two or more people can "get around the data." The LX situation called for an individual workplace large enough to allow two or three people to grapple with data and ideas. This, and shared spaces next to the fixture, were seen as important to the culture of experimentalists and engineers and conducive to productive problem-solving.

Face-to-face meeting places generally provide a useful informational redundancy in which workers can determine whether they and their co-workers are, for example, reading off the same instruments. They also provide workers with opportunities to combine their experiences in understanding raw data. These face-to-face meeting places also offer opportunities for new insights. One person whose experiences are different than those of his or her colleagues may hear or see something different than the others would. This sharing of multiple representations of the findings, where each can be checked against the others, allows the development of a robust understanding of the problem.

5. *Information overload is a problem:* Management of information flow was an important issue for the project team. As one manager wrote in a memo to Greg Zack:

> More and more information is being received by the individual every day, and more and more time is spent reading mail, sorting through documents, filing, etc. This means less time doing other work. It sometimes gets to the point where so much information is being sent to individuals in an effort to keep them informed, that the individual turns off and stops processing, which defeats the purpose. . . .

6. *Dialogue is needed:* The nature of work in the LX lab also required that collaborating researchers have opportunities to meet spontaneously and engage in dialogue regarding events occurring in the lab. Collaboration in the form of more formal meetings was already happening in people's offices. More often, though, it was happening in the lab or in front of a malfunctioning machine.

7. *It is important to meet in the middle of the work:* The conference room used by two of the platform teams had the traditional setup: a wall for projector displays at one end, chairs along the wall at the opposite end, and an oval table in the center. During regular sunrise meetings, the more senior people would sit at one end of the table, while less senior personnel would occupy the other end. The technicians—the people who had actually observed a problem in the first place—would sit in the chairs along the wall, out of the main flow of the meeting. They had no way to display any information about the problem. The apparatus and artifacts actually connected to the problem, or the parts that were the cause of the breakdown, would not be present. This conference room was used for the platform team's daily morning meetings and for periodic problem-solving meetings. Team members cited the lack of immediacy in these meetings; it might take two or three days to assemble the people with the authority or

knowledge to solve an important problem. And once these people were assembled, it was difficult to recreate the situation in which the problem had occurred. Efficient problem-solving, as experience indicated, did not happen in the conference room but at the machine or in the corridor outside the laboratory, where the right people could be gathered and the problem examined in the presence of the equipment or fixture under discussion. The design challenge, then, was to either (1) bring the work into the conference room or (2) bring the conference into the middle of the work.

Shaping the LX Common

The understanding about the nature of work just cited contributed to the idea of an innovation node work area, with its central open room in the former corridor, as the focal point for face-to-face and remote collaboration. This area would be equipped with information technology (LiveBoards, video technology, PCs electronically net-worked with other labs, and also traditional low technology such as whiteboards). It was to be surrounded by active laboratories and open office spaces. Based on the metaphor of the New England common, this space, dubbed the *LX Common,* would be located in the midst of the LX work area and electronically networked with other labs of LX members that were spread over three floors of an adjacent building. The Common would represent the home of the lab, where every matter from technical problems among lab members to research policy problems between leadership and the lab would be discussed out in the open.

The design of the Common happened piecemeal, evolving through a series of discussions, conjectures, and conflicts (Figure 6.1). The sketches, developed during the LARC workshop in August 1994, represent both a spatial and a technological conclusion of the evaluation/design workshops: (1) There was a need for a lab center (what later became the LX Common) electronically linked to other

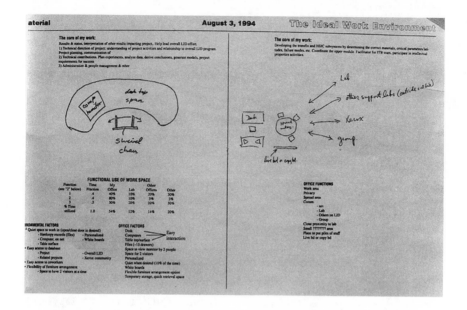

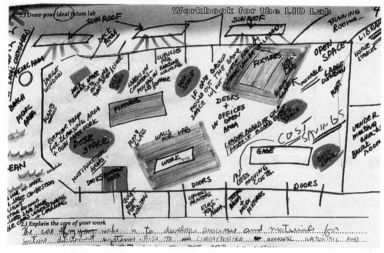

Figure 6.1   Sketching the LX Common.

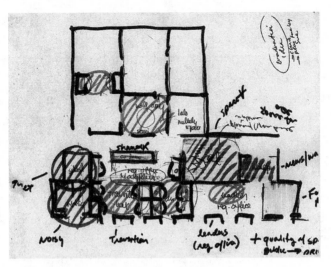

Figure 6.1 *(continued)*

labs in the lab group and other Competence Centers within the Wilson Center. (2) There was a need for continuous, open meeting areas in the center of the lab work area. Several months after the LARC workshops, the LX Common stood as an empty room waiting to be filled with some kind of activity—what kind being as yet unclear. This incomplete workplace, with its ambiguous and permeable boundaries, stimulated a kind of working interaction among the researchers that was new to the research group. The ambiguous, incomplete work environment seemed to lend itself to tasks of collaborative inquiry in which problems were unclear and needed to be framed and where data were being explored whose meanings were as yet unclear.

SPACE

The workshops revealed the need for informal and formal meeting places. Informal meeting places were described as unscheduled and open to anyone. Workshop drawing sessions identified several possible locations for informal meetings in and around the lab: the kitchen area, the space around copy machines and printers, the spaces immediately adjacent to work cubicles, and the intellectual property area. Formal meetings, by contrast, were by invitation only and took place in defined areas such as the enclosed conference room.

Workshop participants also identified the need for a *situation room* as an alternative to a formal enclosed conference room. Unlike the sunrise meeting room described earlier, equipped with a whiteboard, an overhead projector, electronic media devices, and a large oval table, this situation room would be an open work area and would enable people to retrieve all the information they needed at any time. Space would be available for the display of charts, photographs, and other visual representations. The work area would also afford direct visual or electronic access to information in people's laboratories or offices.

Innovation depends upon communication across disciplines and across different levels of the organization. To succeed, the LX lab manager needed to be able to sell changes in strategy, or results of work, to management in a more direct way than before. Like researchers elsewhere, team members felt that their ability to make a case for their work to others—particularly to the Xerox managers who controlled resource allocations—was constrained by the current workplace. This was particularly important for the LX lab, which was working on a technology that had the potential to give high-quality color to the marketplace but that was not within the dominant family of technologies for the traditional Xerox copier and printer. Engineers needed opportunities to showcase the innovative technologies on which they were working. Furthermore, they wanted a forum within which to sell changes in research strategy and the results of their work to management. The innovation showcase would also facilitate meetings with outside vendors and possible business partners representing companies other than Xerox, regarding such matters as testing new products for production or developing spin-offs from the research.

The LX Common was eventually configured as a semienclosed area that could be extended into the corridor (Figure 6.2). It could permanently provide for a set of different activities or meetings that

The empty work area
The LARC workshops were held in a portion of the space the LX lab was later to inhabit (around the small, dark table at the far end). By moving the table around, trying different configurations of meeting arrangements, the participants gradually occupied the corridor, and defined it as part of their "conference room" or "situation room."

The empty LX Common
In February 1995 the LX common is still an empty room, located between four labs, opening toward the corridor—actually the corridor becomes part of the common area. The two LiveBoards, still crated, sit in the back corner.

Open work area outside the lab

The populated corridor
Leadership meetings are held in the open, where people can pass by in the corridor. Here an internal lab meeting among senior scientists discusses progress-evaluation approaches.

Meeting space outside the office

Traditional conference room

A variety of meeting spaces
"What they said about the space was that it had really changed the learning structure of this group. . . . It wasn't an office space where you did your private work, it was a communal space where you worked in an organic way around creating, communicating and interacting with regard to the transmission of knowledge. . . . There was a whole new set of social rules. . . ." (Gordon Moore)

Kitchen area

Figure 6.2 How the LX Common came into being.

previously would have required separate, dedicated places. At the top of Figure 6.3 is a view of the original plan, with its narrow corridor lined by prebuilt carrels, offices, and cubicles. In contrast, the new plan (shown at the bottom of Figure 6.3) indicated a widened corridor that allowed for spillover from adjacent laboratories, meeting

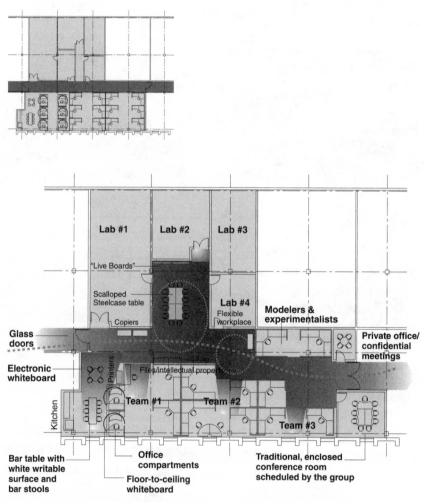

Figure 6.3 Original and new plans for the LX work area.

rooms, and service areas. The boundaries to this area were, unlike those in the original, blurred; individual offices were replaced by cubicles that fed energy into the common area and fostered communication and collaboration. This LX Common could be a showcase and demonstration area for people outside the situation. At other times it could be a problem-solving area inside the situation. Each of these activities was to occur in the same space on different days or in different ways, and with different participants (Color plate 19).

The LX Common would have a very open feel. It would be partly open to the main path of circulation, with windows and a door leading off to adjacent LX work areas. The space itself would be only loosely defined, designed to change in response to the size of the group occupying it and how it was being used. The result would be an area whose boundaries could be defined by different agendas.

TECHNOLOGY

The union of work space and technology was the goal of LX workplace experiment change strategy. Shortly after the LARC workshops, Greg Zack initiated an architecture committee, consisting of people from DRI, the LX group, the Wilson Center computer support staff, and Digital (Chuck Kukla), to work on computing and information architecture to support some of the ideas and the needs that came out of the workshops.

Personal computers were installed in the LX lab in November 1994, in the first wave of a corporate shift to a standard PC platform. The original network based on Windows for Workgroups (WFWG) did not work. But, with the aid of a consultant and a conscious decision to move outside the realm of the Xerox-standard WFWG solutions, Windows NT was adopted. Installation of the new PCs occurred at the same time the organization was being moved and restructured, destabilizing the computer infrastructure and causing serious anxiety during the early months of the pilot. The technical staff of Wilson Center Services had no experience in NT, so for the most part the LX lab had to devise its own system.

The most important technological tool for the LX lab, however, was to be a central information presentation system. This idea had its genesis in one of the platform workshops, where a researcher sketched what he considered to be the ideal laboratory environment (see Figure 6.4). The sketch showed the four core labs of the group, shared work areas, and, in the center, a situation room. The researcher conceived the idea of channeling information generated in the labs into the situation room via a central information system for presentation and joint discussion. Based on this drawing, Greg Zack and Chuck Kukla developed the concept of the Active Project Information Center (APIC). The APIC concept was to have a very large interactive electronic display of project information that used Xerox LiveBoards. It would be an interactive data archive for the LX lab, updated continuously and accessible to all members at all times both at the Common and through their PCs (Figure 6.5). Two people outside the

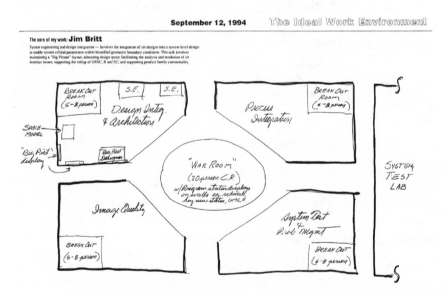

Figure 6.4 Drawing of the ideal lab environment.

Figure 6.5　APIC as a focus, conversation, and discussion area.

situation discuss a problem with the aid of displays on two LiveBoards, which help them go back into the situation, retrieving data and pointing at aspects of the problem.

From the workshops and discussions, LARC got an idea of what some of that information content could be. Greg Zack did much of the thinking and led the brainstorming work to develop the content areas to be posted on APIC. Many categories of information were to be displayed, including status and data from lab experiments, a calendar and meeting reminder, a "who's out" list, a problem area giving status on important issues, notices of upcoming milestones, a video tunnel into the conference room across the street, video from the lab, and bulletins such as "six days since the last invention proposal." Information would be laid out in a consistent format day to day, as in a newspaper, so that lab members would know where to look for each category. The system would also automatically save all information to produce a history. If a lab worker missed a day, he or she could click on the display and see the previous day's newsletter or newspaper, or go back to any other date or hour in the past. Small stars on the Live-Board indicated places where additional information was available and accessible through a click of the pen. Among other things, these annotations might indicate who was responsible for a particular task and its current status. Lab workers could add comments and update information easily, creating an extended conversation.

Zack quickly saw that the APIC system could ameliorate some of the communications problems caused by having people spread across several buildings. Frustrated with the slow speed of implementation of the APIC concept, he went ahead with a usable mockup of it, placing two LiveBoards in the LX Common for experimentation. There the lab members quickly started using the LiveBoards in unanticipated ways. By changing the mode of design from design by committee to design by doing, the group not only got different results, but played on the strength of the existing work practice in the LX group: the experience of performing experiments, testing, validating results, and framing the problems in new ways. Using APIC as a playground for experiments was much more productive than the expert approach first tried.

One engineer recalls talking with Zack about using

> . . . those interactive boards in this common area, so that we could have problem-solving activities and team activities going on in there. And then, communicate that directly to our computers or to other people from the LiveBoards. And it seems as if that has turned into using those boards for a different use than we originally had planned. . . . Like you have a screen so you can do a problem-solving exercise . . .

Coupled with the unanticipated use of the LiveBoards by the lab members, the amazing explosion of the World Wide Web in late 1994 was the other major surprise in the development of technology in support of LX work practice. This led to the architecture committee's decision in April 1995 to adopt the Web as the universal user interface for LX information. The various information types planned for APIC became Web pages.[5] The LiveBoard would simply run Netscape and have easy access to any information.[6] The key part of this decision was the discovery in April 1995 by Kukla and Zack at Digital of a prototype system named Workgroup Web. Its concept was simple and powerful: It was a document repository fully accessible from the World Wide Web, with no client software required except a Web browser. Documents could be stored and retrieved simply, using Netscape as the user interface, and hence easily shared with others or retrieved from home, the LiveBoards in the Common, or anywhere else (Figure 6.6). Through a video camera connected to

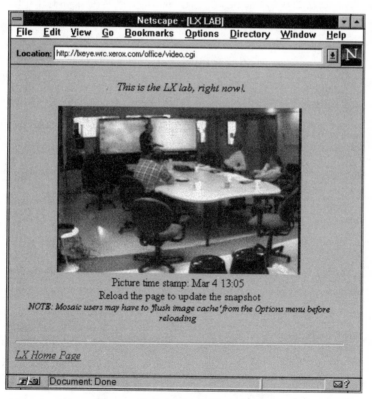

Figure 6.6 The LX snapshot.

a Web server, anyone in LX or in another city may, using the Web browser in his or her office, drop in on the LX Common in real time. Kukla and Zack saw Workgroup Web as a direct but much more powerful replacement for the shared file system LX had been using.[7]

Its work no longer needed, the architecture committee was disbanded in early summer of 1995. The LX members had taken over the LiveBoards and enjoyed their ability to drive them. Zack readily gave up the idea of trying to make the system behave as in the original concept. The complete version of APIC was never implemented, but it inspired and guided the idea of information flowing into and being accessible from the Common and helped make real use of the Common for information, discussion, and hence innovation (Figure 6.7). The photo at right (top) shows the LX Common in March 1995, still an uninhabited, empty area. The wall between the conference room and the corridor has been removed. The workplace invention is built but not yet populated. The two LiveBoards sit in the rear, not yet unwrapped. The photo at right (bottom) shows the LX Common four months later, with the innovation node and the marketplace as conceived now in use—a place for information exchange, formal and informal meetings, confrontation, and learning.

From the outset some senior LX researchers were dubious about the effectiveness of LiveBoards and of remote collaboration in general. When they needed to communicate, they were more apt to go to the people they needed and speak with them directly. As one scientist put it:

> The thing I've always found very, very useful was to get four or five people together who were fairly knowledgeable about xerography or whatever the problem happens to be. Then you start talking and having ideas. And pretty soon my idea sparks another idea. You end up with a whole different concept than when you started with. Or you've got several different paths that you could follow that you wouldn't have had by yourself. Can you achieve that with the LiveBoards? How interactive is it?

Figure 6.7 Before and after installation of the LiveBoards.

The researchers' use of communications technology also revealed something important about what was happening in the LX group. Given his awareness of the dilemmas inherent in the sharing of incomplete work (you don't want to share the "noise," you don't want to look bad, and you also don't want to give your ideas away before you've secured them as yours), Knapp and his colleagues had created a computerized communications network with three separate disk drives corresponding roughly to the sequence *data, information, knowledge.* The P drive was for personal data to be kept private. (The importance of such privacy had been underlined for Knapp by a visiting anthropologist who had spent several months in the lab.) The W drive, which had existed for some time but had been little used, was for information meant to be shared by only a few people. After the common space was inhabited, Knapp reported finding the W drive in very high use, with about half the people in the laboratory putting data into it and reading out of it on any given afternoon. The K drive was for knowledge that was to be used for validated, finished work suitable for public sharing. "Now," Knapp said, "we have the sense of sharing information, and knowledge, as it is being generated."[8]

The LX Lab at Work

By March 1995 most of the spatial and technological elements of the new LX lab were in place, though continual adjustments would follow. Unlike other Wilson Center labs, which were dark, closed, and industrial in appearance, this one was bright and open (Figure 6.8). A visitor entering through the glass doors would first pass the kitchen area—whose wall had a floor-to-ceiling whiteboard and whose tabletop could also be written on—and would next encounter another gathering place, this one equipped with a large conference table and the two LiveBoards, where researchers might be discussing their own data and other data drawn from the boards (Figure 6.9).

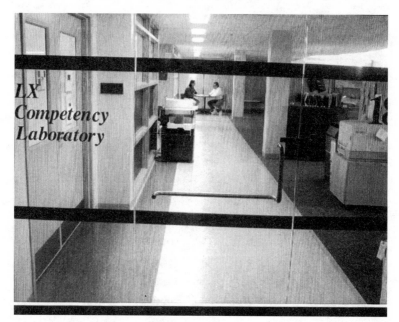

Figure 6.8   The Wilson Center and the LX lab.

The LX Common has a very open feel, being partly open to the main path of circulation and having windows and a door leading off to adjacent LX work areas. The Common is an open window giving the lab members contact with the outside world. Comments and conclusions could be entered through the LiveBoards into the APIC system, which would make them available to other LX researchers located elsewhere on the campus via their office PCs. Information flowed freely, without requiring a need to know. Opposite the space with the LiveBoards was the intellectual property area, with files and desk surfaces. Elsewhere in the LX work area, outside the kitchen area and in corridor locations, team members would likely be seen exchanging information or discussing common problems.

On a typical day, a visitor would likely see people coming and going from the Common area conference table into the adjoining

Figure 6.9   The marketplace for research.

laboratories. Proximity made it easy to quickly duck inside one of the labs to inspect a machine or process under discussion. Meetings in the space took on qualities of informality and shifting membership. People who passed by a group at work in the Common felt free to listen in and, from time to time, to join the work at hand. Some work previously confined to the adjacent labs could now be done in the common area, where it could be viewed, critiqued, and demonstrated to a wider range of people. Ideas for how the new space could be used expanded as people became familiar with it. The Common eventually developed as a multipurpose area providing space for the actual work of project subgroups within the project (Figure 6.10). The LX Common is the locus for innovations in the new work practices and technology, and also the arena for confrontation of ideas. Since the space itself is only loosely defined, boundaries can be determined by

Figure 6.10   The conference room in the corridor.

the agenda of the day. Meetings in the space take on qualities of informality and shifting membership. Project management meetings took place in this new location, as did training and meetings designed to showcase LX work. Jim Larson, the lab manager, did not have his own office in the area, but would always conduct his meetings there and would speak of the LX Common as the "family table." John Knapp once observed fourteen meetings occurring at the same time in the LX work area! The first operations review was conducted in the LX Common in June 1995, and it was then that most of the lab members first started seeing the power this meeting area had in its ability to cross professional as well as hierarchical boundaries.[9]

In contrast to past practice, those huddled at the conference table might represent a number of different levels in the Xerox hierarchy and a number of different scientific specialties. Suppliers, Xerox marketing personnel, and general managers might also be present. People would enter and leave meetings as time permitted, or when they felt they had something to learn or to contribute (Figure 6.11). In

Figure 6.11 The mobile and open meeting.

this sense, the Common was an open window, giving LX staffers contact with the outside world and vice versa. As one visitor to the site remarked:

> You'd be having a conversation and somebody would come up from behind and enter the conversation. And he would stay for five minutes, and then he'd drift off into a lab or someplace else. Nobody said, "Hey, wait a second. You're not in this meeting." People just floated in and out.

In the conference area were two LiveBoards where researchers would be discussing their own data and other data drawn from the boards. Comments and conclusions would be entered through the LiveBoards into the APIC system, which would make them available to other LX researchers via their office PCs. Information flowed freely, without a need to know. Elsewhere in the Common, outside the kitchen area and in corridor locations, team members would likely be seen exchanging information or discussing common problems.

The LX lab had the same people and the same research responsibilities, but the new team-based organization, the new technology, and the new spatial arrangements were having a tangible effect on the way work was done and how lab members interacted with each other and with non-LX personnel. "What's really changed in the laboratory," according to John Knapp, "was a change in the work culture. There was something different happening to the group, as opposed to just change in the facilities." The new arrangements stimulated a subtle democratization that took several forms.

Exposed to the qualities of this work environment, the researchers invented a new kind of meeting, the *LX share meeting*, which differed dramatically from the researchers' traditional seminars. The LX share meetings would be devoted to presentation and discussion of unfinished work in progress where the group as a whole could be involved in the further development of incomplete ideas. The idea of LX share meetings grew out of a typical drop-in-and-out conversation in the common space. The participants came up with the idea of meetings about ideas not yet finished, illustrating what they had in mind by reference to what they were doing in the common space at that very moment. People would come to those meetings with work in progress, incomplete ideas, and information whose importance was not yet fully apparent; those who brought the information would be responsible for raising the first round of questions. As Knapp put it, "everyone in the lab would walk away from that experience learning something." Weekly share meetings became a regular Friday event. Previous meetings of this type were essentially one-way forums through which research findings were presented to the larger group. The share meetings, by contrast, were give-and-take problem-solving sessions in which the insights of the many were added to the findings of particular individuals.

The new system required personal adaptation. For example, meeting manners appropriate for traditional closed conference rooms were not entirely appropriate for an open-space meeting. At first, people were reluctant to walk through the Common if a meeting was in progress. In one case, technicians trying to reach their lab a few feet away via the Common—where a meeting was under way— detoured several hundred feet to enter the lab through a rear door. The laboratory manager eventually recognized what was happening and declared three simple rules: (1) Traffic through the Common was acceptable at any time. (2) Anyone was free to join any meeting in the Common. (3) Anyone was free to leave any meeting in the Common at any time.

The LX Common became the exclusive territory of LX personnel. Other laboratories did not have such a central home base, only a name and a collection of labs and offices. Ownership of space, in the sense that the lab members themselves could take the initiative of calling a meeting, were free to play with technology, and could organize lab tours (which had never happened before the workshops)— in short, could make decisions on the lowest possible level about what was necessary to get the work done—had a dramatic effect on the work culture in the lab. The lab went from a culture of hierarchical control to a culture of responsiveness and self-organized work. There was a sense of collective ownership of the lab and its individual components. One scientist remarked that his territory had been expanded; he named several spaces in the larger territory, like the LX Common and the kitchen area, that he felt he had the right to consider his own. This was someone who previously had not been willing to give up his large offices in favor of a cubicle located near the Common.

The LX group took ownership of its place with great pride. Champions for such activities as LX share meetings and lab tours, computer networks, an LX library for intellectual property, and so forth, made this place into a bright, lively research center. No space at the Wilson Center, except the LX work area with its Common, contained all the ingredients: open meeting area, conversation technology, and group ownership. Young scientists would say: "I used to look forward to Fridays. In this lab I stay until I have done the job. This is the kind of work environment Xerox needs to develop in order to attract and recruit young, talented people."

REFLECTIONS ON THE LX CASE

Within Xerox the LX workplace experiment has been broadly recognized as successful, and it has become the focus for thought about new and more productive ways of working elsewhere in the organization. Though the productivity of R&D work—and even time to market—is difficult to measure, it was nevertheless clear to Xerox managers that the changes in space, technology, and organization had presented a promising potential for the company. During the year following the establishment of the new LX lab and Common, for instance, five of the eight awards for outstanding performance at the whole Wilson Center went to individuals in the LX lab. The lab was credited with producing three times as many patents as the much larger laboratories of Xerox's competitors. And after two years John Knapp reported that the lab had been able to develop its first product for market, from the original concept to the introduction of the finished product, in a period of eighteen months, while under normal circumstances five years would have been required.

Throughout the LX workplace experiment neither the space nor the technologies were totally suitable, but continual adjustments by lab personnel moved the various components toward increased support of work practice. Some noteworthy qualities of the experiment are:

- It violated conventions for meeting places, putting them inside the very heart of the work and making their boundaries permeable and flexible.

- ⊙ It required behavioral changes, such as new meeting manners.

- ⊙ It overthrew conventions about office size and location being dictated by organizational status.

- ⊙ Traditional office carrels were abandoned in favor of communal space where people could better innovate and share information.

- ⊙ Information technologies were used to bring people and their work together in new ways.

- ⊙ The path of development followed a course that none of the participants advocated or anticipated.

This last point may be the most telling of all. None of the key players in this design game would see his or her initial image of the LX lab prevail. Each, in fact, had to abandon those initial images during the course of the design process. Knapp, for example, had started the experiment with a very traditional view of space and organization. To him, joining the LARC pilot project was simply an opportunity to obtain space and computers. But as the project played out, his view changed and his vision expanded.

Greg Zack's view changed as well. What for him had been a straightforward information systems problem gradually took on other dimensions—namely, the sense of "family identity" for a lab and the feeling of ownership of a place. The LiveBoards, the centerpiece of Zack's technology intervention, were originally thought of as a way to facilitate group work and to provide a communications and presentation instrument for management. By virtue of their location in the LX Common—reachable by anybody who wanted to use them and not in a formal conference room—the LiveBoards became vehicles for communication among the LX technicians in connection with their day-to-day work, thus picking up on the traditionally valued face-to-face method of getting sparks to fly. But the presence of the LiveBoards also reflected a fundamental shift in approach to the design of technology tools for work, from designing by committee to designing by doing, from an expert approach to a co-invention approach.

Horgen relates that she learned how profound an effect an intervention can have in an organization. When the participants held their workshops in the presence of ongoing work and in an incomplete workplace, and were asked to treat their new place and its tools as an experiment, they then adopted this style of inquiry in their work itself. She had seen this happen before, but had never seen so clearly the linkage between workplace-making and the transformation of the work practice.

These and other adaptations illustrate the uneven course of development through which dynamically coherent workplaces are formed. Indeed, if we revisit the SOFT diagram presented in the first chapter of this book, we are reminded of how a change in one dimension of workplace-making—be it space, organization, finance, or technology—creates pressure for change in one or more of the other dimensions. For example, the new spatial and organizational changes that promoted teamwork in research stimulated thinking about new financial incentives better suited to a team-based environment. Likewise, the introduction of new technology, which had been seen as the centerpiece of LARC's initial change strategy, merged with the spatial change strategy and altered the way members of the organization interacted with each other and with their work. The fact that each dimension of workplace-making impacted the others resulted in an iterative progression of development in the LX lab. The new space was not created through a single, well-planned stroke but through a long series of interactive adjustments, each leading by degrees to a higher state of perfection.

LARC members attributed the project's success to the fact that it was guided and championed throughout—an important factor in any intervention. The leadership did not allow the project to be held hostage to any particular narrow agenda. Jim Larson and John Knapp's attitude toward experimentation in their own and the LX

group's research program had accustomed them to the need to constantly drive the change process and to take well-thought-out risks.
These attitudes toward research became part of the space and technology change process, and enabled the LARC consultants and the
LX lab members to co-invent both the process of change and the
actual changes themselves.

> In the beginning we thought somebody would "LARC-ize"
> us . . . after a while we understood that we had to become LARC.
> (John Knapp, LX lab)

7

Process Architecture Revisited

P rocess architecture is a strategy for helping organizations better shape their workplaces as they seek to improve productivity and competitive advantage. Within this context, process architecture's promise is to mount an active, collaborative process of design inquiry in order to create dynamically coherent workplaces. In light of this claim and the challenges that process architects face, we bring three main questions to bear on the analysis of our case studies:

1. How well does process architecture deliver on its promise? More specifically, is it possible to transform an organization's game of interests and powers to achieve active, collaborative design inquiry? When such a transformation is brought about, does it yield a dynamically coherent workplace, including integration of space, organization, finance, and technology (SOFT)? When design inquiry becomes active and collaborative, and when the workplace becomes dynamically coherent, does the desired improvement in work practice occur?

2. When process architecture delivers on its promises, how does it do so? What are the causal mechanisms by which active, collaborative design inquiry comes into being? Just how does such inquiry yield a workplace matched to desired changes in work practice? How does a dynamically coherent workplace entrain improvements in the work that goes on within it?

3. What kinds of knowledge, skills, and attitudes are required of a competent process architect?

Our cases tell us that there are affirmative answers to these questions and illustrate what it is like to achieve—to a greater or lesser degree—an active, collaborative process of design inquiry, a dynamically coherent workplace, and improved work practices. The cases illustrate particular features of these transformations—for example, the creation of a group of stakeholders who can actively collaborate in the design process, or a spatial arrangement well matched to a desired work practice. Two of the cases—those of the Bank of Boston and the LX laboratory—reflect fully realized examples of effective process architecture achieved through the combined efforts of consultants, organizational leaders, and workers.

Not all of our cases are success stories. Even when they succeed, they reveal only a partial fulfillment of their promise. Nevertheless, there is something to be learned from failure, and much to be learned from partial success. But is this evidence and learning enough to satisfy corporate and institutional executives whose goal is greater productivity? The answer may be yes, but only if the role of process architecture in achieving those goals is understood to be a significant part of a larger plan. Ultimately, greater productivity is achieved through improved business strategy and, at the operational level, the skillful design and management of key business processes. Process architecture contributes to the extent that it supports both.

TRANSFORMING THE DESIGN GAME

The hallmark of successful process architecture is the transformation of the design game (Figure 7.1). Neither the Ainsley case nor the InterCorp case is an example of that transformation. The formal reference process of the university in the Ainsley case was subverted by two powerful figures, the dean and the donor. The university's space planners and facilities managers tried to play by the rules, but were unable to bell the cat. In the end, they were marginalized by the two dominant players. These workplace professionals were unsuccessful in impressing the dean and donor with the likely costs of their last-minute design decisions and change orders; nor did they present any more effective options. The result was a workplace that mirrored the process that created it: compartmentalized and compromised. The

Ainsley Building

The design game stalemated: The instigators remain isolated, while the users—though concerned and active within the formally agreed-on reference process—never manage to get their concerns into the actual game as played. The more powerful players leave the reference process behind. The result is a less than optimal building that reflects separately the agendas of the instigators and the recipients.

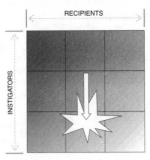

Ainsley Building

InterCorp

Even with a potentially active recipient group, the efforts of the consultant are stifled by the internal power battle. The consultant eventually is ejected from the game.

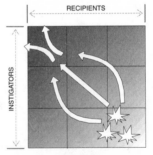

InterCorp

Research University Labs

The new reference process—in the hands of members of the space administration—reveals that most of the space gridlock can be solved through the renovation of one specific research unit. Though emerging with an agreed-upon master plan, the consultants are not able to help the stakeholders involved to see the benefit of the first action step or of the process that had just been successfully completed. The joint effort dissolves and the master plan is never implemented.

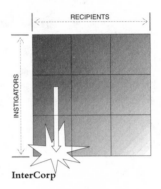

Research University Labs

Bank of Boston

The design game is orchestrated by the internal manager, set out to involve the right knowledge in the right task. At all levels in the bank, the employees are involved in shaping their new work life in a complex design game that is tightly controlled but nevertheless responsive to anyone's ideas and open for redesign.

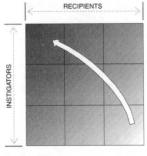

Bank of Boston

Figure 7.1   Design games.

(continued)

Cluster Design

The design game begins as a fairly conventional design process. But as the cluster design idea suddenly emerges, the interactive game begins. The resolution and the refinement of the design are worked out in collaboration with the recipients in a way that drastically changes how work is carried out in the hospital.

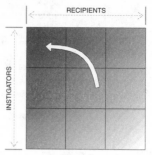

Cluster Design

The LX Common

The consultants demonstrate a design game that not only produces a new and surprising work space but informs the transformation of the actual work process from isolated research work within individual labs ("foxholes") to an open, collaborative place for innovation and learning.

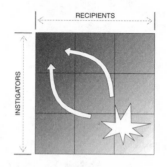

The LX Common

Green Hills

The consultant enters a fragmented game in disarray, and is able to reframe the problem and construct a new design coalition.

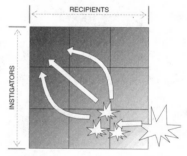

Green Hills

Radiation Therapy

The consultants are faced with deciphering a hidden client system, understanding partially competing agendas that the actors are unwilling to voice in public, and detecting what organizational and political issues underlie the solution the clients present to their consultants as an answer to their problem.

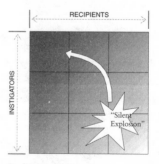

Radiation Therapy

Figure 7.1   *(continued)*

224

Ainsley building was suboptimal from the point of view of both sets of values—the planners' view of a building that would house academic research, favor public spaces for interaction, and look like an academic facility, and the donor's views of elegance, polish, luxury, and status.

The InterCorp design game was equally untransformed. Robert Oliver was caught in the internal battles between facility managers and physical planners, between office staff and corporate management, and between one division and another. Oliver's understanding of the expert's role—that of applied social scientist—depended on the presence of a unitary and rational decision-maker who would receive and act on the information provided by the expert. But there was no such decision-maker, only a mélange of contending players whose conflicts created dilemmas for Oliver that remained unresolvable as long as he framed his role within the technical-rational approach.

We see the existing design game transformed in the radiation therapy, Green Hills, and University Research Laboratories cases. In all three of these instances, the process architects recognized the existence of the game and diagnosed it. In the radiation therapy case, the process architects had to decipher a hidden client system, understand the competing agendas that the actors themselves were unwilling to voice in public, and make sense of underlying organizational and political issues. Once the hidden client system and agendas were decoded, the process architects used technical information and financial scenarios—about costs, investments, and financial burdens associated with the new center—to induce the competing client institutions to arrive at a more or less consensual decision on the location of the new medical facility.

At Green Hills, the process architect joined the game as an architect/physical planner. As Stanley Nobel came to understand the situation and the contending players, he expanded his role to include a diagnostic analysis and transformation of the existing design game, and he came to play multiple roles as process designer, facilitator, and organizational developer. Using his legitimacy as a spatial planner as a springboard, he transformed the game as he found it. He created a client system he could work with, then helped those clients to discover for themselves the values of the Green Hills site. Those values became the basis for a development program that was responsive to the potentials of the site and to the values people held for it.

In the University Research Laboratories case we observed how process architects generated an improved method for resolving inter-group conflicts over space allocation, as well as a process for space utilization that more nearly matched the actual preferences of the research groups involved. Here the process architects used their repertoire of tools—and invented new ones—to achieve cooperation among the research groups rather than forcing each to appeal to a higher authority to resolve conflicts.

In the Bank of Boston and LX lab cases, we see two interestingly different examples of the conversion of an existing design game to an active, collaborative process of co-design. In both cases the transformation of the design process was closely intertwined with the transformation of the workplace. The Bank of Boston case stands out for several reasons. First, the design of the Canton facility was integral to the redesign of the back-office business the new facility was intended to serve. From the very beginning, performance criteria for the new workplace were derived from a new business vision and strategy, which Peter Manning and his team developed as they fought to fulfill their mandate: Make the business profitable or get rid of it. The salient features of the Canton facility—the bare-bones sawhorse tables, the flexibility built into the spatial arrangements and technological infrastructure, the opening up the shop floor for regular tours by prospective clients—all derived from a leading business idea, the visible accounting factory, which became the leading design idea. Manning orchestrated a wide-ranging group of active collaborators in the design process: the internal Wings Team of business section heads, technical analysts of the accounting processes, marketers, internal facility managers, an external team of consultants, and prospective users of the facility.

In spite of Manning's orchestration, the process of workplace creation had the character of good jazz—it was full of surprises and on-the-spot improvisation. For example:

- The marketing staff's rejection of level-status offices
- The discovered need to invent flexible conduits for electricity and data cables
- The failure of the basic furniture (pinwheel tables without storage capacity)
- The adoption of just-in-time work flow and a paperless office format

In each of these instances, the inside-outside cross-professional design team responded with rapid, on-the-spot invention and adjustment. The design process was itself a process of on-the-spot development achieved through agile management and execution.

In the case of the LX lab, the process architects entered the picture just when lab researchers were most disturbed at the prospect of moving to a new space designed and equipped with premanufactured office carrels. This design was actively resisted. In two workshops, the process architects used walk-throughs, workbooks, and slide shows to encourage the LX workers to describe how they actually conducted their work and to sketch their impressions of an ideal work environment. The idea of a common grew out of these sessions. The LX Common would be a "spread-out place" for collaboration and communication, where drawings and data could be made visible all at once and where people would be able to think together "with their hands as well as their brains." The Common became an energizing concept, generating and guiding subsequent design work in which the researchers were the main actors. The empty space built as a result of the workshop and into which the researchers ultimately moved became the locus for further design. The two LiveBoards, originally intended as a means of remote collaboration, were incorporated into the new space and came to be used as vehicles for enhanced face-to-face communication.

A year or more into this design process, it became clear to the Xerox research managers—especially John Knapp, the day-to-day leader of the LX lab—that some combination of the new workplace and the new design process had been responsible for inducing a new and highly desirable mode of collaboration into the regular work practice.

The two versions of process architecture displayed in the Bank of Boston and LX cases make an interesting comparison. In each we see the crucial importance of commitment to the design process by the internal leadership. In the Bank of Boston case, Manning acted as an internal process architect, contributing his accounting knowledge to the final result. In the LX case, the external LARC consultants—especially Horgen—catalyzed the collaborative design process; but they would have been unable to do so had they not received strong support from the two internal project champions, John Knapp and Jim Larson.

Both cases demonstrate the power of an idea: in the one, the accounting factory, in the other, the common. Each energized and guided a design process that was fast-paced and driven by the need to inhabit the new work environment. Significant elements of the design process were accomplished on the ground, in the surroundings of the new work environment. There was also a strong element of reflective conversation with the situation in each case: an element of incompleteness and surprise against a background of preset intentions, to which the designers responded by on-the-spot reframing of problems and invention of new design ideas.

Uneven development, a key feature of process architecture, is visible in each case, particularly in the LX case. There, changes in work process triggered changes in work environment (as in the initial call for a common place), and changes in work environment triggered changes in work process (as in the invention of the LX share meetings).

How Process Architects Manage Transformation of an Existing Design Game

The protagonists in our successful cases met the second challenge of process architecture by getting different interests, languages, views, images, and values on the table. They also helped to create behavioral worlds and physical settings conducive to the resolution of these differences.

The transformation of the design game is a story of the practitioners' use or invention, within a custom-tailored process of design inquiry, of certain structured events and instruments and ways of using them:

- Encouraging inhabitants of a work space to become more aware of what the existing workplace means to them, and which of its features serve or frustrate their purposes.

- Engaging space users in characterizing the core of their work and imagining an idealized environment.

- Doing these things collectively, so that individuals (or specialized groups) become aware of the idealized images held by others (University Research Laboratories, LX lab).

- Close observation of how work is actually done, represented by images and stories, as a basis for workplace design (DEC/Monsanto).

- Rapid visualization of workplace design ideas; rapid synthesis of the workplace images held by individuals or subgroups. These can be fed back into the collaborative design process. Similarly, rapid detailed design (yellow trace) or mock-up of facilities, so that users and other stakeholders can quickly see and respond to the features of the new workplace (Bank of Boston, cluster design, University Research Laboratories, LX lab).

- The use of these and other methods to draw participants out of themselves and encourage them to objectify the site and think about it in its own terms (as in Nobel's drafting board sessions and Horgen's walk-throughs, slide shows, and drawing sessions).

- The use of a mocked up or partially realized work environment as a setting in which to engage in collaborative workplace evaluation and design. This gives participants a vivid sense of the setting they seek to develop and creates a prototype of collaborative inquiry that can be transferred to the work itself (LX lab).

- The use of concrete design games as vehicles for collaborative workplace design—progressively sharing and synthesizing the idealized images of groups of participants (the envelope game) or creating in the participants an understanding of the work process they will be enacting in the new work environment (the sailboat game).

ACHIEVING A DYNAMICALLY COHERENT WORKPLACE

In the DEC/Monsanto case we saw the achievement of dynamic coherence and the revelation of its consequences for the improved performance of work. The nursing cluster design case provides only fragmentary information about the process of design inquiry that achieves dynamic coherence; however, the case tells us a great deal about the ways in which the nursing cluster design enhances the performance of nurses, the interaction of nurses and patients, and the experience of the patients. The Bank of Boston and LX cases provide rather full descriptions of the entire cycle of process architecture: how a more active, collaborative design process is achieved, how that process generates a work environment that matches the way work is actually done, and how the process moves the environment toward a desired image of work practice.

When we explore just how an enhanced work environment supports the emergence of enhanced work practice, we uncover certain key qualities of the spatial, technological, and organizational environments for work. In the following list, we stress spatial qualities; in the subsequent section, we discuss technology's role in a dynamically coherent workplace. The list of spatial qualities reflects our particular mix of case studies and is not exhaustive.

Incompleteness. There are attributes or features that make a place appear incomplete in form, material, or extent. In terms of form, this might be a shape (a J, for example) that is somehow not complete either as a geometric form or as a conventional room. Regarding material, there might be a high-quality finish on one wall but framing showing through on another. In terms of extent, the place might somehow imply its full dimension through the marking out of its ultimate footprint, but the superstructure might be only partly built.

Incompleteness may also result from the implication that the form must be completed outside itself, as a room partially open to the corridor may demand completion by the appropriation of space in the corridor. This is like a partially finished sentence uttered by one individual that demands completion on the lips of another. The mind is invited to fill in the missing part. In a group, each person may do this in a way that relates to his or her own work practice. This phenomenon is best illustrated by the responses of the LX lab researchers to the incompleteness of the common space as it was when they first occupied it.

Blurred territorial boundaries. The boundaries of the LX Common overlapped the boundaries of the adjoining corridor. The result was an area where boundaries could be defined in relation to different claims, creating open, indefinite, and sometimes disputed territory. Some problems require many different disciplines for their resolution. It is often impossible to see where boundaries should arise between disciplines, and sometimes one discipline will yield insights in unexpected areas. Blurring of territorial boundaries creates areas of ambiguity and fosters the development of communities of practice that promote communication and collaboration across disciplines.

Flexibility. This refers to the capacity of a place to support, with low-cost adjustments, a variety of activities that make different demands on the space. As work evolves in unexpected ways, or as new participants bring new requirements, the participants can easily redeploy their space, themselves, and their resources to undertake new actions. In the Bank of Boston's facility, flexible spatial and technological arrangements made it possible for the work process to change in response to evolving needs and goals.

Size and shape. These terms refer to the dimensions, proportions, and exact geometric configuration of a place. Size and shape will either constrain or support work. For example, the new spatial arrangements of the hospital wing in the cluster design case directly supported nursing activities. In contrast, space standards dictated by prestige, rank, or seniority may fail to support effective problem-solving teams, as the LX case suggests.

Reciprocal visibility. This refers to the ability of individuals located at different points within a space to view one another; high reciprocal visibility enhances opportunities for exchange. The LX Common afforded just such opportunities. The people conducting a meeting in the Common and those passing by in the former corridor could see one another and reciprocally decide whether the passers-by should join the meeting. In the nursing clusters case, the reciprocal visibility of nurses and patients enabled nurses to monitor patients continually without special effort; patients could keep their nurses continuously in view, relieving their anxiety and enabling them to make their needs known immediately.

Transparency. Transparency is the property of place that permits one-way inspection of its contents. When transparency is high, an individual outside the place can look in, or an individual within the place can look from one part into another. This form of visual access may or may not be accompanied by acoustical privacy. By virtue of transparency, one can see what is going on elsewhere; in doing so, one is reminded of the many elements and people that make up the work process or the problem-solving situation. In the Bank of Boston's facility, for example, the transparency of workers' activities to their adjacent supervisors enhanced supervisory control. The transparency of the work space in the bank's new mailing facility allowed viewers to look down from a gallery, supporting the use of the work space as a stage for the display of services to be sold.

Artifactual presence. Artifacts embody individual and group memories, often in ways that are essential to the performance of organized work. In the cluster design case, equipment visible in the patient's room and materials on the mobile supply cart reminded the nurses of tasks to be performed, and may also have symbolized for the nurses the nature and importance of the service they were rendering. In the DEC/Monsanto case, the idea of a design room derived from the need for a large space, positioned next to the production line, that would permit display of engineering blueprints to facilitate the diagnostic activities of the process engineers. The LX Common with its nearby fixtures is another example. The fixtures were a regular reminder of accumulated knowledge, work that had been done, and work that remained to be done. Similarly, being able to see into adjacent laboratories brought to mind the range of operations and disciplines needed to create xerographic equipment. Arguably, the presence of such artifacts creates a richer field for purposeful thought and innovation. They become "things to think with," in Seymour Papert's memorable phrase.[1]

Departing from workplace stereotypes. Departing from the conventional images associated with certain workplaces (e.g., a wet lab, a nursing station, a paper processing operation) helps us challenge conventional approaches to work practice, enabling imaginative solutions. Consider, for example, the stereotypical wet lab versus the wet lab designed to include multiple uses of computers, as described in Chapter 3. Or contrast the LX Common with the more conventional double-loaded corridor with offices next to laboratory space.

When we depart from stereotypes of place, we make way for the development of leading ideas for workplace design—powerful images that guide the design process through all of its phases. These may be developed in ways that cut across projects and become adapted and refined in each new project. The nursing cluster concept developed in this way over a period of years. Or the leading idea may be created in the course of the design process itself—as occurred in the image of the accounting factory in the Bank of Boston facility. Employing these ideas, participants use their experience to name what they want to produce even before they design it. In the LX case, the LARC consultants used the New England town with its common to explain their idea for the Wilson Center. This idea suggested boundaries between towns as overlapping. The consultants could then identify and attack the contrast between volatile organizations and stiff infrastructure, showing how it was possible to inhabit several laboratories—or "towns"—at once, suggesting that each of the nine competency centers or labs could be focused around one common, with shared communication among the commons.

Technology and the Dynamically Coherent Workplace

Our discussion of the dynamically coherent workplace has thus far emphasized the interaction of spatial arrangements with the organization of work. What happens when we add technology to the equation? What do our cases tell us about integrating technology with spatial and organizational features?

Technology appeared in several of our cases: the Bank of Boston, nursing clusters, DEC/Monsanto, and the LX lab. In the nursing cluster case, low technology played a minor but essential role. The folded corridor that made it possible to create the clusters also reduced storage space, creating a demand for a new storage technology. The mobile supply carts, designed on the basis of a careful study of nurses' needs for supplies and just-in-time principles, were key to the viability of the cluster design.

In the DEC/Monsanto case, ethnographic studies of actual work methods provided a basis for inventing computational tools that would match and enhance the work process. DEC@aGlance, to take one example, grew out of Chuck Kukla's insight into the informational needs of production engineering practitioners. Here we saw in operation the strategy of inventing applications of information technology not to automate existing patterns of work but to support collaborative activities and problem-solving on the part of informal work teams.

In the Bank of Boston case, we observed how architects, engineers, and facilities managers invented a new technological infrastructure (the cable trays) to provide power, data, and telecommunications to prewired pinwheel tables, complementing the new spatial/organizational value of flexibility in the work process and its workplace. As in the nursing clusters case, this technological invention dealt with the infrastructure (channels for flow of supplies and information) that proved necessary for the new work environment. At this stage of uneven development, the invention of new technology responded to demands created by a new spatial/organizational configuration. Earlier in the design process, however, the causality had been the opposite. Gail King's systems development analysis and accounting software meshed with Peter Manning's prior idea of the accounting factory, and joined with the Coopers & Lybrand just-in-time approach to inform the spatial work flow structure.

In the LX lab case, technology was central to the design process in at least three ways. First, the core work process was itself a process of technological development. The creation of the next generation of xerographic technology required a cross-disciplinary process in which the practitioners of specialized disciplines would solve problems lying between, rather than within, their fields. This requirement for cross-disciplinary dialogue informed the performance criteria that guided the design of the LX lab's new work environment. Second, the centerpiece of the LX lab's cross-disciplinary work and environment was the integrated fixture, a model of the as yet unbuilt machine. The fixture provided the setting for numerous iterative experiments, each of which had the potential to require changes in each of the fixture's subsystems. Finally, the LiveBoards originally intended to facilitate work at a distance found unanticipated uses in the Common area, where researchers interacted directly.

Every work process has its characteristic technology that places its own demands on the work environment. In an unstable organizational milieu, a change in the technology of work portends a change in the spatial and organizational dimensions of the work environment. In addition, the work environment has a technological dimension, one aspect of which is infrastructure technology that accommodates the flows of materials, power, information, money, and communications. Process architecture often presses the limits of existing infrastructure, generating demands for technological invention. Conversely—and this is especially true of the rapidly developing field of information technology—the availability of innovative infrastructure technology creates opportunities for change in the workplace. Process architecture stresses the intimate co-design of such technology in interaction with the development of new spatial and organizational configurations. The story of the LX workplace experiment suggests how this process of co-design can evolve in surprising ways, and also suggests that in the future the functions of space will not be understood without an intimate knowledge of the interconnections between space use and information technology.

WHAT PROCESS ARCHITECTURE REQUIRES OF ITS PRACTITIONERS

We have described ways in which competent process architects have been able to move an existing design game toward active, collaborative design. Now we turn to the competencies on which effective process architecture depends.

Skillful Use of Tools

Effective use of the tools within the layered framework of process architecture, as illustrated in our cases, depends on particular skills, values, and attitudes. A competent process architect uses these tools flexibly, adapting them to different organizational settings and learning to use them in new ways. In the University Research Laboratories case, for example, Browning and Voysey used several familiar procedures—survey questionnaire, walk-through, workbook, and slide show—to resolve the space wars being waged among the different groups of researchers. In the LX case, Horgen was engaged by the LX group to use a version of the process she had developed for the wet lab. She quickly realized, however, that the new situation did not lend itself to a replication of any process. From the very first workshop, the LX group members took hold of the process and used it to pursue their own design agenda. The idea of the Common gradually presented itself, and the group began to develop it. The LARC consultants were able to live with sustained confusion about what was going on and to allow the participants to declare and develop their own framing of the workplace problem and elaborate their own design intentions.

Process architects must be able to use tools to promote rapid, iterative collaborative design, emphasizing fast reduction to practice and the rapid creation of multiple representations of spaces and artifacts. The emphasis is on rapid visualization of design ideas and views of the problem, so as to promote recognition and critique, which means that the process architect must be able to hold ideas loosely, treating them more as vehicles for communication than as final products. Even design tools familiar to practitioners of the technical-rational approach, such as the user surveys associated with post-occupancy evaluation (POE), can be used in ways congenial to process architecture. In the University Research Laboratories case, POE survey data were used not as findings to be presented to management but as tools to surface user preferences in group meetings and to foster ongoing collaborative inquiry.

Knowing and Not Knowing

A skillful process architect is not an expert in the conventional sense. He or she understands the process of design inquiry and the tools that support it, but depends on others for contributions of expertise in the form of local knowledge. This interplay of knowing and not knowing is suggested by a deeper look into process architecture's conception of collaborative design. Jan Åke Granath has written:

> A collective design process is a participatory design activity where the people, or the actors, concerned and affected by the design result, take part and with their respective expertise, knowledge, values, and interests, in a collective way formulate the design result. They affect each other's knowledge and values in such a way that the common knowledge and objectives of the organization are both questioned and developed. The design activity also generates new knowledge and goals. Collective design is something more than contributory influence and just participation. It is not a process aimed at compromising in order to find the smallest common denominator. Rather, it is a process where knowledge and values confront, complete and modify each other, leading to something new.[2]

In process architecture, there is sometimes an advantage in not knowing too much, so that one can shape situations in which one is able to confront different kinds of knowledge. For example, a process architect who conducted a walk-through in a health care facility invited an experienced senior physician to participate in the initial meetings. But the process architect asked the physician to stay in the background and not take the lead in asking questions. She did this because she wanted to create an atmosphere of talking to the inhabitants about things that might seem obvious to them, things that they would never talk about or even see, things that they take for granted without ever thinking how they might be done differently. The process architect told the physician, "You know too much," and she could actually see how this was so, because when the physician entered the discussion the dynamic shifted. The physician became the teacher and the residents became the students who did not know enough and therefore didn't want to reveal what they didn't know. But toward the process architect—the innocent outsider—residents and other staff members could play the role of experts in their own environment and therefore think harder about their own future responsibilities. They looked to the senior physician for answers. With the process architect, they gradually saw that they needed to develop answers to questions about the changing workplace together, and they perceived that they would share responsibility for the work-ability of those answers.

For this process architect, knowing what was going on within the health care facility was beside the point. Her expertise was an ability to recognize how the understandings of the facility's inhabitants were, or could be, reflected in architecture, and an ability to design a process in which these same individuals could develop alternatives. The point was to *recognize*—not to *know*—what was going on.

Skills and Attitudes Specific to Collaborative Design

To the extent that our cases reveal effective process architecture, they show process managers who are able to foster active, collaborative processes of workplace design. What kinds of attitudes does this require? The ability to combine knowing and not knowing, described in the preceding text, is a key element, but not the only one.

Process architecture demands patience. Listening and recognition are necessarily slow and therefore often frustrating to people who "want to get the damn thing built." By comparison, technical-rational expertise operates at a faster pace. Figuring out what is dysfunctional in a given environment takes time. It also takes time for new concepts to ripen and for everyone to find out what works and what does not.

Process architecture also requires openness to creative tension between users and practitioners. This approach is much more complex and demanding than traditional programming (sometimes called the writing of the architectural brief), which typically depends primarily on established space standards and on fitting concerns expressed by the user into preexisting categories. A program is supposed to give a description of all the elements that go into the future building or product, in terms as accurate as possible, in order to guide the designer. This is quite possible if one is building more of the same thing one already has; for example, when expanding a facility that supports work processes perfectly well. But if there is a problem with the work process, or if one has installed new technology that dramatically changes the way of working, it is not so clear whether the old type of building works any more, and it is not so straightforward to just buy another one. One cannot write a program for something if one does not yet conceptually know what it is or what it will look like. Most approaches to programming build on the assumption that you know what the end result will be, at least conceptually. So how does one go about building something that has not been built before—solving a problem that has not been dealt with, or even acknowledged, before? In a more limited approach to participatory planning, the consultant's role is defined as that of an expert on buildings or computer systems who seeks to get the users to provide needed information about an already defined problem. The consultant asks the users how many wastebaskets they need, for example, or gets them to describe their work process, but only in order to understand and build a shelter around those processes, not to improve or change them. The users tend to treat the building expert with a kind of distant respect, believing that he or she will figure out what they need. Unfortunately, the users are almost always disappointed when the space is built, exclaiming in despair, "This is not what we asked for." The building expert shrugs and says, "They don't know what they want. I spent hours and hours listening to their complaints and requirements, and I tried to meet their specifications. They always just want the moon."

The architect in such a case believes that he or she has been engaged in a truly participatory design process. There is one major problem: The users (as well as the architect) have difficulty describing anything outside what they already know or have seen before. In contrast, process architecture aims to create a design collective where the end result is owned by all involved. The dynamic between the building expert and the user is different from one-way participation and allows for a different kind of collaboration between user and architect. Experts tend to treat other experts with deference, in the sense that they will not question each other's expertise or authority of knowledge. A nonexpert or user—defined as somebody who doesn't know and is allowed not to know—can ask whatever question he or she wants, or have views on anything outside his or her own knowledge. This kind of situation releases an interesting creative duality, because each person becomes both an expert and an amateur at the same time. This enables the design collective to challenge the expert view, break it apart, and use local expert knowledge to create something that falls between, rather than within, existing competencies.

Process architecture demands a tolerance or zeal for open-endedness and persistent uncertainty. For the process architect, the design is never entirely complete. Change in one aspect (e.g., technology) naturally demands change in one or several others. And loose ends and uncertainty invite the contributions of others in addition to the design practitioners involved in the design process. In contrast, loose ends and uncertainty make the traditional designer uncomfortable; he or she attempts to complete the design, leaving nothing open or unfinished. However, one of the characteristics of the design process is that one rips apart what has been, looks at it with different eyes, and puts it together in a way it has not been put together before.

Finally, the process architect does not fixate on building as a test of success. The result of the collective design process may be that nothing needs to be built, or that the solution lies in new technology or new modes of organization. The process architect must be open to—indeed, welcoming of—such an outcome.

Cognizant of the Design Game and Zestful for Its Play

Effective process architecture depends on the practitioner's ability to understand, play, and transform an existing design game. This means that the game of interests, powers, and freedoms is not ignored as "organizational politics" and outside the circle of professional practice. The competent process architect puts the dynamics of the existing design game on a par with spatial, technological, and financial aspects of the situation. Understanding the game in play is an essential component of professional knowledge. The competent practitioner must be able to identify the decision-makers, the users whose work processes and workplace will be affected, and members of the stakeholder group who understand the political process and work practices.

The sharper the process architect's understanding of the game, the players, and the stakes, the more effective he or she can be in framing the issues, confronting them, and transforming them into a new design game that leads in a more constructive direction.

8

Learning Process Architecture

In the previous chapter we looked back over our case studies to describe the practices, skills, attitudes, and values of process architecture. In this chapter we explore how these capabilities and qualities are learned by individuals and organizations. What did the individual participants in the projects we studied learn or fail to learn about process architecture? What obstacles did they encounter? What were the significant variations in what and how they learned?

We find it useful to distinguish three phases in the process by which individuals learn a new practice:

1. *Discovery:* by which we mean coming to understand or reunderstand something—for example, grasping in conceptual terms the meaning of process architecture.
2. *Invention:* by which we mean imagining what to do in a situation and recognizing a new strategy of action.
3. *Production:* by which we mean delivering in actual behavior the invented strategy of action.

Learning a new practice like process architecture requires moving through these phases not once but many times, in different contexts and different combinations.[1] The passage from discovery through invention to production moves us as individuals from concept to action, from idea to behavior.

We also explore in this chapter how organizations learn the concepts and practices of process architecture. Organizations cannot learn unless their individual members learn new ways of thinking and acting on the organization's behalf. But individual learning is insufficient. New ideas and practices generated by the inquiry of individuals in interaction with one another must enter into the organization's store of knowledge and routines and must become embedded in organizational artifacts such as actual written records, memories, and programs. Therefore, we distinguish a three-stage learning sequence for organizations:

1. *Planting.* The project is initiated, developed, and completed.
2. *Taking root.* Learning from the project enters into the thinking and action of individuals and into the store of individual and organizational knowledge and routines.
3. *Dissemination.* Innovative practices of design and work are reinvented in new situations within the larger organization or across organizational boundaries.

Our approach to individual and organizational learning draws on several sources: First, we relied on retrospective studies of workplace creation, such as the InterCorp, nursing clusters, DEC/Monsanto, radiation therapy, and Green Hills cases. For some of these we have done follow-up studies with process managers or participants. Second, we utilized the University Research Laboratories and Xerox LX lab projects, where we tracked processes of intervention as they unfolded and later conducted follow-up interviews and group meetings with some participants.

INDIVIDUAL LEARNING

Our cases and follow-up discussions offer examples of individuals who were exposed to process architecture and who grasped its important features. Other individuals had at least as much exposure, yet did not come to understand these key concepts and principles or, having understood them at some level, were unable or unwilling to convert them into practice. When individuals are exposed to the practice of process architecture, what enables them to grasp what it is about? What experiences are most helpful to them? What is it, on the other hand, that makes the essential principles of process architecture so difficult for others to grasp or practice?

We have examples of individuals who, upon exposure to process architecture—either through talks about it or direct experience— became interested in sponsoring process architecture projects in their own organizations. For example, Zack Rosenfield described the reactions of a nurse who heard one of his talks about nursing clusters:

> In explaining this to some folks in Pittsburgh, somebody "got it" and said, "Oh, I see, if you do this, then you're going to get this kind of self-reinforcing loop behavior where you get a result far greater than you've just described to us!" The person I was talking to was a nurse. She understood, without my having said so, that behavior was going to change. The atmosphere would change the unit. The notion that the atmosphere could change and that that would have specific, tangible results—it was the first time I'd seen anybody else get it. But I conclude from that that it is possible.

Even more impressive were the reactions of the owner-manager of Menorah Park nursing home in Buffalo, New York, where Rosenfield undertook the design of new and expanded facilities. Initially, this individual embraced the idea of cluster design in the name of efficiency. Cluster units and some services, such as food, were to be arranged on one floor, so that patients could easily move from one to the other, while other services, such as physical therapy, would be brought to the units themselves. Observing and learning from the operation of the clusters, and its measurably beneficial effects on elderly patients, the owner-manager perceived that the nursing assistants who had responsibility for these units were capable of far greater autonomy in the responsible provision of care than the organization had ever assumed. Gradually he removed intermediate layers of nursing supervision and extended vastly greater levels of control and trust to the nursing assistants. An intervention that had initially been justified as a way of bringing services into spatial proximity on one floor came to be redefined as a way of radically decentralizing responsibility for the provision of care and of flattening the organization and thereby reducing its costs of operation.

In the Xerox LX lab case, different research managers appear to have learned different things from their interactions with the LARC consultants (though there was a general tendency for people to focus on the LX Common and the look of the resulting workplace rather than the process that produced it). For example, the business manager of the LX group, a former chemist new to research management at that time, seemed mostly interested in the LX Common as a show-place for selling the group's research. But John Knapp, day-to-day leader of the group, understood quickly the potential benefits of both the dynamically coherent workplace and the active, collaborative design process the consultants were trying to bring into being.

In the University Research Laboratories case, follow-up inter-views conducted more than a year after the end of the project revealed polarized responses. With one notable exception, the heads of the research groups dismissed the project. They felt it had been too time consuming, and, although it had led to consensus on the out-lines of a new master plan, it was seen as having come to nothing since the university had committed no new funds to it. Space admin-istrators of the individual schools and of the university, on the other hand, had a different view. They thought the consultants had done a thorough job of examining space issues and the university's planning processes (or lack thereof). They admired the objectivity and impar-tiality the consultants brought to the process, as well as their ability to get faculty members from different schools to talk to one another and find common ground. One administrator grasped the nature of the process architecture approach rather fully. This was the first time, she pointed out, that the group had looked at the building as a whole, sorted out all competing needs, and tried to satisfy as many of those needs as possible. In her opinion, the process had been effective in getting the heads of the research groups to sit in the same room, articulate what each group's ideal workplace would be, discuss prior-ities, and work out solutions together.

In this project, a sense of collegiality developed as people sat down together to learn what others did in their spaces. People were generally fair and willing to negotiate with their colleagues. Researchers even agreed that they could fit into a much smaller spatial envelope—something that never occurred before or since. The walk-throughs had brought all participants into direct contact with crowded and unused spaces. For the first time, the administrator said, people who had previously been extremely unrealistic became more realistic about what they needed. It was also one of the few occasions on which space administrators "went into a meeting armed with a thorough understanding of how people did business in the space."

This administrator attributed the project's success to both the time the consultants had invested and the trust they had built up. The consultants had begun the project with no preconceived notions; they did not seek to impose their own values. As a result, people were honest with them. The administrator hoped other people could be trained to do the same: "Supposedly, these are real principles they're following, a real process; you could train people to do that just the way you train people to be mediators." But the administrator ended her interview with the observation that the people who were following the tenets of process architecture would have to build up some examples of "success"—actual physical construction—to get others to really buy the approach.

Unlike the individuals described above, some workplace professionals have trouble understanding what process architecture is about, even after they've seen it firsthand. Others are intrigued by process architecture but have difficulty progressing from the cycle of discovery through the cycles of invention and production. The major roadblock for them is not what they need to learn, but what they already know—what they must unlearn. This problem of unlearning is underscored by Zack Rosenfield's experience in working with architects and administrators to promote the nursing cluster design his firm had pioneered at the Somerville and Hackensack hospitals:

We wrote articles. I gave seminars. I scheduled speaking appearances before groups of administrators and nurses—anybody I could get to listen to me. A lot of architects came. The architects jeered and asked snide questions. It has something to do with our training . . . it's a very individualistic profession. . . . By and large it's "bad" for you to copy someone else's work, [though] we do it all the time, of course. But we don't like to think of it that way. So from architects, contempt. The administrators said, "I don't believe you. I think you're just another salesman trying to sell us a piece of work, and I don't want to hire you."

According to Rosenfield, his greatest success in developing clustered nursing units occurs when he and his associates have project control. "When we have to work through another architect, our success is almost zero. They just don't get it."

Once in a while I see published plans—very few nursing home plans, but mostly hospital plans—that incorporate some piece of the cluster concept, but they never seem to get [all of] it. . . . I've had many people say, "This is a cluster," and then show me something [about which] I say, "Well, you got this half, but you didn't get this half." Why don't they get the whole thing? It beats me.

If the architects don't "get it," people who have working experience in a hospital or nursing environment do. When a team of nurses visits Hackensack or Somerville or both, according to Rosenfield, they get the point. "The moment they walk in the door, they get the feeling of the place. They know that it is different."

Rosenfield's comments suggest an explanation for his frustration. The architects' obsession with originality is an obstacle to learning from what works. They resist innovations "not invented here." But the best way for people to learn is to observe what is working in existing sites. By contrasting direct exposure to a new site with their own experience, and by combining the best elements from both, people discover new possibilities for their own workplaces. In contrast to the architect, the people who will actually use a given work environment—nurses, in this instance—are the ones who have the least to unlearn. They have no hang-ups about originality or qualms about the source of an innovation that results in a more effective workplace. The people most sensitive to the shortcomings of their existing environments are the ones most likely to grasp and respond to a useful innovation.

The theme of unlearning is central to the stories of two other individuals involved in our cases.

Robert Oliver: Tenacious Professionalism

When Robert Oliver emerged from his chastening experience with InterCorp, he seriously attempted to broaden his consulting approach. Having experienced the limits of his technical-rational approach and the organizational traps into which it led him, he wanted to go beyond it. But he found that difficult to do. The stages he passed through in his effort are revealing.

In the first instance, Oliver framed the problem as one of educating his client. "They want our data," he said, "but they don't respond to us. How can we educate them?" Later, he wrote a new account of his work at InterCorp, treating it as a puzzle that he sought to explain. In this document, he attempted to come to terms with what he saw as "irrationalities" in InterCorp's behavior. He wrote, for example, that when the corporate staff applied their usual cost/benefit analysis methodology to the selection of a site for the new headquarters building, they did not select "the most cost-effective of the four options." Rather, "InterCorp's image-makers determined that the location of the headquarters was a more important consideration than the cost of the project."

Describing his problems in trying to win support for his survey methodology, Oliver explained how "naive" he had been to imagine that his method of post-occupancy evaluation was "a simple information-gathering tool that could be used by clients to learn something about their buildings." He had learned that "this model of consultancy is unrealistic; generating information in the form of feedback is a politically loaded act for which the experienced consultant has to take responsibility as an agent of change."

Oliver first became aware of his naiveté as he attempted to organize workshops to train InterCorp facilities staff in his methodology. He succeeded in attracting only a few people to these workshops. Nor could he instill any enthusiasm for his methods. Caught up in conflicts among his powerful client managers, Oliver became increasingly isolated and frustrated. He ran afoul of facilities staff members when he conveyed information concerning ventilation problems directly to the group that had responsibility for ventilation systems only to discover that he was seen as violating the trust of the lower-level staff who had given him the information. His findings were distorted by what he described as "disorganized and ineffectual patterns of communication within the organization." When he took on an associate from within InterCorp, he quickly discovered that she saw her main responsibility as toward her bosses: "It was to them that she expressed her concerns and reservations about the way she had seen the survey results processed." In the end, Oliver concluded that his POE methodology "no longer had any attention in InterCorp's facilities group." In a bitter epilogue, Oliver wrote that

> InterCorp will continue to use its consultants as scapegoats as long as it is caught in the dilemma of attempting participatory space-use dialogue with users in the context of an authoritarian, hierarchical organization. The facilities organization dispatches these consultants as would a serial killer, dismembering their reputations and burying them in shallow graves; in doing so, it protects the status quo and itself.

Through the process of his reflecting on his experience, we see Oliver coming to important insights. We also see him frankly detailing the traps and frustrations into which he has fallen. He attributes these outcomes to pathologies in the client organization—its authoritarian structure, its internecine conflicts, and its disposition to scape-goat its consultants. Such interpretations leave little room for an alternative professionalism, from the perspective of which some of the frustrating outcomes of the InterCorp project could be attributed to limitations inherent in Oliver's approach to practice. Nevertheless, he does not shrink from describing the negative results of his work in ways that leave the listener free to form his or her own interpretations. And, between the lines of this document, Oliver reveals an awareness of things yet to be explained.

Shortly after writing this memorandum, Oliver joined a workplace practitioner familiar with the process architecture approach in a project in which they aimed to combine their methodologies. The process architect's reflections on that experience suggest how Oliver, now seriously interested in adopting some elements of process architecture in his approach to workplace development, nevertheless found it difficult to act in a manner consistent with that aim. For example, he would use workplace photographs in meetings with groups of users, but would use them only to gather information, not to provoke feedback for further design inquiry.

The process architect wrote Oliver a letter in which she contrasted her approach to the project with his, underlining features of process architecture that Oliver found mystifying or disturbing. Her letter began with a general rule: When a process architect makes contact with clients, she never starts by presenting what *she* knows about *them* and their work, or the system *they* are supposed to serve. Rather, she begins by trying to understand who they are, what they are concerned about, and what they think it is important to know about. The meaning of objective feedback presented by an outsider will be determined by the specific social context in which it is presented. The process architect observed further that in their client organization professional employees held themselves above plant personnel, whom they regard as "their servants." "If we begin our relationship with them [the physical plant personnel] by presenting data from the professional occupants, we will merely reinforce the status quo, the 'view from above.' Such a presentation would stand in the way of treating all employees as experts on their own environment, and undermine our attempts to establish a relationship of mutual respect with them. . . . We cannot be wedded to one particular tool that we happen to master, [but should also] discover and get hold of the tools *they* already have in use, and learn which ones work well."

Oliver's colleague wanted to develop a strategy for parallel processes of intervention and to create events within this process that would provide opportunities for dialogue between people who usually do not talk to one another. She also sought a "safe environment" in which these parties could meet to clarify their concerns and goals to their colleagues and counterparts. She tried to explain to Oliver that data alone do not produce change, nor does the exercise of familiar technical expertise. What counts, rather, is whether people are willing to listen. And this, in turn, depends on building a relationship that begins with the process architect seeking to understand what people within the organization already know, treating them as experts on their own work and work environment, and learning "where they are" so as to help them move on from there. This stance, in turn, means that each client situation is unique, needs to be understood in its own terms, and thereby demands from the process architect an ability to respond to surprise and uncertainty through reflection in action.

Walter Deming: A Reductionist Interpretation of Process Architecture

In the University Research Laboratories project, Walter Deming, a new employee in the office of space planning, was positioned to learn from the practice he had observed, and might have aided its dissemination to other university space allocation situations had he come closer to grasping the fundamental ideas of process architecture. In a follow-up interview, Deming said that the most valuable thing he had learned from the project was not "getting the users in a room and talking about their space," but what it revealed about the university's space allocation process: how complicated it was, the number of different people who were in on the act, and how senior professors bypassed him and the formal reference process and went directly to the provost with their demands.

The process that Voysey and Browning initiated was, in Deming's view, exceedingly time consuming. He acknowledged that the outcome—getting people to resolve their issues together in the same room—was valuable, "but not to the level of detail where the process architects were taking it." He observed that the cast of players and their needs and priorities had changed dramatically since the study ended over a year before, whereas the study seemed to him to "assume a static environment." He pointed out that people "just hate dealing with space issues," and that the university "bends over backward to accommodate people," which he interpreted as a weakness in the system. Yet people perceived a building as "theirs," when in fact it was the university's building.

"Space planning is a war," Deming remarked, picking up an image familiar to the university's space planners. Agreements are made, but they change as soon as directors change, and things fall apart. People are continually proclaiming, "Me, me, me!" and "My needs are more important than yours. . . . And every time you go down the pyramid the interests get split, and more split."

One of the university's chief space administrators threw a different light on Walter Deming's experience. According to her:

> Walter doesn't think the techniques work. That is what he told me while we were working on the project. He said that he tried it on one of his own space changes, and that it didn't work for him. But frankly, I don't think he really understands how process architecture works. You don't build trust with people in three days, or a week, or two weeks. It's a very serious social process that takes time. As the plan builds up through the process, people see their ideas in it. That's when they begin to trust the process. That is what Walter tried to shorthand. You know, you can't just say, "Well, I'm going

to try it. I'm going to ask people what they want." It's not the same thing. It didn't work for Walter because he didn't really do it.

Explaining Variations in Individual Learning

What makes process architecture difficult for individual practitioners to understand—and even more difficult to practice—is not its novelty or complexity; the difficulty is in its requirement that people unlearn familiar, ingrained concepts of professionalism. They must see new skills as relevant and revise their established systems of expectations.

Robert Oliver and Walter Deming were trained in technical-rational approaches to spatial programming and planning. Process architecture challenged the paradigm of their taken-for-granted professional behavior. Oliver, who had been socialized to think of his profession as one of gathering, processing, and feeding back technical information on the performance of buildings, had begun to understand the inevitably political dimension of that activity, noting for the first time the need to understand the organization's prevailing design game. Still, he did not grasp the social meaning of his work. Nor could he wean himself from close identification with the tool kit he had spent years mastering. Walter Deming, who observed process architecture firsthand, saw its potential for resolving the space wars endemic to his institution. Still, he did not recognize the time element required to get to know the inhabitants of a place, learn their ways, and cultivate their trust. Constructing a simplistic interpretation of process architecture (namely, getting a group of workplace users to sit around a table to resolve their differences), Deming proved to himself that the new approach did not work—thereby demonstrating to the space administrator who observed him that he had never really grasped the essence of the idea.

It is consistent with our findings that the individuals in our cases who seemed most readily to see and internalize the critical ideas of process architecture were not workplace professionals. For the most part they were space users such as Rosenfield's Pittsburgh nurse or managers like the owner-manager of the Menorah Park nursing home in Buffalo, the space administrator in the University Research laboratories case, or the research manager of the Xerox LX lab. These individuals were not held back by a conflicting image of professionalism, nor were they disposed to construct a reductionist interpretation of process architecture. Rather, they were alert to what was going on in the project at hand, seeing it, in some instances, better than could the professional. These individuals could discern answers to questions they were just beginning to ask; they could recognize outcomes that exceeded their initial expectations and, on that basis, revise their expectations.

ORGANIZATIONAL LEARNING

To understand how organizations learn the concepts and practices of process architecture, we must explore how the results of inquiry conducted by individuals in interaction with one another become part of the stock of organizational knowledge. The questions then become:

1. *How does a project of process architecture get planted in an organization in the first place?* What kinds of learning must occur within such a project in order for it to begin, to be fully implemented, and to succeed as success is defined within the confines of the organization?

2. *How does a project of process architecture take root in an organization?* How robust is the learning derived from project experience, as evidenced by the ability of individuals and groups in the organization to maintain the values contained in the project's intentions and to set and solve new problems created by the realization of the project's goals? What kinds of learning are involved in these processes, and what factors impede or support them?

3. *Once a project of process architecture is planted and takes root, how does learning from the project become disseminated throughout the organization?* Disseminating the innovative ideas and practices of process architecture requires, at a minimum, that individuals throughout the

organization pick these ideas and processes up, first at the level of dis-covery and then at the levels of invention and production. What are the organizational resistance and impediments to such dissemination? How, and under what conditions, may such resistance be overcome?

The several subprocesses through which process architecture is planted, takes root, and is disseminated are affected by the fact that an organization learns to enact principles of collaborative inquiry not only in its way of designing its workplace but also in the uneven development of its substantive work processes. This dual effect heightens the challenge of organizational learning. At the same time, it presents alternative opportunities for entry and development. Both factors come across clearly in Zack Rosenfield's conception of the nursing cluster.

Rosenfield linked his idea of the cluster workplace to the values of Total Quality Management (TQM). He saw the cluster workplace as a setting for continual and collaborative incremental improvement in work performance. For a workplace to function in this way, Rosenfield knew that workers had to be free to make decisions and take actions, to run experiments and learn both from their own experience and from the observed or documented experience of others—all within the broad parameters of the global task for which they were responsible and for which they would receive fast, public feedback in the form of performance data. Furthermore, workers had to understand how their individual activities fitted into the larger task, and had to have access to the information they needed (medical records, in the nursing example) to carry them out.

These are the conditions of the cogwheel experiment and the building blocks of TQM.[2] The spatial arrangements of Rosenfield's nursing clusters fostered cogwheel conditions: Nurses and their patients could interact and respond to online demands because they had one another in view. The small scale of the cluster suited the number of patients a nurse could handle, and the number of nurses in a cluster was about the right size for a group devoted to continual learning. The artifactual surround was likewise appropriate: Patient beds, mobile supply carts, communications devices and the like supported the work and provided cues to the tasks to be performed. Furthermore, the large and complex task of patient care was broken down into smaller units of measurable performance, making it possible for nurses to see the causal connections between particular actions and their outcomes.

The nursing cluster idea was centered on the devolution of responsibility for performance and for continual instrumental—that is, single-loop—learning. To create the desired environment, however, the hospital or nursing home would have to engage in double-loop learning:[3] Some of the fundamental assumptions and values in organizational theory in use had to be changed, and greater trust, responsibility, and freedom had to be extended to frontline workers, thereby reducing intermediate layers of bureaucratic authority. For this to happen, managers had to give up their view that workers are primarily motivated by carrots ("bribes") or sticks ("kicks in the ass") in favor of the view that workers are self-motivated when they belong to a collective with responsibility and freedom to learn from the performance of the larger tasks with which they are charged.[4]

Here, then, we see how a design process can create a workplace conducive to ongoing improvement in performance relatively free of external interference, while at the same time that process creates in its own operation a model of the kind of active, collaborative inquiry that is desired for the work itself. Thus workplace-making becomes a model for the actual work practice of the organization. In similar fashion, we observed in the LX lab case how researchers came to work more openly and collaboratively than before. Their doing so was attributable to the collaborative design workshops in which they had participated and to certain features of the new workplace they had helped design.

Planting a Project of Process Architecture

For a process architecture project of workplace-making to get started, be completed, and succeed, that is, to be planted, several conditions must be met. One or more members of the organization must grasp, at least dimly, what the project is about, and must give it the backing and sponsorship it needs. The larger organization must be at least minimally receptive to the project. If there is resistance—and there is always at least some, sometimes a great deal—that resistance must be overcome. In the previous section we focused on individual grasp and learning; now we concentrate on organizational receptivity and resistance.

Robert Oliver's description of the authoritarian, hierarchical, and tradition-bound world of InterCorp suggests one form of organizational resistance. We have seen another in the polarized world of the University Research Laboratories, where, in Voysey's words, "We set out to revise the reference process and we failed." The University Research Laboratories project polarized a slice of the university organization, affecting the biomedical researchers in one way, the space administrators in another. As already noted, administrators were receptive to the project; to them it represented an alternative to the continual space wars with which they had to contend. Among the researchers, one "loved" Voysey's and Browning's process, which made perfect sense to him. Another saw it as "an exercise in futility," since, as he put it, any solution to a current problem would soon be nullified by change. Other researchers, who declined to be interviewed, reportedly believed that the process was a waste of time since "nothing came of it."

In both of these cases, organizational resistance was active. Perceiving the projects as foreign intrusions, different individuals worked actively to reject them. Moreover, resistance had multiple sources. Some individuals and groups responded defensively because they perceived threats to their territories, to their power and status, or to their ability to navigate freely along the bypass routes of the organization. To some extent, the projects represented new forms of uncertainty; various people were more disposed to stay with their familiar messes and stalemates. To paraphrase Hamlet, they were more inclined to accept the ills they had than "fly to others we know not of."

The Bank of Boston case, in contrast, highlighted the energizing effects of Peter Manning's new business vision. People understood that the business was supposed to inspect itself constantly and come up with ways to improve operations. When pockets of resistance were encountered, Manning laid down the law: "You will do this—take the costs out!" In the absence of such a champion, the process architect has to work out an alliance with the organizational leader—as happened in the LX lab case, but not in the University Research Laboratories case.

Perhaps nothing overcomes the natural resistance to change more effectively than the threat of annihilation. "Change or die!" The power of these words has been observed over time and across industries. Faced with imminent demise, organizations in crisis are generally more open to radical change. The Bank of Boston case is a prime example. Manning had a mandate to "fix it or kill it." Zack Rosenfield heard similar signals among nursing homes that were beginning to fear threats from new forms of competition in the health care field.

It is also clear that, whereas the introduction of a new workplace-making process can unleash a win/lose game of interests and powers, the institutional status of the organization can be crucial to the outcomes of such a game. For example, middle- and upper-level nurses in the nursing homes can legitimately perceive that a cluster design, with its devolution of responsibility for care to lower levels and its consequent flattening of the organization, represents a serious threat to their own security. The director of a private nursing home, whether for profit or not for profit, is likely to be able to manage the staff pressures that result from perception of such threats, whereas the manager of a *county* nursing home, subject to civil service rules, may be unable to do so.

To be planted, a new project of process architecture must be completed, implemented, and viewed as a success according to local organizational criteria. The University Research Laboratories case featured great initial excitement about a common plan developed for the long-range, global use of space. Yet this plan was never funded, the university's space committee having decided that the consensual solution would be too expensive. An attempt to get external funding for a piece of the solution also came to naught. This result, in the words of one of the space administrators, was "the kiss of death" for collaborative design at the university.

The university's initial commitment was to demonstrate, not to make the test project happen, which would have enabled it to be seen as a success. Nor did the consultants press their clients to implement the results. In retrospect it became clear for the initiators and the consultants that in order for a new reference process to be seeded or planted in the organization the first project had to be seen as successful.

Taking Root

As we first noted in Chapter 2, a process architecture project often functions as an episode in the uneven development of the organization as a whole. A change in the work environment creates a new opportunity for the redesign of work, or a change in one dimension of the workplace—spatial, social, or technological—triggers change in one of its other dimensions. For a project to take root, it must be effectively implemented and members of the organization must engage the new challenges that arise in the wake of that implementation. These new challenges may be of several different kinds, as illustrated by our follow-up discussions with participants in the Bank of Boston case. That project was never "finished." In the spirit of process architecture, it just kept going, as change in one area created pressure for responses elsewhere. But project participants had to fight to maintain the ideas and values of the process; the facility's wiring system provides one example of this. As the reader will remember from Chapter 2, the spatial flexibility of the facility required complementary flexibility in the network of electrical and data transmission cables. This was threatened when new wiring standards appeared. These new standards were linked to the faster data transmission speeds needed to support the facility's local area network (LAN). Unfortunately, wires consistent with the new standards were incompatible with the flexible wiring system developed by the project team.

> The new wires had to terminate at a standard wiring box. If we did that, we could no longer pull the cables back up the hoses. Every time we wanted to reconfigure, we'd have to get wiring people in here to disconnect, bring the wires back down, and reconnect them. With the initial system, all we had to do was release one connection, pull the wire back, and then pull it through to make that one connection again. We're currently trying to see if we can jerry-rig a system to both maintain our flexibility and meet data requirements.

Evolutions in the work process also required continual readjustment. Once the basic design elements of the Canton facility were in place, there was a need to fine-tune the work flow. This fine-tuning was done, as another participant said, in a way that "learned from the earlier process."

> It's the work flows that really need revisiting [and] . . . continuous incremental improvement. It's no longer comprehensive front-end design, but piecemeal design. For example, the problem of the big TVs with screens big enough to get 8½ by 11 in full view—they stretched the workstations by about 20 percent, so now [the workstations] need to be replaced.

At the time of our follow-up interviews, the process managers at Canton were about to begin a nine- to twelve-month reengineering project. This time, they planned "a concurrent circle of activity instead of a linear process." Marketing, engineering, and manufacturing would work together from start to finish, and frontline workers would "pipe up with bright ideas on a regular basis," suggesting what was right or wrong with the work flows in their areas. One of the new process managers commented that he continued to be absolutely amazed by the insights of employees who were routinely ignored in the past. He offered this example:

> One employee suggested a new approach to handling questions from investors' phone calls that require a department research specialist who can take questions that the phone operator cannot handle. This would free up operators from doing that research, making it possible for them to take more calls. The by-product of this process change is that responsibility for researching and responding is shifted back to the operations area that originated the work. It becomes a quality control intervention, motivating workers to minimize the number of calls they're getting.

Another example had to do with document handling:

> We send an awful lot of correspondence to shareholders that we know they're going to send back to us. Right now we handle it blindly: We send it out, and when it comes back in, we go through a sorting process, determining where it needs to be handled. Today, we're planning to bar-code our correspondence so that any piece that comes back can be quickly scanned to determine the account it applies to and what needs to be done. This could eliminate the current process of "open, read, interpret, sort."

Here, peer pressure, not dictatorial management pressure, motivated process improvements.

The very success of the Bank of Boston Canton project created new problems of a different order. Success in signing on new clients caused the work volume to triple. At first, managers attempted to deal with this crush of business by tweaking the system. It took them three years, they said, to realize that "instead of just trying to get people to run faster, we needed to revisit the whole work flow."

Even more daunting was the role played by new, big clients, who were now dictating not only what they wanted Bank of Boston to do but how they wanted the work done. For example, PacTel, a huge new customer, said, "You can't possibly do our printings and mailings in this small facility." So the division established a mailing facility on the model of the Canton work environment in nearby Westwood, Massachusetts. PacTel also demanded that the bank create a new printing facility to produce its annual report.

As time went on, the bank discovered that it would have to make continual alterations in the system it had created for its big customers. Initially it set up a high-volume operation exclusively for major customers like PacTel. Later, operations managers realized that it made more sense to have elements of stock transfer operations embedded in an integrated transfer-operations floor. These managers needed, as they put it, to "educate PacTel to the fact that the way we're doing it is better than what they're asking for—and we can't meet their standards consistently unless we allocate our resources variably throughout the day." The operations managers created "floater groups" that could shift rapidly to wherever demand was heaviest. And they learned, as part of this reeducation, to show PacTel that the bank could anticipate and respond to its needs for service. For example, PacTel was currently splitting in two, which would create new demands, and the operations managers were then gearing up to meet the expectation that their phone lines would be "burning up over the next couple of months." Moreover, as these managers pointed out, they had learned from their experience with PacTel. They had partnerships where they played the role of the customer to others in the role of vendors—"and we're just as aggressive with them as PacTel is with us."

New project managers were brought in to handle the division's new facilities and the new problems that resulted from the creation of those facilities. Managers credited their experience with the sailboat game with helping them to deal with change and the need to respond quickly. "It created a language for us, freed us from our biases and assumptions, and it showed our clients that you left your title at the door when you sat down to a brainstorming session."

The Canton experience indicates how a project can take root in an organization. It also illustrates uneven development at work in continuations of design inquiry that incorporate learning from the previous rounds. The design of a new work environment, undertaken to accommodate changes in the behavior of users and customers, changes the nature of the game being played in the workplace. A new organization of work begins to make itself evident, generating a new set of occasions for interaction. At the same time, new problems come into view—newly visible after the first round of problem solving, or triggered by the new solutions—that call for new rounds of inquiry and learning.

Disseminating Principles and Practices

The perceived success of a project of workplace creation, even when accompanied by evidence of organizational learning, by no means guarantees effective dissemination.

LIMITED DISSEMINATION IN THE BANK OF BOSTON CASE

It is clear from this case study that Peter Manning and his team learned a great deal about both the workplace they were envisioning and the process for bringing it into being. But their experience had very little impact on the rest of the organization. Follow-up interviews and meetings with people at the Bank of Boston indicated that, with the notable exception of the Westwood mailing facility, the bank as a whole acquired little or no understanding of the significance of the Canton project despite its perceived success both as a workplace and as the physical manifestation of an effective strategy for revitalizing the stock processing business. Process managers at Canton and Westwood claimed that the principles of redesign they learned and put into action were applicable to many other areas of the business, in operations and in administration as well. Yet they readily admitted that the dissemination of the Canton model went only as far in the bank as pressures generated by Canton's success forced it to go. In other parts of the bank, people "didn't really understand what the Canton process was about."

LEARNING FROM SUCCESS

What conditions are necessary for effective dissemination of a project of process architecture? What are the distinguishing features of an effective practice of dissemination? Our most insightful answers to these questions emerged when members of SPORG joined several members of the LARC team and the Xerox LX group in an effort to reflect on just what had given rise to the common space and to the new work practice. John Knapp, day-to-day leader of the research group, played the role of lead inquirer in these sessions. Knapp was convinced that something important linked to the creation of the new space had happened—something that had not only altered the group's physical work environment but had significantly affected its ways of working. Knapp wanted to clarify this conviction in order to figure out how better to spread the benefits of the project more widely throughout the Xerox laboratories and impart a new working culture to the Wilson Center as a whole.

THE PARADOX OF REPLICABILITY

The participants in these discussions commented on the confusion and uncertainty that had shrouded the beginnings of the project. "Had you asked us then," Knapp pointed out, "you would have gotten six different stories." Moreover, Turid Horgen, who had been called into the LARC project with a vague mandate to reproduce the sort of process she had led in other places—to create a space planning process for combatants embroiled in conventional space wars— quickly discovered that that mission would be incorrect in the Xerox case. Here researchers were not fighting over limited space, but were up in arms over the idea of being forced into semienclosed office compartments that substituted for private offices. Horgen led this group through a process similar to the evolution of the wet lab described in Chapter 3: an appreciation of the existing work environment, making use of building walk-throughs and workbooks, and a collaborative exercise of ideal-seeking design inquiry, exploring what a more ideal work environment would be like. But the participants in the Xerox workshops quickly took control. They moved directly to a redesign of the new space and developed the image of what came to be known as the LX Common, which enabled both new social patterns of communication and collaboration and new spatial and technological supports.

At one point in this retrospective discussion, Knapp told Horgen that he remembered a time about a third of the way through the project when Horgen had told him what the common space would be for. He recollected turning to her with some irritation and asking, "Why didn't you just tell us in the beginning? It would have saved all this trouble!" But, of course, Horgen could not have done that at the beginning, any more than Knapp and his colleagues could have given a clear and consensual account of their objectives for the project. A clear image of the common space and its multiple purposes only emerged in the course of the workshops, mostly through the contributions of the researchers themselves, with the LARC consultants using their design expertise to shape the final form.

The confusion that marked the initial stages of the project was indispensable. It signified on the part of the client a willingness to proceed on the basis of a sense of something important to be done and a dimly seen image of the goals to be achieved—business contribution, decreased time to market, increased research productivity—but no clear sense of how those goals could be crystallized in the situation at hand. On the consultants' part, the confusion signified a willingness to let go of a preconceived picture of the consulting mission and the procedures by which it would be carried out, without as yet having anything to take the place of that picture.

In short, the specific version of the process architecture approach that had been developed in the University laboratories project could not be replicated in the Xerox project. It had to be reinvented.

As with any complex approach to thought and action, dissemination of the principles and practices of process architecture goes beyond the mechanical replication of methods and procedures. It requires that essential ideas be grasped in such a way that projects embodying them *can* be reinvented in new contexts. For this reason, the projects that best represent the principles of institutional change may be ones that on the surface resemble it least.

The importance of reinvention rather than replication might also be expressed in a paradox of replication, rather like Groucho Marx's quip that "I would never join any club that would accept me as a member." In this instance, "No process worth replicating is replicable." Put in less jarring terms: "A worthwhile process must be reinvented rather than mechanically reproduced."

THE DEMAND FOR SIMPLE SOLUTIONS

Would-be agents of dissemination are continually faced with dilemmas generated by demands for simple solutions and procedural recipes. Several of the practitioners featured in our case studies have long attempted to promote their own versions of the practice of process architecture, and they have had to struggle with the problem of getting people who are thirsty for simple solutions to understand what they mean. In the Xerox LX lab case, however, the client leaders were unusually tolerant of uncertainty and receptive to the idea that they themselves had to be active in defining both the mission and methods of the new project. "After months of waiting for LARC to do something for us," Knapp said, "we finally realized that we were LARC ourselves . . . that LARC was only a collection of hardware and people tools whose use we had to select and initiate." Knapp's group would have to select from that collection and initiate its own agenda. Once this was clear, according to Knapp, people in the LX lab took the initiative and shifted from drawing up lists of complaints to asking, "Why don't we try this?"

ELEMENTS OF REINVENTION

Once people discover that dissemination requires reinvention rather than mechanical replication, good things follow. Everything that was important to the earlier stages of organizational learning—planting and taking root—contributes to the process of dissemination: the uses of past experience, the readiness of individuals to learn, the evaluation of the earlier success in terms of its effectiveness and implications for future action, and the interaction of workplace design and substantive workplace experience.

EVALUATING SUCCESS

The issue of disseminating learning from projects of process architecture raises the question of evaluation: Did the project give rise to a better workplace outcome, more effective working practices, and greater business contribution? These questions are pertinent when decisions must be made about allocating resources to future projects of process architecture. Did a success occur? If it did, what aspect of the process architecture approach caused it to work that might be carried over and appropriately reinvented in another situation?

In our review of the Xerox LX lab project, we asked the client participants and LARC consultants why they believed something important had happened in the LX lab. Gregory Zack, one of the LARC consultants who visited the LX group most often, said the feeling in John Knapp's laboratory was strikingly different from that in other Wilson Center labs. For example, researchers were in the little kitchen area in the LX work area all the time, talking in different, shifting groups of twos and threes about their work and using the whiteboards.

John Knapp pointed to other indicators of success. After several months, "when we began to get collaborative," he said, people in other research groups began to ask what was going on. Members of the LX group who had resisted moving to the new research space now asked to move there. And groups located at a distance from the LX Common began to hold their meetings at the Common.

Greater access to information is another indicator of success. One of Xerox's upper-level research managers held an operations review in the common area. This was, as Knapp put it, a "difficult technical review" that would previously have been held in a private conference room and attended by higher-level managers only. Once important meetings like this began to be held in the LX Common, researchers gained access to top-level information at the same time as their bosses. This would not have happened without the new facility. As Knapp said of the new common space, "Our lab has a place, a home. It's not just a name or an organization. And if you're going to talk about tough subjects about your family, why don't you say it in your home?" This represented a change in the social rules that governed the use of the territory: Anyone, no matter who, could walk by, sit down, and decide whether he or she should be there or not.

USING WHAT WE ALREADY KNOW

If dissemination is reinvention rather than replication, how can process architects and their clients make use of their past experience? The answer to this question has to do on the one hand with how process architects use patterns and themes they have experienced before, adapting and recombining them in new situations. On the other hand, the answer is linked to how process architects can help clients to rediscover and adapt what they have already done—what the clients themselves already know but cannot articulate. The LX project experience illustrates these points in several ways. The development of the Common had grown out of a number of different experiences, each representing something already known. Horgen recalled a building walk-through in which participants encountered a place in the Wilson Center that worked very much like the new Common. It was a room surrounded by laboratories. The table in this room acted as a semipublic place. This arrangement cropped up as a prototype in a subsequent workshop that developed the idea of the LX Common, and Horgen detected in it "a model that could work." (Knapp professed surprise at this story: He said he would have described the room as "dysfunctional space that just 'grew up' in the old labs.")

Another source of the concept of the LX Common was the idea, put forward by one of the researchers who made simulation models, of a space he could use to demonstrate his models for other researchers, and get fast feedback on his modeling experiments, without having to invite the other researchers to formal meetings for that purpose. This notion, which the researcher called "the simulation room," also helped to shape the image of the LX Common.

Finally, Horgen had observed patterns of work in other projects that were recalled by her own observations of the LX researchers. Early in the project she emphasized to Knapp that "the really exciting moments are happening in the hallways." As she tried to explain what she saw as an important work pattern that should have consequences for the spatial design, Horgen said:

> Around the outside of this building there are offices, and in the inside there are laboratories. And while there are people who go from office to laboratory, there are also some people who spend 90 percent of their time in their laboratory and 10 percent of their time in their office. And then there are people who are 90 percent in their office and 10 percent in the laboratory. And then there are modelers who are never in the laboratory, they're only in the offices. And the technicians who are only in the lab and are never in their offices. And the really exciting moments were really happening in the hallway.

"What we'll do," Knapp responded, "is populate the hallway with the important things that promote this kind of interaction." Noting that the inventions and innovations were coming from the interactions of people from the offices and from the laboratories, Knapp was concerned that what was working be added to the new space. "That is, having noticed something we're doing that's working as we would like the new space to work, though we've never taken notice of it or tried to analyze it before, we'll now deliberately pick it up and add to it, in a new setting, features we believe will enhance it."

Once the idea of the new common space had emerged in the workshops, the LARC consultants and the LX group members began having their meetings in the new building, in the place where the Common would later be built (even though an existing wall, which would have to be removed, kept the space from being used exactly as it ultimately would be). And these people said, as Horgen remembers: "The exciting moments happen around the machinery, so this place can't be too far away from the lab." This, as Knapp recalls, was where the vision came from that saw "offices, laboratory, hallway, where the whole thing becomes the workplace."

It was in the common space, once it was inhabited by members of the LX group, that LX share meetings were invented. As Knapp tells the story, and as we have recounted it at greater length in Chapter 6, he had left the new LX space for a time, and when he returned he was struck by the differences he found in the degree of interaction and collaboration among researchers in the group. In this observation, "recognizing what we were already doing," Knapp saw "some of the things we needed to do to improve what we now had."

John Knapp and his colleagues saw in the new common space an informal model of what they might come to do more deliberately and systematically in their substantive work practice. The presence of their joint thinking activity within the new setting served for them as a "piton" they could use to pull themselves up to the image of the LX Common. Here Knapp was doing what he so frequently did with his researchers: helping them to see patterns in the rough data they were accumulating and to recognize the leaps they might already be making without quite being aware of it.

❂

CONCLUSION

The permeable boundary between designing and learning, which we observe in the uneven development of a workplace, is a key feature of process architecture. Learning, individual and organizational, arises not only from but within the processes of design. Designers are often surprised by the unanticipated effects of their changes to the work environment. These cause them to reframe the problem they are trying to solve and begin the design process once again. Thus, one episode of design serves as a prelude to another.

In several of our cases—the LX lab and the nursing cluster cases in particular—occupancy of the newly designed space caused the actors to see design solutions with new eyes. The nursing cluster, for example, came to be seen as solving problems that had not previously been framed: improving patient well-being, shortening recovery time, and reducing stress and the intake of medications. That the cluster design solved these problems was only understood after people had worked within the cluster.

The practice of process architecture is inherently open-ended and context specific. This makes learning more difficult, but also more essential. The nature of work is different in every different setting, and the demands of dynamic coherence change from one type of work to another. Process architecture's emphasis on the active, collaborative involvement of stakeholders in workplace design leaves it open to discoveries of new purposes and priorities and to the invention of new methods for achieving them. This is unlike learning the methods of technical-rational expertise—such as POE or conventional approaches to spatial programming—where one learns a fixed set of methods and tools. The process architect must continuously learn and adapt, applying certain tools when they make sense and inventing others as needed.

Any institution that seeks to promote organizational learning of process architecture must be able to do for itself what it endeavors to do for those it serves: It must extend freedom and responsibility to frontline workers, mobilize collaborative processes of design, and flatten the organization. These changes are essential to a dynamically coherent workplace and to the open-ended learning that process architecture demands.

For those who have participated in the six years of case studies and organizational interventions described in these chapters, there is no more vivid illustration of an environment for learning than

SPORG itself, which has been a fruitful setting for continued, open-ended inquiry into the meaning and methods of process architecture. Membership in SPORG has been steady at the core and variable at the periphery. Some have joined the enterprise for brief intervals, while others have formed long-term relationships with the group and its members. Its modes of inquiry are argumentation and active research. Working sessions are characterized by vigorous argument over the meanings of case material, the definition of important terms, and the relationships among key ideas. One of the early participants referred to the group as "the SPORG cauldron."

SPORG has been a setting for the essential work of retrospective reflection, as project participants ask themselves, "What have we really done?" "What have we learned?" "How should we frame the next project?" At other times the group has been a consulting resource for practitioners who pause in mid-project to take stock and consider their next moves.

We don't anticipate achieving a final framework for process architecture. This approach to workplace-making—like any activity in this time beyond the stable state—is subject to an environment of continuous and largely unpredictable change to which it must respond. We are confident, however, that the approach can fundamentally contribute to an organization's well-being by creating more coherent, dynamic workplaces while helping the organization to learn about itself and apply that learning to the improvement of work process. Process architects have a double challenge: to create more effective workplaces and to implant ongoing learning and design process improvement within organizations.

Epilogue

Our professional experience in creating workplaces in a variety of organizational settings led us to explore and then to conceptualize an approach to workplace-making that we call process architecture. Our work and that of a relatively small number of our colleagues often has a transforming impact on organizations with which we collaborate. What is it about what we do or how we do it that contributes to organizational transformation and changes in work practice? How do these changes happen, and what is it about what we do that makes them happen?

We practice as process architects, even though we differ in professional training, use different intervention strategies, and prefer to use different tools. A common theme of our work is a focus on the improvement of work practice and organizational design; our work is not limited to just the physical workplace. Consequently, we manage the workplace-making process in the context of its being an intervention for organizational change. It is this orientation that is the essence of process architecture.

Process architecture is both radical and familiar. Many professionals focus their practice around an understanding of how work is done and then design the workplace to accommodate that work. But process architecture aims at a larger objective: It seeks to co-invent the workplace and work practice in a dynamically coherent way.

Today the watchword of organizations is agility to adapt quickly to changes while ensuring that all the pieces of the organization work together effectively without the need for a long chain of command

and rigid procedures. Engaging managers and workers in a design inquiry–oriented workplace-making process significantly adds to their change management skills, and this can carry over to the design of work itself. The experience shakes people out of the assumption that every management challenge lends itself to be translated into a clearly defined problem for which an optimal solution can be designed. And it teaches the work group to rely on itself to solve its own problems and grab its own opportunities.

Our framework for process architecture is still a work in progress. We see several basic challenges facing its development and application; perhaps the greatest is the need to shift an organization's narrow attention from creating a singular workplace product to the more comprehensive transformational nature of the workplace-making process. Three of the other paramount challenges are transporting lessons from one group to another, building responsibility and capability for process architecture, and keeping its processes unfrozen.

We are now in the process of looking more closely at this last issue, especially to discover how organizations can broaden a successful workplace experiment beyond the area where it first occurred. The cases in this book are about work groups within larger organizations. When these groups achieve a dynamically coherent workplace through process architecture, there is inevitable interest in how that positive experience can be replicated in other parts of the organization. This raises several questions for which we do not yet have answers. When does a process have to be reinvented, as compared with being replicated in a new situation? To what parts of the organization can the experience be transported directly? Is the scale of the work group an issue? What is the impact of differences in organizational culture among groups? What kinds of conditions need to exist within the potential host organization to enable it to learn from its own experiment?

What we know about these questions is largely anecdotal, and the answers await further reflection by ourselves and others. We believe, however, that the best soil for process architecture is in an organizational unit that knows it must transform itself and that has the leadership to drive the exploration.

Process architecture prepares an organization to both design and manage ongoing transformation and to be agile. But the approach can be a hard sell to business managers who have little patience for a process that goes beyond "Tell me what the best practice is, adjust it for me, and let's get on with it now!" It is ironic that process architecture, which is designed to serve organizations buffeted by the rapidity of change, takes time. The achievements of process architecture rest on its ability to play out complicated design games, to build truly collaborative teams, and to reiterate steps of the process while learning from actions taken. Time is actually an ally of process architecture because it provides the organization an opportunity to reflect on and thereby more effectively frame its challenges and opportunities.

We are persuaded that process architecture requires more than a skilled process architect: Success depends on the active collaboration of the stakeholders, and it demands cross-disciplinary teams. Moreover, it should be seen as a collaborative effort rather than the result of a few individuals working together.

Ellen Schön, artist (and daughter of the late Don Schön), upon reviewing a draft of our manuscript, correctly cautioned us about the demanding task we might be placing on one individual: "Entering a messy situation as an outsider, alone, to think on your feet, generate confidence in yourself and the process, mediate and transform conflict, be both a leader and a participant in facilitating consensus for designs that adapt to fast-paced changes, designs that intimately affect the organization's bottom line, is a big challenge; it is a job for more than one, otherwise it seems an almost unattainable alternative to the traditional technical-rational approach." Ellen is, of course, right. In different ways and at different times the process architect may be leader, coach, or supportive teammate. Leadership, creative energy, and active supporting roles move from one to another, then to yet another in often unpredictable ways: Roles have to be assumed and then let go.

In keeping with the notion that process architecture is bigger than process architects, it is important to emphasize that we aim for teachable skills and the modification of the professional behavior of many, rather than looking for all attributes of professional skills to be contained in a single individual or even a single profession. Our cases illustrate effective use of tools drawn from those already in good currency by professionals based in the different quadrants of our SOFT diagram. We need to dig more deeply into these quadrants to add to the repertoire of tools, and we need to create new tools to help shape workplaces whose dimensions are as yet unforeseen and strengthen workplace-making as conditions continue to evolve and change.

Breaking out of stereotypes of the workplace is always a difficult task; it is even more complicated today, when work practices are in transition and when the technology that supports work is moving into the unknown. What is clear is that the three-dimensional world represented by physical space is just one of the networked, interrelated environments in which individuals and teams work. Equally important, for example, is the virtual environment—or cyberspace—that enables people to find, refine, create, recombine, express, and apply the information and interactions on which their work rests.

A change in the workplace, or a proposal for such a change, usually brings forth demands for proof that the change will positively impact productivity and employee satisfaction. Posed in this way, the challenge is not particularly useful: It is actually misleading because it puts a burden of proof on the workplace that more legitimately belongs on the work group's business processes and work practices. The question is more effectively posed: How does the workplace create the conditions that allow more effective work? How can the workplace-making process enable the group to continue to effectively redesign work and workplace as conditions change? Posing the question in this way puts the business mission and work practice at the center of concern. Once strategies and evaluation criteria are established for these, then strategies for the supporting workplace-making process and for the workplace itself can be described, and only then can an evaluation schema about the workplace be put into place. That schema needs to look into all four SOFT quadrants (finance being the least examined) to create an architecture of evaluation.

We have discussed how an organization's reference process for workplace-making, like its evaluation framework, can become outdated or calcified, outliving its usefulness and creating a drag on creativity and transformation. However, continuity in change can be important. The challenge is to determine which ingredients of successful past ventures can be shared and built upon without freezing the process. The building of a common language for discourse about workplace-making will help; other ingredients are articulating and committing to ground rules, and cyclical evaluation carried out according to explicitly understood procedures, with opportunities for participation that guarantee each stakeholder the chance to have a voice in the future.

Any process in this time beyond the stable state is subject to change. Process architecture is no exception. As we and others move forward to transform workplaces and work practices, we need to keep our ideas open and our minds receptive to the demands of the situation.

It is hard to turn one's back on something that has proven successful, but, as in workplace-making itself, the first task for further developing the approach of process architecture is to respond to the situation at hand. Continuous refinement is necessary. Creating process architecture teams with skills and outlooks to experiment in a widening variety of organizational settings, and then to reflect rigorously on these interventions, will be the keys to further learning.

Notes

❀

CHAPTER 1   WORKPLACE-MAKING MOVES BEYOND THE STABLE STATE

1. W. B. Kleeman, Francis Dotty, K. P. Williams, and M. K. Williams, *Interior Design of the Electronic Office* (New York: Van Nostrand Reinhold, 1991).

2. Donald A. Schön, *Beyond the Stable State* (New York: Random House, 1971).

3. See the DEC/Monsanto case in Chapter 5.

4. See our description of the DEC/Monsanto case later in Chapter 5.

5. The Bank of Boston case was prepared by Turid Horgen, Bonné Smith, and Jacqueline Vischer. Between June 1992 and March 1993, Horgen, Smith, and Vischer made four visits to the Canton facility, conducted and audiotaped extensive interviews with key actors in the PDBM process, and drew on working memos and articles from the business press. Analysis of the data was carried out in conjunction with members of MIT's Space and Organizational Research Group (SPORG). Frank Becker participated in one of these meetings, contributing to our reflection on and analysis of the case. Scott Petersen and Jon Stein of the Bank of Boston, Nancy Harrod of Sasaki Associates, and Karen Monks of

Coopers & Lybrand, all members of the design team, participated in a SPORG seminar to reflect on and summarize what lessons could be drawn from their experience. Some of this material is presented in Chapters 7 and 8. Anne Townes analyzed and wrote an account of the sailboat game, presented in Chapter 5.

CHAPTER 2   CONCEPTS OF PROCESS ARCHITECTURE

1. See, for example, Everett Hughes, "The Study of Occupations," in Robert K. Morton et al. (eds.) *Sociology Today* (New York: Basic Books, 1959).

2. The philosopher Ludwig Wittgenstein used the concept of language games in his *Philosophical Investigations* to reshape our understandings of ordinary language and remake the foundations of contemporary philosophy. Inspired by their regular poker games at Princeton in the 1940s, John Von Neumann, Oscar Morgenstern, and their colleagues devised the mathematical techniques of game theory that have since exerted a profound influence on operations research, economics, and social science. In the 1950s, Merrill Flood began to explore the prisoner's dilemma game, which has become fundamental to contemporary social-scientific understandings of the interplay of cooperation and competition. Howard Raiffa, Duncan Luce, Thomas Schelling, and many others have fruitfully explored the theory and application of the idea of games to human situations of politics, games, wars, and other matters.

3. John Habraken et al., *Concept Design Games, Books One and Two* (Cambridge, MA: Department of Architecture, MIT, 1987).

4. The growing profession of mediated negotiation, promoted by Roger Fisher, Lawrence Susskind, and others, aims to invent

structures and skills of negotiation for joint gains. Increasingly, theorists and practitioners influenced by the game metaphor manifest an interest in the conversion of win/lose to win/win games. Bower and Sabel suggest games in which cooperation and competition can coexist.

5. Of these, one of the best known is based on Karl Jung's research on personality types, further developed as an analytical tool and action-oriented framework by Isabel Myers and Katherine Briggs. The Myers-Briggs methodology demonstrates how people bring very different approaches to issue-framing, decision-making, and interpersonal relations. As the experience of research and practice makes clear, personality type does affect organizational behavior.

6. William Bridges, a consultant to organizations in transition, recognized that entire organizations differ in how they deal with change. Bridges found Jungian theories useful in understanding how organizations, as well as individuals, behave. After experimenting with ways to assess an organization's type, he evolved what he called the Organizational Character Index.

7. The differences in cultures that exist in organizations, influencing their creative and political processes, are central to Charles Handy's theories about organizational approaches to the management of change. In Handy's book, *Gods of Management* (New York: Oxford University Press, 1995), organizations are presented as having one of four basic cultures. In *club organizations,* power radiates from the top boss, and a personal relationship with that individual matters more than any formal title or position. This Handy sees most often in small, entrepreneurial companies, especially investment banks and brokerages. A *role culture* exists in highly structured, stable companies and public bureaucracies with precise job descriptions. Life insurance companies, or firms with a long history of success with a single product, often fall into this category. The *task culture* emphasizes talent and

youth and promotes continuous, successful team problem-solving. This style Handy sees most often in consulting organizations, advertising agencies, and start-up firms, where it serves mainly to enable individual members to achieve their own purposes. Universities, architectural firms, and medical group practices are likely to be examples of this kind of organization. Handy's descriptions of organizational cultures are lucid and insightful. But, like Bridges, Handy holds his concepts loosely, treating them as a "low definition theory" that "suggests rather than prescribes . . . [allowing] room for the intuitive and creative interpretation."

8. Albert O. Hirschman, *The Strategy of Economic Development* (Cambridge, MA: Harvard University Press, 1958). Hirschman described several mechanisms of unbalanced growth: *backward linkage,* through which, for example, a new manufacturing enterprise creates demands for raw material supply; *forward linkage,* through which a new resource, such as electrical power, entrains new downstream uses of that resource; and the paradoxical process by which highly demanding *tasks of narrow latitude,* such as the maintenance of aircraft equipment, which, in Hirschman's words, "must be done well if they are to be done at all," create new kinds of capability.

9. John Dewey, *Logic: The Theory of Inquiry* (New York: Holt & Rinehart, 1938).

10. The American management theorist Russell Ackoff has used the term *messy* in very much the same way.

11. Refer to the elements of the SOFT diagrams in Figures 1.1 and 1.2.

12. Our idea of *event* is strongly related to the idea of *occasion* developed by Roger Barker. Barker found it useful to describe the meaningful episodes of life in ways that took account of purpose, physical setting, social rules, and other factors that had to be encompassed in a single term.

CHAPTER 3 FROM STEREOTYPE TO DYNAMIC COHERENCE

1. The cluster design case, which focuses in detail on the design of the nursing clusters, is based on two SPORG meetings that were held with Zack Rosenfield: one in the spring of 1992 and one in the late winter of 1993. During these meetings, Rosenfield told the story of the development of the Somerville and Hackensack Hospitals' nursing units—examples of NBBJ's cluster design. Most of the information from these meetings was descriptive, although important analyses of various parts of the design process were initiated as well. Additional descriptive information was gathered from health care journals that ran accounts of the nursing units, a report on a study of the Hackensack nursing unit, and telephone interviews with the architect. The case was originally researched and written by David de Sola.

CHAPTER 5 THE PRACTICE AND TOOLS OF PROCESS ARCHITECTURE

1. William Coaldrake, *The Way of the Carpenter: Tools and Japanese Architecture* (New York: Weatherhill, 1991).

2. The DEC/Monsanto story was brought to the attention of SPORG by Anne Clemens, formerly a DEC staff member and now a principal of the Da Vinci Group, a human factors consulting firm, and Charles Kukla of the Integrated Manufacturing and Product Development Group at DEC. Clemens and Kukla spoke of their experiences during a SPORG seminar in November of 1992. The case describes two linked research projects that were carried out between 1988 and 1993 by Kukla and Clemens.

Both projects were undertaken in collaboration with the Monsanto Company—the first at its nylon production unit in Pensacola, Florida, the second at its Saflex (car window adhesive) plant at Indian Orchard, Massachusetts. In each of these chemical process manufacturing facilities, the DEC researchers focused their studies on the process control function with the aim of designing new software systems for improvement through an ethnographic study. The SPORG seminar functioned to distill a series of themes and theories about the events related by Clemens and Kukla. As these ideas were pursued and elucidated further in a series of interviews with Clemens, Kukla, and others involved, the story evolved into the present case.

3. "The semilattice in our study was quite crucial. The semilattice was used by C. Alexander in a study of cities. Alexander's analysis provided us with a model that could describe what we found and provided us with some confidence and validation that our discovery was not unique to our particular approach or specific to this site and project. We used the semilattice model to represent the informal organization structure in a way we could map to the more formal structure. That mapping allowed us to understand how stable the informal structure was compared to the formal structure. The formal structure changed many times during the course of the project but the informal structure stayed the same. In some sense the semilattice model was a tool used to model the organizational structure." Comments by Chuck Kukla, January 12, 1998.

4. Comments by Chuck Kukla, January 12, 1998.

5. Shoshana Zuboff, *The Age of the Smart Machine* (New York: Basic Books, 1988).

6. The full game takes up to four hours. The Coopers & Lybrand personnel who pioneered the sailboat game begin with a session on business process redesign, showing what it is, where it fits into the work, and what a company can expect to gain from it. They

then stage the game, with its ten-minute rounds of play and twenty- to thirty-minute caucuses between rounds.

CHAPTER 6   A SYNTHESIS OF IDEAS AND PRACTICES: THE LX WORKPLACE EXPERIMENT

1. Illustrating the complexity of this proposition, one researcher describes his test fixture: "This lower fixture is an optical table. And it is damped to minimize vibrations, coupling into it from the floor. It is being used in another mode, however, here, and that is as a precision underlay to all the various subsystem components. The optical table is pretty precise, but it's not that precise and if you were—and it weighs several hundred pounds. If you were to move it, you will torque the thing in several dimensions, and it will not relax completely. It was three months for us to do it the first time. I would strongly recommend against moving this particular fixture, just because of the mechanical alignment problems that would certainly entail if it were moved. We have requirements for about 50 amps of power to run all the various componentry around it. We require compressed air to run some of the fixtures. Some of the materials that we use in the process, we know have their characteristics change with temperature. So we do need to at least monitor what the temperature is around here and keep a good record of that. Ah, some process characteristics are also affected by the amount of humidity that's in the air. There are a number of subcomponents that we operate at high voltage. So we have to manage some effluents from there. There's some ozone generation that takes place. The volume of the laboratory here pretty much sops that up, but it would be a concern if it were moved to a smaller physical space. We are sensitive to the amount of work space that we have around here. If one of these things comes out to make adjust-

ments inside, we have to obviously have a place to put it." Transcript of workshop, August 1994.

2. The Laboratory for Remote Collaboration (LARC) project was created as a collaborative research and development project between Digital Equipment Corporation and the Xerox Corporation, through Xerox's Design Research Institute at Cornell University; later SPORG, at the MIT School of Architecture, also became a partner in the project. The participants from within the Xerox organization who were instrumental in instigating and defining this initiative, and in implementing changes in it, include the Joseph C. Wilson Center for Research and Technology, the LX laboratory within the Wilson Center, and the Wilson Center computer and facilities service organizations. Individuals from these groups converged in what became known as the LARC team. The LARC workplace pilot illustrated in this case was conceived as a testing ground for collaborative technology developed by LARC. The vice presidents for research of the two corporations, Xerox's Mark Myers and DEC's Sam Fuller, initiated the LARC workplace pilot, and Mark Myers suggested that a research group central to the business of the Xerox Corporation in the newly formed Wilson Center in Webster would be the place to establish a test bed for remote collaboration as a real-time experiment.

3. The LARC team consists of Greg Zack, Chuck Kukla, and Turid Horgen, representing, respectively, Xerox's Design Research Institute at Cornell University, Digital Research and Architecture in Littleton, Massachusetts, and MIT's Space and Organizational Research Group (SPORG) in Cambridge, Massachusetts. Bill Porter, a member of SPORG, as part of their community of practice helped develop some of the key concepts that formed a part of the intervention. Suon Cheng and Xiaofang Tu worked as research assistants on the project, and Suon Cheng wrote his master's thesis as part of it. Cheng worked in the LX lab as a participant-

observer for the summer of 1995 and interviewed several of the lab members about their experience, working closely with Bob Lechner, head of facilities services for the Wilson Center. Chuck Kukla, through his own approach based on ethnographic studies of work, has contributed to the analysis of the relationship between workplace and work practice. In addition to being active in the design of the workplace experiment, Greg Zack has written comprehensively about the development of computational tools during the workplace experiment, and has contributed to our understanding of the interdependence between space and technology. John Knapp and Joe Mort have written an account of the LX experiment, and John Knapp and Greg Zack have together participated in several SPORG seminars, trying to understand the implications of the LARC intervention and the LX workplace experiment.

4. Kukla had been associated with SPORG at MIT and had observed its process, taken extensive notes, and participated in the review of some of its projects. He suggested that SPORG be involved in the LARC pilot and that the methodology used in the Research University building project be duplicated by means of organizing evaluation and design workshops with three of the laboratories at the Wilson Research Center.

5. The LX Network news server, implemented by Harry Barshatzky at DRI, was an interesting hybrid of push and pull technology. It constructed and presented through Netscape a sequence of pages derived from an industry news subscription and from announcements or updates by the LX lab secretary (or anyone else wishing to broadcast a news item). The pages were cycled automatically with the intention that they be running continually on the APIC whenever no one was actively doing anything else there.

6. The Web paradigm instantly removed any need for a Visual Basic layer. The flexibility of this design and its ease of implementation

outweighed the functional benefit of a programmed newspaper layout of Visual Basic-driven windows.

7. The group made arrangements to install a beta version at LX. The Workgroup Web led to a second version, named Workgroup Web Forum, which, with a more scalable, server-based architecture, proved to be a huge benefit to LX. It transformed the way people could save and share documents, and since Forum supported any format—not just HTML—it was friendly to the Wilson Center infrastructure based on Word and Power-Point. Two special Web servers based on the APIC functional concept were built in the summer and fall of 1995 at DRI. Mike Cavanaugh adapted some Web freeware to build the Web Snapshot server that gives a real-time picture taken from a video camera in the LX Common.

8. The original network based on Windows for Workgroups did not work. But, with the aid of a consultant and a conscious decision to move outside the realm of the Xerox standard solutions, Windows NT was adopted. The new PCs were installed at the same time the organization was being moved and restructured, destabilizing the computer infrastructure and causing serious anxiety during the early months of the pilot. The technical staff of Wilson Center Services had no experience in NT, so the LX lab had to devise its own system for the most part.

9. Gordon Moore, a physician and former director of the Harvard Community Health Plan Residency Program, visited the LX lab on December 2, 1995—sixteen months into the experiment—together with a group of researchers from MIT, the Lego Corporation of Denmark, the Danfoss Corporation of Denmark, and the Norwegian Building Research Institute. Moore's way of inquiring into the LX experience became an unexpectedly important event in which the LX lab members themselves discovered that they had a story to tell and invested quite an amount of time in understanding what made this workplace experiment

so successful. This point, at which a newly formed work group saw the necessity of developing the story of its history and was able to articulate a coherent idea of that story—which it then named the LX experiment—became an important part of building the group's identity and ownership of the problems members grapple with daily as well as of group members' commitment to their research work in future technology.

❂

CHAPTER 7   PROCESS ARCHITECTURE REVISITED

1. See Seymour Papert, *Mindstorms* (New York: Basic Books, 1980).

2. Niclas Adler, Jan Åke Granath, and Göran Lindahl, "Organizational Learning Supported by Collective Design of Production Systems and Products," in Sven Åke Hörte (ed.) *Organisatorisk lärande: En antologi frå projektet, Utveckling av nyckelkompetenser för individer och företag* (Institute for Management of Innovation and Technology, Chalmers Tekniska Högskola, Tekniska Högskolan i Luleå, 1955).

❂

CHAPTER 8   LEARNING PROCESS ARCHITECTURE

1. Chris Argyris and Donald A. Schön, *Organizational Learning II: Practice, Theory, Method* (Reading, MA: Addison-Wesley, 1995).

2. See Robert L. Chapman and John L. Kennedy, *The Background and Implications of the Systems Research Laboratory Studies* (Systems Development Corporation, 1956). Kennedy's development of the cogwheel experiment at the Systems Development Corpora-

tion in the late 1950s was initially applied to the task of training teams that operated the SAGE system responsible for spotting and shooting down enemy aircraft. Kennedy's training methods—basically, methods for instituting a setting for continuous, collaborative inquiry into the improvement of task performance—were subsequently applied to many fields of endeavor, from business management to health care. See also Harold Leavitt, "Some Effects of Feedback on Communications." *Human Relations* 4 (1956): 401–410.

3. Argyris and Schön, *Organizational Learning II.*

4. This view of the motivating power of collective responsibility and freedom of performance is what W. Edwards Deming, the father of the quality movement, declared most vividly in his writing and teaching.

Index